This work: "Thoughts and Ways of Thinking", was originally published by Ubiquity Press and is being sold pursuant to a Creative Commons license permitting commercial use. All rights not granted by the work's license are retained by the author or authors.

Cover Image Credit/Copyright Attribution: IIIerlok_Xolms/Shutterstock

Thoughts and Ways of Thinking: Source Theory and Its Applications

Benjamin Brown

Published by
Ubiquity Press Ltd.
6 Windmill Street
London W1T 2JB

Text © Benjamin Brown 2017

First published 2017

DOI: https://doi.org/10.5334/bbh

This work is licensed under the Creative Commons Attribution 4.0 International License (unless stated otherwise within the content of the work). To view a copy of this license, visit http://creativecommons.org/licenses/by/4.0/ or send a letter to Creative Commons, 444 Castro Street, Suite 900, Mountain View, California, 94041, USA. This license allows for copying any part of the work for personal and commercial use, providing author attribution is clearly stated.

The full text of this book has been peer-reviewed to ensure high academic standards. For full review policies, see http://www.ubiquitypress.com/

Suggested citation:
Brown, B 2017 *Thoughts and Ways of Thinking: Source Theory and Its Applications*. London: Ubiquity Press. DOI: https://doi.org/10.5334/bbh. License: CC-BY 4.0

To Assaf, "my firstborn, my might, and the beginning of my strength, the excellency of dignity, and the excellency of power", with tremendous love and deep appreciation.

Contents

Introduction	vii
Chapter One: On Method	1
Chapter Two: Initial Definitions and Preliminary Clarifications	5
Chapter Three: Source Calculus – The Formalist Line of Argumentation	11
Chapter Four: Cultural Systems – The Pragmatist Line of Argumentation	43
Chapter Five: Source Theory and the Philosophy of Religion	73
Chapter Six: Source Theory and the Philosophy of Law	103
Chapter Seven: Source Theory and the Philosophy of Language	119
Chapter Eight: Summary and Perspective	137
Appendices	143
Appendix I: Sentential and Non-sentential Expressions of Data	145
Appendix II: Forgetting as a Creative Function	147
Appendix III: Creating Null Data Out of Null Data	151
Appendix IV: Manipulative Changes in the Meanings of Words	153
Bibliography	155
Index	163

Introduction

Many of the important revolutions in philosophy occurred not by taking a step forward, but rather by taking a step backward. The great question that every philosophy hopes to answer is "What are the basic elements of the world?" When it makes progress in presenting answers to this question, it is challenged by the next philosophical revolution, which asks whether the very inquiry about these elements is possible at all. It therefore poses even more basic questions and presents answers containing even more basic elements. And so it goes. The Greeks tried to describe the world, and were so bold as to present definite propositions about it. Then Descartes came and said that before we can describe the world and its elements, we must ask whether we are even capable of knowing anything about it. This question heralded the development of epistemology, which tried to provide answers to this more basic question. But then Frege, Russell and the other pioneers of analytic philosophy arrived on the scene and stated that before we can describe the world, including the boundaries of knowledge, we should remind ourselves that all our assertions about the world are made through language. Let us then try to find out to what

---

How to cite this book chapter:
Brown, B 2017 *Thoughts and Ways of Thinking: Source Theory and Its Applications.*
    Pp. vii–xiv. London: Ubiquity Press. DOI: https://doi.org/10.5334/bbh.a. License: CC-BY 4.0

extent our language represents the objects it is meant to represent, to what extent we are able to say meaningful things, and about what. Thus began the "linguistic turn" in philosophy, which attempts to provide answers to this more basic question.

Source Theory, which I present in this book, is an attempt to take yet another step backward. This theory claims that every datum – whether mental or linguistic – has a source. The set of data transmitted by a particular source or set of sources constitutes a database. The way the data are managed according to their sources is the source model, and all of these are parts of a system. This poses a challenge to modern philosophy, asserting that before we try to describe the world, including the boundaries of knowledge and the relationship between world, mind and language, we should remind ourselves that our entire discussion is within a system, and sometimes about a system.

Indeed, Source Theory is a branch of epistemology, and thus seems to return the discussion to the stage before Frege and Russell. However, it understands epistemology in the broadest sense. Contemporary epistemology enquires into the rational justification of belief, while Source Theory reminds us that the rational system is only one of many possible systems; contemporary epistemology examines our beliefs about the *is*, while Source Theory gives us tools that can work for the *ought* as well. Contemporary epistemology treats our knowledge of language as distinct from our knowledge of the world, while Source Theory applies the basic scheme of the latter to the former as well. As we shall see, it actually deals with more basic questions of philosophical discourse in general, and also helps clarify – and sometimes even solve – questions that have occupied numerous branches of philosophy for centuries. At the same time, it evokes new questions which have not been raised before, or at least have not been sufficiently refined. Thus, although the main purpose of Source Theory is to illuminate the discourse in epistemology, it also has fruitful applications in almost every branch of philosophy. Moreover, it attempts to provide a primary theoretical foundation for discussion in many of these areas.

In addition, Source Theory presents an innovative approach within epistemology proper. Traditional epistemology took for granted a list of belief sources, including "(1) external perception; (2) memory; (3) self awareness (reflection, or inner consciousness); (4) reason" (Chisholm 1977: 122; Steup 1996: 9. see also Chisholm 1964: 245), and discussed their interrelations. It did not account for the nature of a source per se. Modern epistemology has followed the same path, and has kept moving in circles around the well-known debates among internalists versus externalists and foundationalists versus coherentists. These discussions did yield a few important elucidations, but they ignored other important directions of enquiry. The innovative idea in Source Theory is that it takes the human mechanism of knowledge as if it were an information system or, better, a variety of information systems. Instead of speaking about senses, reason and the like, it begins with the concept of "source" as such; instead of speaking about ideas and beliefs, it speaks about "data"; instead of speaking about experience, deduction and other "belief-forming processes", it speaks about inputs, outputs, the creation of data and their transmission. This approach may sound similar to the Turing-inspired approaches of the computational cognitive sciences, in particular computational epistemology (see summary at Rugai 2013), or possibly to Dretske's epistemological theory (Dretske 1995). However, this book takes a much more fundamental and therefore much more abstract and more intuitive path than both lines of thought. It does not presume to claim that human understanding is computer-like. Nor does it attempt to quantify the content and scope of information transmitted to the human brain or explain how the brain processes it. Rather, this book focuses on the formal logic of what it means to receive data and to determine whether or not to accept them as true. Source Theory does not undermine these theories nor corroborate them, but addresses a much more fundamental level of analysis.

Through all these changes, it explicates the concept of source as such, on an abstract theoretical level, while using the four classical sources merely as examples. To reach this abstract theoretical level, Source Theory presents a new logical tool – the Source Calculus – that helps us treat the issue "algebraically", beyond the concrete "figures" of senses, reason and the like. As we shall see, this tool – the formalist line of argumentation – sharpens the edge of the age-old "infinite regress" problem, and brings it to what we will call "nihilistic absurdities", which necessitate the adoption of a different, pragmatist line of argumentation.

The pragmatist line of argumentation leads us to a theory that might be wrongly identified, in contemporary terminology, as a form of accessibilist internalism. In my discussion, however, I will not go into the existing literature about this theory, nor elaborate the differences between my version and previous versions of it, nor engage myself in polemics with its critics. The argument, I believe, should stand by its own right and receive the response it deserves according to its own flow from the premises to the conclusions.

Although the present essay is an attempt to take philosophy one step backward, it nonetheless strives to take it several steps forward as well. The backward step is necessary because every discussion in Western philosophy uses rational tools. The rational system is large and important, and can boast many achievements. Nevertheless, it is only one system, and other systems offer alternative ways of thinking, and consequently different data. This book comes to say: Before you discuss issues of any sort, you should be aware of the question of which system you are using, and why you are using this particular system. To be sure, this point has been raised, occasionally and marginally, in various academic areas, especially postmodern discourse, but the issue needs to be placed in a philosophical context and discussed with the use of rigorous analytic tools. At the same time, the present essay also takes several steps forward by using these new tools to return to old, and sometimes even ancient, problems, and to critique deeply-rooted ideas of modern analytic philosophy. While this philosophy has generally been scholastic and involved in meticulous but unhelpful discussions, Source Theory promises to help clear up many matters and illuminate them with a new light, by considering several classical problems within one unified system. I am aware that this is a very ambitious plan, but I hope to demonstrate that it is justified.

* * *

In our daily life, we often argue about various issues. Sometimes these arguments are fruitful, but at other times it seems that we are arguing past each other. In the latter type of case, we tend to say that the two sides disagree not only about the issues, but also about something deeper.

An example of a dialogue of this sort can be found in the correspondence between Baruch Spinoza and Hugo Boxel in 1674. Boxel writes to Spinoza, "I should like to know your opinion of apparitions and specters, or ghosts; and if they exist, what you think regarding them, and how long they live" (Spinoza 1995, Letter 51: 261). Boxel himself believed that they existed, supporting his belief with the claim that "there are to be found throughout antiquity so many instances and stories of them that it would indeed be difficult either to deny them or to call them into doubt" (ibid.). Spinoza, as one might expect, disparaged Boxel, expressing doubt about the authenticity of the stories and even made the almost-modern claim that the words for these supposed entities are meaningless (ibid., Letter 52: 262–263). Boxel insisted on his view, trying to provide a basis for these stories with four pseudo-philosophical and pseudo-rational arguments (ibid., 53, pp. 264–266). Spinoza did not have any trouble refuting them as based on incorrect assumptions and using invalid methods of proof (ibid., Letter 54: 267–271). Boxel, for his part, continued to insist on his view, writing that Spinoza had too high a standard of proof, and that he ought to make do with less decisive proofs than those used in mathematics: "In this world we are less demanding; to some extent we rely on conjecture, and in our reasoning we accept the probable in default to demonstrative proof" (ibid., Letter 55: 273). Spinoza answered once again, this time discussing the issue of the level of proof (ibid., Letter 56: 277–279). He understood, however, that this was not the source of the controversy between them. He apparently wanted to get rid of this bothersome correspondent, ending his letter with the following remark:

> In conclusion, most esteemed Sir, I find that I have gone further than I intended, and I will trouble you no longer with matters which I know I will not concede, your first principles being far different from my own (ibid.: 279).

It is clear from this correspondence that Boxel's belief in devils and ghosts was not based on the philosophical arguments he used to try to convince his interlocutor, but rather on religious, mystical or occult traditions. His attempt to use his opponent's methods to support his arguments is pathetic, and we can see clearly why Spinoza refused to take them seriously.

Spinoza thought that the difference between him and his opponent was a matter of "first principles". If these principles are axioms, then different principles will lead to different conclusions. But from where does the difference between the principles stem?

Wittgenstein described a similar situation when he discussed the modern debate between science and religion about how the universe came into being. The scientific theory is apparently more reasonable than the Scriptural description, but Wittgenstein knew that this reasonableness is not enough to convince believers in the Bible:

> [W]hat men consider reasonable or unreasonable alters. At certain periods men find reasonable what at other periods they found unreasonable. And vice-versa. But is there no objective character here?
>
> *Very* intelligent and well-educated people believe in the story of creation in the Bible, while others hold it as proven false, and the grounds of the latter are well known to the former (Wittgenstein 1969: 336).

Wittgenstein thus believed that the cause of the difference between the two views is a different conception of "reasonableness". While "reasonableness" may not be the right word here, if we decide to use it we come up against a question similar to the previous ones: "From where does this difference in people's conceptions of reasonableness derive?"

When I first became interested in these questions, about thirty years ago, I tended to believe that it is important to distinguish between *thoughts* and *ways of thinking* – that is, between the "what" and the "how". Spinoza and Boxel not only thought different things, but also reasoned in different ways; and the same is true of believers in the Bible in contrast to believers in science such as Wittgenstein. Over the years, however, as I continued to consider this problem and develop my ideas about it, I became increasingly convinced that the "how" can be reduced to a "what" – that the different ways of thinking about things do not stem from differences in some mysterious processes in different people's minds, but simply from the fact that they are thinking within different systems. These truth systems are different because they are based on different sources – that is, different types of objects that provide their agents with the data they use to form their beliefs – or even with same truth sources ordered in different hierarchies. The latter theory does not negate the previous one – there are indeed different ways of thinking which lead to different types of thoughts – but the basis of these ways of thinking is the difference between their sources of data.

Indeed, along with the classic questions of epistemology, the question of the relationship between religion and rationality was a major factor in the development of Source Theory. Since, on the one hand, I have devoted many years to research on Jewish religious thought, it seems to me that I have had the opportunity to digest its internal logic as a system. On the other hand, since I have continued to my philosophical inquiry (including my research on Jewish thought) with Western-style rational tools, I have deepened my sense of the distinct internal logic of the Western rational system as another system. To be sure, one of the prominent applications of Source Theory, which I develop in the Chapter Five of the present essay, is in the field of the philosophy of religion. It would be a mistake, however, to think that this is its main purpose or its main use.

* * *

I did not publish my findings right away because I preferred to support and develop them properly first. I tried to support my theory by formulating it with the most rigorous tools of analytic philosophy, and I tried to develop it by considering its potential applications to a variety of areas, most of which are not directly connected with epistemology.

To present Source Theory rigorously, I developed Source Calculus, which is introduced in Chapter Three, after the preliminary clarifications of Chapters One and Two. This chapter presents the formalist line of argumentation for Source Theory. As demonstrated in this argumentation, the consistent application of Source Calculus leads us to three nihilistic absurdities, which seem to show that it is impossible to have any justifiable thoughts. These skeptical absurdities show that it is necessary to replace the formalist line of argumentation with an alternative line that limits the range of possible systems. This is the pragmatist line of argumentation, which is presented in Chapter Four. If the third chapter can be considered as an earthquake, then the fourth one is intended to give us the tools needed to rebuild the ruins. From this point on, I abandoned rigorous logical arguments in favor of ordinary verbal ones. Nevertheless, as I explained in Chapter One, the self-destruction of the formalist line of argumentation does not negate the usefulness of Source Calculus for other purposes. Chapters 2–4 together form the basic core of Source Theory, and it is impossible to understand the theory without reading all of them.

The rigorous use of a logical calculus to prove the central argument of a philosophical thesis is quite rare in philosophical literature, even in the analytic tradition. Although analytic philosophers created logical calculi and had fruitful discussions about them, only a few used them to prove their substantive claims (Gödel being one of the rare exceptions).

One might argue that if the nihilistic absurdities are proven by a logical – that is, rational – method, this should limit their validity to the rational system alone; moreover, if the argument undermines the justification for the rational system itself – or at least its absolute validity – then we are faced with a classic skeptical paradox. However, as the reader will see, the formalist line of argumentation has only been used to provide the reader with a bird's eye view of the variety of systems. Thus it is like Wittgenstein's (or Schopenhauer's) ladder, which one must climb only to throw it away afterwards.

The remaining chapters present some applications of Source Theory. As I considered various possibilities, I came to realize that the theory is applicable to almost all areas of knowledge, especially the various branches of philosophy. I chose three of these as examples: the philosophies of religion, law and language. Chapter Five, on the philosophy of religion, exemplifies the applicability of Source Theory to full, "big" systems; Chapter Six, on the philosophy of law, exemplifies its applicability to a "small" subsystem within a larger system. Chapter Seven, on the philosophy of language, exemplifies its applicability to an untypical subsystem within a larger system. However, there are also some other justifications for the choice of these three fields: The philosophy of religion, as mentioned, was one of the fields (together with epistemology) that first awakened my interest in this issue, and therefore can serve as a convenient example of its applicability; law is one of the areas in which the term "sources" ("the sources of the law") has been used since ancient times, in a sense quite close to that of Source Theory; and the philosophy of language posed the most burning philosophical questions in the previous century, which often were too far detached from the problems of epistemology. It is therefore important, in my opinion, to put them back into this larger context.

As mentioned, the first four chapters of the book must be read as a precondition for the most elementary understanding of Source Theory. Afterwards, readers may choose one or more of the chapters on the applications of the theory according to the areas that most interest them. However, it is worth reading all three of these chapters because this demonstrates the broad range of applicability of the theory. To be sure, the selection is not exhaustive, but I will leave it to others to apply the theory to other areas of philosophy (moral philosophy seems particularly appropriate).

* * *

I am indebted to nearly all the great philosophers who have written about the areas I discuss in the book, especially the great analytic philosophers and epistemologists of the twentieth century. I cannot mention all of them during the discussion, as such mentions are liable to interrupt the flow of the argument and make it more complicated, but I am sure that their imprint will be recognized.

Similarly, I am indebted to the many people who have helped me in my personal and professional life. There are so many of them that I cannot thank even a small minority of them here. However, I must at least thank the people to whom I am most indebted – my parents, Hana and Joseph, who brought me up and encouraged my learning; my wife, Iris, who helped me in every respect and even held discussions with me over the years about some of the ideas in this book; my children, Assaf, Yehoash, Renana and Na'ama, whom I am enjoying raising. I likewise thank my teachers, colleagues and students, from various times and various areas. Prof. Zeev (Warren) Harvey read an early version of this book and wrote helpful comments on it. I am grateful to him as well. Similarly helpful were the comments made by Yair Lorberbaum and Juan Toro, who dedicated time and energy to reading the book and making suggestions that helped me improve some of the arguments. Dr. Naomi Goldblum assisted me with the translation and language editing of the book. Last but not least, I would like to thank Tim Wakeford and all the other supportive and highly professional staff members of Ubiquity Press who worked to develop this book. It has been a pleasure working with you!

CHAPTER ONE

On Method

An ideal philosophy is one that is built as a logical calculus, structured axiomatically. It is perfect not because it is necessarily true – its definitions might be unfruitful, its axioms false and its inferences fallacious – but because it is transparent, and allows the reader to follow the arguments. Indeed, particularly because of the many potential mistakes, the formal, logical path is the ideal one: It forces the author to reveal his building blocks and offer them to the readers' judgment. He can much less easily hide behind lofty words or vague phrasings. When readers are acquainted with the definitions, the axioms and the inferences, they can criticize them, and, if they are not good enough, suggest others instead.

But in addition to the clarity of the text and its openness to criticism, this method has another value – the investigation of the foundations of the issues. Philosophy, *any* philosophy, aspires to take different segments of the world and explore their underlying foundations. These foundations are primitive, irreducible, and therefore arbitrary to some degree. The construction of a logical calculus, as well as the *more geometrico* manner of writing, impel the author to declare his foundations at the outset, and show how all the rest follows from them. If he finds that they are not sufficient, he will need to add more; if he learns that some of them are superfluous, he will reduce them to others. The author himself, and not just the reader, is thus more aware of the foundations. Thus, in a utopian philosophical world where we discover the foundations of all the branches of philosophy – namely, of all the various segments of the world – all these foundations will be able to cohere into a single unified set that will be the underlying foundations of the world as a whole.

Indeed, there are issues for which the formal logical tools seem absolutely inappropriate. An essay in political philosophy, for instance, would seem weird if written *more geometrico*. But even there, scholars can and should aspire to set clear definitions and infer their arguments as much as possible from the simple

---

How to cite this book chapter:
Brown, B 2017 *Thoughts and Ways of Thinking: Source Theory and Its Applications.*
Pp. 1–4. London: Ubiquity Press. DOI: https://doi.org/10.5334/bbh.b. License: CC-BY 4.0

and agreed-upon to the complex and question-begging. Even if this style still falls short of the perfect exploration of the underlying foundations, it will at least come closer to this ideal.

But what happens when such formal argumentation leads to a dead end? Should we then give up all the achievements of the formal line of argumentation and discard the philosophical construction founded on it? The best example of such an "accident" is a paradox. If a formal calculus leads to paradox, does it render the whole calculus valueless? Frege thought it does. For years he toiled on his logical formalism, using it to discover the foundations of arithmetic. But in 1902, shortly before he completed his *Grudlagen der Arithmetik*, Russell sent him a letter with his famous paradox. Frege added an appendix to his book, but nearly discarded his entire project. The paradox similarly threatened Russell's own logic in *The Principles of Mathematics* which he co-authored with Whitehead, and therefore he too added an appendix to the book. Whether or not he, or others after him, succeeded in solving the paradox is disputable. But if they did not, should this be a reason for abandoning Frege's and Russell's logics?

I think we should not abandon them. A single flaw in a system (and I'm using the word *system* freely, not bound to the strict technical sense that appears later in this book), even an axiomatic one, does not have to render the whole system wrong. We should abandon it in those areas directly affected by the paradox, but we do not have to refrain from using it in the areas where it works perfectly well. The paradox may await a solution, or even remain unsolved, but the system can continue.

We all know the problem of the number 0/0 (zero divided by zero). According to one arithmetical rule, 0 divided by any number is equal to 0; according to another rule, any number divided by 0 is equal to infinity, or undefined; according to a third rule, any number divided by itself is equal to 1. Thus we have three different results to the very same fraction, produced by three different valid rules! This flaw undoubtedly undermines the universal validity of all three rules, but does this mean that we have to discard all our arithmetic? Should we say that from now on 0/5 will not be 0, and 5/5 will no longer be 1? Obviously, the whole system will continue to be useful, because it has proven itself useful – and true – in all other areas aside from these special irregularities. We will keep employing it, then, in all the areas where it works, and will abandon it only in the areas where it does not.

Some will surely say that this is a pragmatist move, and indeed it is. It does not demand that the logical calculus have an all-embracing flawless purity; it only requires that it work – and this is the main test of the calculus. It is the pragmatists' test for truth, and especially for the correctness of systems and theories that transcend the scope of an isolated assertion. When strict formalism fails, but our healthy intuition insists that there is no need to give up the whole system for this reason, we may well use the pragmatist approach as an alternative.

We can conclude, then, that once the formalist line of argumentation comes to a dead end, the way out is to use a pragmatist line of argumentation. We may hope that this method will be accepted to some degree by both formalists ("rationalists") and pragmatists. The formalists may agree to give up the dominance of logic where logic itself declares its own helplessness, while the pragmatists will may agree to comply with the demotion of pragmatism to a lower priority or no priority at all, which is used only when logic fails to give an answer. Indeed, even the founders of pragmatism admitted the supremacy of logic as a first priority, although some of them justified logic through psychologistic reasons and refused to acknowledge its absoluteness.

The pragmatist test – whether or not "it works"– is not restricted to the rehabilitation of formal calculi flawed by paradoxes. We may employ it whenever and wherever strict "rationalist" tools lead us to dead end.

When should we say that a system works? It depends very much on the system at issue. When it is a logical calculus, we will be satisfied if it's intuitive and consistent in all the areas where the flaw does not appear; but when richer and more complex systems – such as the ones we discuss in the coming chapters – are involved it is likely that we will have to consider different tests. This question is addressed at the beginning of Chapter Four. At any rate, it is noteworthy that among the founders of pragmatism – in particular William James and F. C .S. Schiller – two tests appear interchangeably, without sufficient distinction between them. One may call them the test of pleasure and the test of functioning. The test of pleasure, which is basically a psychological, utilitarian test, suggests that we should choose one system over another if it provides more pleasure to its users, while the test of functioning is a socio-cultural test, and determines that we should choose one system over another if it has been tested and proven workable by many users, on a variety of occasions, for long periods of time, and provides them with more or less coherent answers, applicable to life. Even if the test of functioning also has some sort of utility, this utility is not defined in subjective, "hedonistic" terms, but rather in objective, "intellectual" ones. As far as we are concerned, we will certainly apply the pragmatist line of argumentation by using the test of functioning. The test of pleasure might lead to ridiculous consequences, such that whoever is more pleased holds a greater amount of truths. Thus we could invent a pleasurometer to isolate pleasures and match them one-to-one to the stimuli that evoke them, and so, in every case of principled controversy between two people about two competing theories, connect both of them to the device, examine who is more pleased and so determine whose theory is right. This is an intolerable absurdity for anyone who takes philosophy, science or any other discipline seriously. True, the test of functioning is not altogether acquitted of the same charge, either, but it is clear that it would look for more objective "truth signs" in the theories presented to it than just a subjective feeling of their holders.

We can summarize as follows: A well-conducted philosophical inquiry is one that seeks to develop as many formal, logical systems as possible to suit the various fields of philosophy, and prove its arguments through those systems; in branches of philosophy where this path is not suitable, we should at least take a path that is as close as possible to this ideal, enables us to the arguments critically and avoids rhetorical vaguenesses. However, when the rigorous path leads to a dead end – in cases of paradoxes and similar problems – we should use the pragmatist line of argumentation, and apply it by the test of functioning.

Having said all that, we can now attempt to build a new calculus, aimed at epistemological uses, which we call the *Source Calculus*.

CHAPTER TWO

Initial Definitions and Preliminary Clarifications

Data and sources

This chapter presents the definitions and premises required for constructing Source Theory, including the Source Calculus presented in the following chapter. So as to avoid burdening the reader at the beginning of the book, I have placed the more detailed discussions in the appendices.

A **datum** is an information unit. In a human context, it is an object of the mind that is grasped by an individual and changes that individual's epistemic state when it enters his or her mind. One could say that, in this latter context, a datum is a "thought", in the broad, Cartesian sense of the word. That is, it is anything that can be the object of sensory perception, thinking, asserting, belief, disbelief, or any other epistemic attitude. For the purposes of Source Theory, a datum will always appear in the form of a sentence.

Note 1: For the purposes of Source Theory, a datum is always conscious. Although an unconscious datum can affect a person in many different ways, it cannot be "thought" (in the Cartesian sense), and so it does not change its owner's epistemic state. Therefore it cannot be the object of sensory perception, thinking, asserting, belief, disbelief, or the like.

Note 2: Even though data will appear hereinafter only as sentences, in principle, data are not necessarily propositions, but can be mere objects. A sensual presentation is a datum, and so is a social act. Furthermore, linguistic expressions of data are not necessarily sentences, but can also be words or phrases. For example, not only is "The tower is high" a datum, but so is "a high tower" (I discuss this point at greater length in Appendix I). When dealing with the Source Calculus (in the following chapter), however, we will assume for simplicity that data are propositions, and since the calculus deals with linguistic

How to cite this book chapter:
Brown, B 2017 *Thoughts and Ways of Thinking: Source Theory and Its Applications.* Pp. 5–10. London: Ubiquity Press. DOI: https://doi.org/10.5334/bbh.c. License: CC-BY 4.0

expressions, we will treat the propositions as sentences. In general, our informal discussion will keep in mind that data are not sentences, but the formalist course of argumentation will be limited to those data whose linguistic expressions are sentences. This provides another reason for limiting ourselves to conscious data, since unconscious data are not expressed in sentences.

A **truth source**, or a **source** for short, is an object that supplies a datum. In the human context, a source can be one of the human senses (including introspection), reason, testimony (a person or a text), and the like.

Note: "Testimony" in this context refers to any data whatsoever, and not only to data relating to matters of fact. Thus, a person can attest to a law of logic and a text can attest to a legal obligation, and so on. (Testimony as an epistemic source has recently gained much scholarly attention. See for example: Coady 1992; Dummett 1994; Audi 1997; Lackey and Sosa 2008; Lackey 2008; most of these works, however, focus mainly on questions regarding its justification, which are not at the center of my discussion).

The act of supplying a datum will be called **transmission**. A transmission is carried out if someone might receive it, regardless of whether there actually is a receiver and, if there is, whether the receiver believes its content. Therefore, the existence or nonexistence of the receiver, or the belief or disbelief of the receiver in the transmitted datum, is not an important element in Source Theory, unless the receiver transmits the datum forward. However, if the receiver does transmit the datum further on, thus serving as a source, he thus attests to the truth of that datum, and asks its next receiver to believe it.

Note: Every new transmission is the transmission of a new datum, even if it was already in the receiver's mind, since bringing it up again makes it new. This is true not only for data that have been forgotten and are brought back into memory, but also for the renewal of the very same datum at every moment. Moreover, even the phenomenon of forgetting is itself the transmission of a new datum, since it leads to a condition of absence (this is discussed at length below and in Appendix II).

The basic assumption of Source Theory is that **every datum has a source.** Phrasing this in terms of sentences, it means that a sentence is not uttered in a vacuum; there is a source that transmits it, thus declaring that it is true. A datum cannot exist without a source. In contrast, a source qua object can exist without transmitting any data, but in that case it will not be considered a source.

A **database** is the set of all the data transmitted from a given source or source model (interrelated sources; see below).

A source can transmit a datum directly or indirectly. It transmits it directly when the content transmitted is about the world itself; it transmits it indirectly if the content transmitted is about the fact that a certain source has transmitted a certain datum.

The directly transmitted data are usually transmitted by the sources which we may call the **basic cognitive tools**. There are different views about what these sources are, but the differences are not deep. Descartes enumerated "understanding, imagination, sense and memory" (Descartes 1934: 35); Thomas Reid mentioned "consciousness, memory, external sense and reason" (Reid 1854, Essay VI, Chapter Four: 439); Chisholm, who cited these two philosophers, wrote in agreement with them: "(1) external perception; (2) memory; (3) self awareness (reflection, or inner consciousness); (4) reason" (Chisholm 1977: 122) In my discussion of the human context I will follow the same path, but first I would like to treat this issue more analytically and begin by investigating the functional nature of the sources.

A source can **adopt** another source, either conditionally or fully. A **full** (or **unconditional**) adoption of source b by source a takes place when source a accepts all the data transmitted by source b as true. A **conditional** (or **partial**) adoption takes place when source a accepts the data transmitted by source b as true only if some condition holds (whether it involves the source, the datum, or anything else), and the fact that it does hold is transmitted by a source adopted by source a. This condition will be called **the adoption restriction condition**.

A source can also **reject** another source, either conditionally or fully. A **full** (or **unconditional**) rejection of source b by source a takes place when source a takes all the data transmitted by source b as false. A **conditional** rejection takes place when source a takes the data transmitted by source b as false only if some condition is satisfied, and the fact that it is satisfied is transmitted by a source adopted by source a.

The idea of adoption gives a new meaning to the concept of **belief**, which has always been central to modern epistemology. A belief in a datum is an act that reflects the adoption of the source that transmitted that datum. There is no belief without adoption, and every belief is nothing but the direct modus-ponens-like consequence of the adoption of a source and the transmission of a datum by that source. The belief is evinced by the fact that the adopting source now transmits the same datum.

The idea of adoption also gives a new meaning to the concept of **justification** of belief, which has been no less central than the concept of belief itself. The final justification of all belief is the adoption of the source that transmitted it, or the source(s) that transmitted the data which support it (this disputable claim will be discussed and better proven in Chapter Three below).

A source can adopt more than one source. This means that it accepts the data transmitted to it from these sources. When there is more than one adopted source, each of them is adopted for another type of data. This determination will be called the **division of labor** among the sources. Any two or more sources, together with the division of labor among them, constitute a **source model**. The main source models we discuss are types of compartmentalization, and these are defined below.

In the human context, a person's source model is what constitutes his way of thinking.

A source model together with the data transmitted by its sources is called a **truth system**, or, for short, a **system**.

The types of data

According to the definition of a source, it is an object that transmits new data to their receivers. Thus we can say that sources "produce" data for the receivers. Since sources create data in different ways, we can call each of these ways a **creative function**. A creative function is the relation between the input to the source and the output it produces. I first present the types of creative function *in abstracto*, and only then discuss them in the human context.

A **positive datum** is one that changes a person's epistemic state by adding new content. Most of the data we will discuss are of this type. As mentioned above, for the purposes of Source Theory, a positive datum will be represented by a sentence. Usually I will use atomic sentences, but a conjunction of sentences can also be considered a single datum.

However, there is also another type of datum that I will call a **null datum**, which is actually a non-existent datum. I call it a datum because the absence of information about a certain issue is also a factor that helps determine a person's epistemic state. When you ask a person what his grandfather's birthplace was and he says "I don't know", he possesses a datum, not only about his own knowledge but also about his grandfather's birthplace – but a null one. If he now learns the answer, we will say that the newly acquired positive datum replaced his null datum.

Creation *ex materia* and *ex nihilo*. A source can create a new datum either out of a datum that already exists in the system or with some other origin. Creation of the former type will be called *ex materia*, and from the latter type, *ex nihilo* (these are sometimes referred to in literature as the outcomes of **generative** sources). This terminology is somewhat misleading, as the source that creates a datum ex nihilo does not actually create it out of nothing; it may create it out of the external world or any other origin outside the system, but this origin is out of our reach and far from our interests. In terms of Source Theory, the datum is not created out of any previous datum within the system. The creation is ex materia only when both the input and the output are within the system.

Let us call the null datum 0, and the two different positive data p and q. The possible combinations of the major creative functions are as follows:

1. 0 is the input and 0 is the output.
2. 0 is the input and p is the output.
3. 0 is the input and q is the output.
4. p is the input and 0 is the output.
5. p is the input and p is the output.
6. p is the input and q is the output.
7. q is the input and 0 is the output.
8. q is the input and p is the output.
9. q is the input and q is the output.

If we analyze this list we can easily see that from a combinatorial point of view 2 and 3 exemplify the same function, that of creation ex nihilo; 4 and 7 exemplify the same function, that of turning a positive datum into a null one; 5 and 9 exemplify the same function, that of preserving the datum as it is; and 6 and 8 exemplify the same function, that of creating one datum out of another one, i.e. creation ex materia. The only function that is logically dubious is no. 1, but it is epistemologically less interesting and we can therefore ignore it for the moment (but see Appendix III for some thoughts about it). Thus, we can speak about four chief functions, which we will number F1–F4:

F1: creation ex nihilo
F2: creation ex materia
F3: preservation
F4: elimination

In the human context, F1 appears in sensation, including reflection; F2 appears in reasoning and judgment; F3 appears in memory (I was not convinced by Lackey's arguments for seeing it as a generative source – Lackey 2008: 251–277 – and agree with Audi 1997: 410 and Dummett 1994: 226); F4 appears in forgetting (a faculty often neglected by modern epistemology; see Appendix II for a more detailed discussion).

These functions involve propositions, not objects, because Source Calculus refers to propositions; but, as stated above, this choice was made for convenience alone, while I do not believe that there is a philosophic need for a sharp logical distinction between the two. Thus I will only discuss objects briefly here, and will develop my argument about them elsewhere.

Objects are of two kinds: individual and general. In principle, only individual objects should be called objects, but we will use the word here for both types. General objects are properties or relations, i.e. predicates, and can be of different levels of abstraction.

According to classical empiricist philosophy, sense data objects are created ex nihilo (in the sense defined above), while predicates are created ex materia from them; according to some rationalist philosophers, the opposite is the case.

The functions that hold among objects are the following:

F5: **Abstraction** develops predicates from individuals (or predicates that determine individuals) to general predicates and from lower predicates to higher ones.
F6: **Judgment** determines that a predicate is attributed to an individual and that a lower predicate is subordinate to a higher one.
Of the many predicates that can exist, one relation deserves special attention, because of its basic character, namely, the part-whole relation. Determining this relation requires one of two faculties that have not yet been mentioned, and so have not yet been named:

F7: The **partitionary** faculty is responsible for conceiving wholes as divided to parts.

F8: The **combinatory** faculty is responsible for conceiving objects as parts of a whole.

Physical objects are partitioned into real parts; while combining two predicates leads to the creation of a predicate that includes both of them as disjuncts, as shown in Venn diagrams.

In fact, abstraction occurs when two or more predicates are combined and a new concept is assigned to the new predicate.

Imagination, a faculty mentioned Descartes's and Reid's lists as cited above, is nothing but a use of the combinatory faculty to combine two parts which are not combined into one whole in the world conceived by the senses and reason.

These functions can also be used for propositions. Thus, for instance, when a person sees green grass (a datum created ex nihilo) he may judge that "the grass is green"; he can now divide the grass to its parts, and judge that this blade and that blade are green; he may now make use of abstraction and generalize that "all the blades are green" (datum created ex materia). He can also determine that the property 'green' is a part of the property 'colored', as every colored thing is either green, blue, red, yellow or the like, and so the grass is also colored.

The creation of data, whether ex nihilo or ex materia, requires sources. The question of which human organ is responsible for each of these functions is a scientific one, and is not a part of our present concern. Viewing epistemic systems as information systems on a purely theoretical level, we may hold that each type of function requires a source of its own, even if empirical research tells us that in the human context there are organs which carry out more than one function and organs which carry out fewer than one function. In the human context, however, the faculties mentioned above constitute our basic cognitive tools.

Having discussed the nature of sources and data, we must now consider the degree of trust we have in them and the degree of justification of this trust. To consider this issue we first make use of a rigorous formal method and present our discussion through what I call **the formalist line of argumentation**. Afterwards we consider it from a different angle, through what I call **the pragmatist line of argumentation**.

CHAPTER THREE

Source Calculus – The Formalist Line of Argumentation

The formalist line of argumentation

Source Theory is at an attempt to elucidate the basic concepts of epistemology by creating a formal calculus and using it to draw conclusions in this and other areas. The calculus and its use thus constitute an attempt at a logical procedure in epistemology.

The formal calculus is constructed with the accepted axiomatic structure, with concepts, axioms and theorems. The basic elements of the calculus are: **data**, **sources** and **transmission**. These were defined informally in the previous chapter. Other concepts – including major ones such as **adoption** and **system** – are defined formally, using the basic concepts.

Sources, data and transmission

Some of the basic concepts of Source Calculus were defined above in Chapter Two. Nevertheless, for the sake of clarity I will repeat some of the definitions here briefly, without the explanations and elaborations added above.

A **datum** is an information unit.

A **truth source**, or a **source** for short, is an object that supplies a datum.

Transmission is the act of a source supplying a datum.

A **database** is the set of all the data transmitted from a given source or source model.

How to cite this book chapter:
Brown, B 2017 *Thoughts and Ways of Thinking: Source Theory and Its Applications.* Pp. 11–42. London: Ubiquity Press. DOI: https://doi.org/10.5334/bbh.d. License: CC-BY 4.0

Sources and data are objects. I use the word *object* in its widest sense, i.e., as denoting a "thing" in contrast to a "state of things" or the like. In the Source Calculus data are represented in the form of sentences. These sentences are nevertheless considered objects in that they can be categorized as elements of sets, so that the laws of set theory can be applied to them; and as terms within predicates, so that the laws of predicate calculus can be applied to them (in spite of my reservations about this calculus, which I hope to discuss elsewhere). Therefore, when a sentence (datum) appears in the form of a variable we can quantify it. The quantifiers that are used here are those used in predicate calculus – that is, the existential and the universal quantifiers.

Since sources, too, are objects, this is the case for them as well. When they are discussed in the predicate calculus, they may appear as either variables or constants, and they can be bound by quantifiers.

For brevity, if a variable appears without a quantifier, this means that it is bound by the universal quantifier. Only when both the existential and the universal quantifiers appear in the same sentence will the universal quantifier be used explicitly.

The first four Greek letters, $\alpha, \beta, \gamma, \delta$, are used to represent the variables that denote sources, and so does μ, denoting a particular type of source which will be specified below. These are sometimes followed by a colon, which is the **transmission sign** : $\alpha{:}\ldots, \beta{:}\ldots, \gamma{:}\ldots, \delta{:}\ldots$

The letters a, b, c, d, h, i, m, sometimes indexed, are used to represent the constants, followed by the transmission sign, a colon a:..., b:... c:..., d:.... The first four letters denote ordinary sources, while the letters h, i and m denote particular sources, as specified below.

A few constants should be introduced. At this stage I will describe these sources informally and briefly, but most of them are defined and discussed at greater length below.

The speaking self, denoted by the Latin letter i: The basic "source" is the speaking self. The speaking self is the agent using the calculus, who transmits the rest of the sources and data to a hearer or reader. In the case of this book, the speaking self is the text of the book, or its author, but each reader may well replace it with his or her own "I". (It might be possible to develop the discussion to involve several speaking selves, but we do not need to consider this complicating possibility here.) In practice, the speaking self is not a source and does not function as one, but functions rather as the subject to which all the sources direct their messages. Therefore, when we use a source variable, it is not always possible to posit the speaking self in it, and when this is the case, I will state it explicitly.

A community, denoted by the Latin letter h: A community is an impersonal source representing a group of sources, most often people, or the vast majority of such a group. The letter h, which denotes a community *in abstracto*, is often followed by an index, to denote a particular community, or a bracketed expression, to denote that the members of the community share a common source or sources, Thus, hf can denote the community of French speakers, while h(a) denotes the community of all the sources that adopt a.

The lower-case Greek letters φ (phi), ψ (psi), ρ (rho) and σ (sigma) are used to denote sentence variables, but there are also special sentences that are denoted by τ (tau), which are defined below.

The small Latin letters p, q, r, s are used to denote sentence constants, while t is used to denote a sentence constant for sentences of the τ type.

The sentence a:p is thus to be read as "a transmits the datum p", or "the datum p is transmitted by a". A sentence of this type, i.e., a sentence reporting the fact that a datum is transmitted by a source, is called a **transmission sentence**.

Note 1: All the sources discussed in the Source Calculus are available to the speaking self. This is because in every transmission sentence (say, a:p) the speaking self is the source that transmits the very fact of the transmission (i:a:p).

Note 2: A basic assumption of the Source Calculus is that when a source transmits a sentence, it "claims" that it is true, and thus, if the source is a person, it may be assumed that he or she also "believes" the sentence.

Indeed, in the human context (e.g. when the source is a person), we can speak about claiming and belief without using quotation marks; when we are speaking about a non-human source (e.g., a perceptual sense), however, it obviously cannot claim or believe anything, in the narrow sense of these words. In such cases, what is meant is that the data transmitted by the source appear to the sources that receive them as data that are presumed to be true. For our purposes we will refer to a source as "he" or "she" if the source is clearly a person, and as "it" otherwise.

Just as there can be direct transmissions, there can also be indirect transmissions. A direct transmission is a situation in which the source transmits a "nuclear" datum, such as b:p. An indirect transmission is a situation in which the datum transmitted by the source is itself a transmission sentence, such as a:(b:p), which can actually be written in such instances as a:b:p without the brackets. In other words, indirect transmissions are situations in which one source transmits something that was transmitted to it by another source. Thus, for example, "a:b:p" means "a transmits the datum that b transmits the datum that p", and so on without restriction. In such cases we say that a's transmission of b:p is direct and b's transmission of p is direct, but a's transmission of p is indirect.

In this sort of situation, we call the source that transmits the nuclear datum (here, b) the "primary source", and the source that transmits the sentence transmitted by the primary source (here, a) the "secondary source". If there is another source that transmits the datum of the secondary source, it is called the "tertiary source", and so on. The speaking self is never counted in the ordered list of sources.

The act of transmission is not transitive. In the case under discussion, a is not necessarily claiming that p is true, nor does it necessarily "believe" p, since it is not the one who is transmitting it. Rather, what it is claiming is only that b:p is true. In contrast, b is indeed claiming that p is true. This is the case for all indirect transmission.

We also consider datasets. A **dataset** is a set all of whose members are data. The letters Φ and Ψ denote dataset variables, while the letters P and Q denote dataset constants.

$\Phi = \{\varphi, \psi, \ldots\}$
$P = \{p, q, \ldots\}$

As defined above, a database is a set of all the data transmitted by a particular source or source model. Such a set is indicated by writing the letter denoting it to the right of the letter that denotes the set: $P\alpha \equiv_{def} \{\varphi\} | \alpha{:}\varphi$

For our purposes, the universal set, denoted U, is the set of all sentences transmitted by i or by i's sources.

$U = P(i, \alpha | i{:}\alpha, i{:} \alpha{:} \ldots) = \{\varphi\} | i{:}\varphi, i{:}\alpha{:} \ldots \varphi$

All the sets we discuss are subsets of this set: $\Phi, \Psi \subset U$

Now we can establish the WFF rules.

φ is a WFF if it can be formulated as a meaningful sentence.

If φ is a WFF, then $\neg\varphi$ is a WFF.

If φ is a WFF, then $\alpha{:}\varphi$ and $\alpha{:}\neg\varphi$ are WFFs.

If $\varphi_1, \varphi_2, \varphi_3, \ldots$ are WFFs, and it is given that $\Phi = \{\varphi_1, \varphi_2, \varphi_3, \ldots\}$, then Φ is WFF and therefore $\alpha{:}\Phi$ is also a WFF.

If Φ and Ψ are WFFs, then

$\Phi \cup \Psi$
$\Phi \cap \Psi$
$\Phi - \Psi$
$\Phi \subset \Psi$
$\Phi \not\subset \Psi$
$\varphi \in \Phi$
$\varphi \notin \Phi$

are WFFs, where the connective signs have the meaning assigned to them in set theory.

If φ and ψ are WFFs, then

$\neg\psi; \neg\rho$
$\psi \wedge \rho$
$\psi \vee \rho$
$\psi \oplus \rho$
$\psi \rightarrow \rho$
$\psi \leftrightarrow \rho, \psi \equiv \rho$
$\psi \vdash \rho$

are WFFs, where the connective signs have the meaning assigned to them in predicate calculus.

At this point we can establish a number of axioms:

<u>Axiom 1: The source axiom</u>
$\forall(\varphi)\exists(x)x{:}\varphi$

<u>Axiom 2: The axiom of the speaking self</u>
$\varphi\equiv i{:}\varphi$

Every sentence (in the text at issue) is transmitted by the speaking self (of that text).

Note 1: The axiom refers to the greater sentence, not to the nuclear sentence.

Note 2: In view of the source axiom, φ should not have been considered as UFF, as it seems to present a datum without a source. The only reason it could be recognized as UFF is thanks to the equivalence of the axiom of the speaking self, which states that the apparently sourceless form "φ" is actually an abridged formulation of "i:φ".

Note 3: Note: i:φ is also a sentence, so the axiom of the speaking self implies that i:$\varphi\rightarrow$i:i:φ, and so on *ad infinitum*

<u>Axiom 3: The axiom of the sources of i</u>
$i{:}\varphi\rightarrow\exists(x)(x\neq i)\ i{:}x{:}\varphi$

Every sentence transmitted by i is transmitted to i by a source different from i.

<u>Axiom 4: The axiom of the credibility of the source about itself (in short, the self-credibility axiom).</u>
$\alpha{:}\alpha{:}\varphi\rightarrow\alpha{:}\varphi$

If a source "claims" that it itself is transmitting a particular datum, then it is indeed transmitting that datum (compare: Williamson 2000, Chapter 11).

Can we also establish the opposite, $\alpha{:}\varphi\rightarrow\alpha{:}\alpha{:}\varphi$? This statement means that whenever a source transmits a given datum it also "claims" that it transmits it. In order to make such a claim, it obviously has to be "aware" of the fact that it is transmitting this datum. This is not always true, so we cannot maintain that it is so for all sources. However, we can maintain it for the speaking self:

The theorem of the speaking self's claim of transmission:

$i{:}\varphi\leftrightarrow i{:}i{:}\varphi$

Proof: This follows from the axiom of the speaking self and the self-credibility axiom.

Note: This statement is also intuitively correct, since in the Source Calculus every claim made by the speaking self is a claim that appears as part of the line of argumentation, and since this argumentation is presented (to the reader) by the speaking self, the speaking self must be aware of it.

Axiom 5: The axiom of the distribution of conjunctive transmissions
$\alpha{:}(\varphi \wedge \psi) \equiv \alpha{:}\varphi \wedge \alpha{:}\psi$

Axiom 6: The axiom of the distribution of implicative transmissions
$\alpha{:}(\varphi \rightarrow \psi) \rightarrow (\alpha{:}\varphi \rightarrow \alpha{:}\psi)$

This implies that the same is true in the biconditional as well:

The theorem of the distribution of biconditional transmissions
$\alpha{:}(\varphi \leftrightarrow \psi) \rightarrow (\alpha{:}\varphi \leftrightarrow \alpha{:}\psi)$

This axiom is weaker than the previous one since the connective between the antecedent and the consequent is unidirectional – a material implication – in contrast to the previous one, in which the connective is bidirectional – equivalence.

The reason the connective has to be unidirectional is that if we assumed that it is bidirectional, this would mean that the source α would be subject to the rules of logic, but in Source Calculus the sources (except for the speaking self, as explained below) are not subject to these rules.

Note: The distribution of transmissions does not apply to the connective "or". Consider, for example, the sentence $a{:}(p \vee \neg p)$. This sentence states that a is stating a sentence that is a tautology, and so he is necessarily making a true statement. In contrast, the distributive sentence $a{:}p \vee a{:}\neg p$ says something else entirely – namely, that a may be telling the truth or he may be stating a falsehood. The same is true for the exclusive or. However, the distribution of disjunctive transmissions can take a more banal form:

$\alpha{:}(\varphi \vee \neg \varphi) \equiv \alpha{:}(\alpha{:}\varphi \vee \alpha{:}\neg \varphi)$
$\alpha{:}(\varphi \oplus \neg \varphi) \equiv \alpha{:}(\alpha{:}\varphi \oplus \alpha{:}\neg \varphi)$

When a particular source α does not transmit that φ and does not transmit that $\neg \varphi$, then it can be said to be "silent", and no transmission sentence will appear. However, sometimes a source may state affirmatively that φ is possible and $\neg \varphi$ is also possible. In such a case, the datum will be denoted with an inverted slash between the two possible data. We define this as follows:

$\alpha{:}(\varphi \backslash \neg \varphi) \equiv_{def} \alpha{:}(\alpha{:}\varphi \vee \alpha{:}\neg \varphi)$

Such a state is one of non-decision, and is called ***non liquet.***

In practice, every source can have one of three attitudes to any meaningful datum: to transmit it, not to transmit it, or to avoid making a decision about it (these can be compared to, but do not fully overlap, the classical doxastic position: belief, disbelief and suspension of judgment; Steup 1966: 7). In light of this we can establish the following axiom:

<u>Axiom 7: The axiom of non-transmission</u>
¬α:φ≡α:(¬φ∨(φ\¬φ))

(This could be written without the internal parenthesis, but they are used for clarity).

Note: In this way, a negative transmission sentence can be turned into an affirmative one.

Adoption

The word **adoption** is used to denote a situation in which a source states that he believes data transmitted by another source, sometimes subject to certain conditions. The sentence in which the attitude of adoption is stated is called an **adoption sentence**. Adoption sentence variables are denoted by t and their constants are denoted by t.

Full adoption of a source is an act in which one source transmits the message that he accepts everything that a given source transmits as true. This act is denoted by the **adoption sign**, which is two colons between the adoptive source and the adopted source. α::β (read: alpha adopts beta) is therefore defined as:

α::β≡def α:(β:φ→φ).

The **rejection** of a source is the opposite of adoption. We can use the rejection sign ÷÷ to denote it:

α÷÷β≡def α:(β:φ→¬φ).

A specific type of adoption is **exclusive adoption**, in which the adoptive source adopts one particular other source and rejects all others. This type of adoption is not used very frequently, and is marked by X::

αX:: β≡def α:(β:φ↔φ)

A source can adopt more than one other source. This means that it accepts the data transmitted from these sources. As mentioned above, when there is more than one source, the subject often has to determine the division of labor among them, i.e., which source is responsible for which type of data, and this entire complex (the sources and the division of labor among them) is what we call the source model. A model will be denoted by a small m followed by an indexical number: m1, m2, etc. Just as a source can adopt another source, it can adopt a source model. A model requires conditional adoption, and this issue is addressed below, after the term is explicated.

Our senses can provide good examples of division of labor in the human context. Most of our senses operate automatically on different qualities. Our ears do not see colors, just as our eyes do not hear sounds. However, there are some qualities that are transmitted by two or more sources. These create a conflict, or contradiction, between the sources, which requires the conditioning of at least one of them (as discussed below).

Any adoption of two or more sources requires a source model. When we want to state the model, we will elaborate the relation between the sources, defining it as a model mn (when n denotes a number) and writing that the source adopted mn; when we can allow it to remain unspecified, we will, for brevity's sake, denote it simply by stating that the subject adopted the two sources in common: a::(b,c).

$$\alpha::(\beta,\gamma) \equiv_{def} (\alpha:(\beta:\varphi \to \varphi) \wedge \alpha:(\gamma:\psi \to \psi))$$

This notation denotes that α adopted both β and γ, without specifying what it will transmit in cases of conflict between their data.

If so far we have seen that τ sentences are of the form α::β; now we see that they can also be of the form α::(β1, β2 ...) etc.

When we wish to specify the adoption to which the τ sentence refers we will write it in brackets after the letter t. Thus, t(a::...) will mean any adoption sentence in which the adoptive source is a; t(...::a) will mean any adoption sentence in which the adopted source is a; and t(a::b) will mean the particular adoption sentence a::b.

Note: If a::(b:φ→a:φ) then a fully adopts b. But when a:(a:φ→b:φ) a only claims the full adoption of a by b, to which b itself does not necessarily subscribe.

At this point we can state another axiom.

<u>Axiom 8: The self-adoption axiom</u>
α::α

Every source adopts itself – that is, every source accepts the data it transmits as true.

This can also be formulated as follows: $\alpha:(\alpha:\varphi \to \varphi)$.

Note: The self-adoption axiom resolves the liar paradox. If we formalize the liar paradox in the language of Source Calculus, it states the premise i:(i:φ→¬φ) and the premise i:φ, and then asks whether the conclusion is i:φ or i:¬φ. But according to the axiom of self-adoption, the first premise is necessarily false, and so the question does not arise.

Since adoption sentences are data, the distribution axiom can apply to them, as follows:

<u>The conjunctive adoption distribution theorem</u>:
α:((β:φ→φ)∧(γ:ψ→ψ)) ≡ (α:(β:φ→φ)∧α:(γ:ψ→ψ))

If we reverse the sides, we get:

α::(β,γ)≡(α::β∧α::γ)

<u>The implicative adoption distribution theorem</u>:
α:((β:φ→φ)→(γ:ψ→ψ))→(α:(β:φ→φ)→α:(γ:ψ→ψ))

That is,

α:((β:φ→φ)↔(γ:ψ→ψ))→(α::β↔α::γ)

This implies that the same is true for the biconditional.

<u>The biconditional adoption distribution theorem</u>:
α:((β:φ→φ)↔(γ:ψ→ψ))→(α:(β:φ→φ)↔α:(γ:ψ→ψ))

That is,

α:((β:φ→φ)↔(γ:ψ→ψ))→(α::β↔α::γ)

The last theorem brings us to another issue. So far, we have been discussing full adoption, but the biconditional adoption distribution theorem leads us to a discussion of partial adoption.

Partial or **conditional adoption** occurs when the adoptive source accepts the data transmitted to it by the adopted source as true if and only if a particular condition holds. Let p' be the conditional sentence. This condition will be called **the adoption restriction condition**. Such partial adoption will be denoted by a formula in which the conditional sentence, followed by a slash, is placed between the adoption symbol and the adopted source. Partial adoption is thus defined as follows:

α::(p'/β)≡def α:(p' ↔ (β:φ→φ))

Even an exclusive adoption can be conditional:

$$\alpha X::(p'/\beta) \equiv_{def} \alpha:(p' \leftrightarrow (\beta:\varphi \leftrightarrow \varphi))$$

The definition of partial adoption leads to:

<u>The theorem of the distribution of partial adoption:</u>
$$\alpha::(p'/\beta) \rightarrow (\alpha:p' \leftrightarrow \alpha:(\beta:\varphi \rightarrow \varphi))$$

Proof:

$\alpha:(p' \leftrightarrow (\beta:\varphi \rightarrow \varphi)) \equiv (\alpha:p' \leftrightarrow \alpha:(\beta:\varphi \rightarrow \varphi))$ by the theorem of the distribution of biconditional transmissions
$\alpha:(p' \leftrightarrow (\beta:\varphi \rightarrow \varphi)) \equiv \alpha::(p'/\beta)$ by the definition of partial adoption
$\therefore \alpha::(p'/\beta) \rightarrow (\alpha:p' \leftrightarrow \alpha:(\beta:\varphi \rightarrow \varphi))$

QED

The conditioning can also apply to two or more sources. Moreover, it may be different for each of the sources:

$$\alpha::(p'/\beta, q'/\gamma) \equiv_{def} \alpha:((p' \leftrightarrow (\beta:\varphi \rightarrow \varphi)) \wedge (q' \leftrightarrow (\gamma:\psi \rightarrow \psi)))$$

Note: The distribution of biconditional adoption, as presented above, is an example of partial adoption, according to the definition presented here. In such a situation the adoption of α and β are conditioned on each other.

When the sentence of the condition of restricted adoption p' (or q') is a tautology, the adoption becomes full. This shows that partial adoption includes the possibility of complete adoption, although the reverse is not the case. This implies:

$$\alpha::\beta \rightarrow \alpha::(p'/\beta)$$

In the following discussions we will mostly make use of partial adoption, which has the broadest range of application. In many of the discussions, the concrete content of p' is unimportant. For these cases we will use an abbreviated symbol of partial adoption: /: . We can define this symbol as follows:

$$\alpha/:\beta \equiv_{def} \alpha::(p'/\beta)$$

A conditional exclusive adoption in which the condition is not specified will be denoted by X/:, as following:

$$\alpha X/:\beta \equiv_{def} \alpha X::(p'/\beta)$$

Note: The difference is that in the formula α/:β the condition is not specified. Thus we will use it only in cases where the identity of the condition is not relevant to the issue under discussion, i.e. in cases where only the conditional nature of the adoption is at stake.

In a different formulation we can therefore state:

<u>The adoption relation theorem</u>
$$\alpha::\beta \rightarrow \alpha/:\beta$$

This is also true, *mutatis mutandis*, for the adoption of more than one source.

If, on the other hand, an adoption restriction sentence is a contradiction, then the adoption does not hold. This situation constitutes the rejection of the source under consideration.

Sometimes there is a situation in which the adoption restriction condition establishes that the data transmitted by the adopted source belong to some dataset P. This is called **(ordinary) compartmentalization**. In such a situation the adoption restriction condition is denoted by placing the membership sign, followed by name of the set, before the slash (this is a convenient denotation, even though it is not elegant):

$$\alpha::(\in P/\beta) \equiv_{def} \alpha:((\varphi \in P) \leftrightarrow (\beta:\varphi \rightarrow \varphi))$$

To be sure, the opposite situation, in which *not* belonging to the dataset is the condition, is also possible. In that case the situation will be notated by the non-membership sign:

$$\alpha::(\notin P/\gamma) \equiv_{def} \alpha:((\varphi \notin P) \leftrightarrow (\gamma:\varphi \rightarrow \varphi))$$

Or, if we use U to denote the Universal Set:

$$\alpha::(\notin P/\gamma) \equiv_{def} \alpha:((\varphi \in (U-P)) \leftrightarrow (\gamma:\varphi \rightarrow \varphi))$$

The main benefit of compartmentalization is obtained when it is used for more than one source:

$$\alpha::(\in P/\beta, \in Q/\gamma|(Q \cap P = \emptyset)) \equiv \alpha:(((\varphi \in P) \leftrightarrow (\beta:\varphi \rightarrow \varphi)) \wedge ((\varphi \in Q) \leftrightarrow (\gamma:\psi \rightarrow \psi))|(Q \cap P = \emptyset))$$

Compartmentalization is therefore an excellent example of the division of labor among sources.

Complementary compartmentalization occurs when the two (or more) adopted sources are "authorized" for complementary sets:

$$\alpha::(\in P/\beta, \notin P/\gamma) \equiv \alpha:(((\varphi \in P) \leftrightarrow (\beta:\varphi \rightarrow \varphi)) \wedge ((\varphi \in (U-P)) \leftrightarrow (\gamma:\psi \rightarrow \psi)))$$

Another type of compartmentalization is a **hierarchy**. This is a situation in which a source γ is adopted on the condition that its data do not contradict those of another source β, which has also been adopted. In such a case we will say that beta is a **superior source** in the hierarchy and γ is a **subordinate source**. Such a situation is denoted by having the superior source appear before the slash, and the subordinate source after it. In terms of compartmentalization this means that the adoption of γ is compartmentalized to data that do not contradict β's data.

If the dataset transmitted by β is denoted Pβ (as above), then the hierarchy is defined as follows:

$$\alpha{:}(\beta/\gamma) \equiv_{def} (\alpha{::}\beta \land \alpha{::}(\varphi \notin P\beta \leftrightarrow (\gamma{:}\varphi \rightarrow \varphi)))$$

It can also be defined somewhat more simply:

$$\alpha{::}(\beta/\gamma) \equiv_{def} \alpha{:}((\beta{:}\psi \rightarrow \psi) \land \neg(\gamma{:}\neg\psi) \leftrightarrow (\gamma{:}\varphi \leftrightarrow \varphi))$$

So far I have presented possible interrelations between sources in the form of adoption by another source, α. This serves as a unifying factor, which determines the order of the sources it adopted. However, we can describe this order abstractly and independently as a unit ready for adoption as a whole. This presentation, which allows great brevity, is in the form of a model. As mentioned above, a model is presented by a small m, usually with a numeral index, or, when speaking about a variable, by the Greek μ. For example, if we want to introduce a model of complementary compartmentalization, as mentioned, we may describe it as a model called m1:

$$m1 = (\in P/\beta, \notin P/\gamma).$$

For short, we can simply say that m1 itself is a theoretical source, and write:

$$m1: \forall \varphi (((\varphi \in P) \rightarrow \varphi) \land ((\varphi \notin P) \rightarrow \gamma))$$

If α applies this model, we can simply state that it adopted m1:

$$\alpha{::}m1 \equiv \alpha{::}(\in P/\beta, \notin P/\gamma)$$

And if α adopts m1 exclusively we write: αX::m1

This notation saves us the need to elaborate complex source relations whenever we mention them. In terms of content, we will treat the adoption of a model as an adoption of sources.

Let us continue the discussion of our senses. As I wrote above, most of our senses are compartmentalized. Since they transmit different qualities, they do not have occasion to conflict with one another: Our ears do not see and our eyes do not taste. There are, however, some qualities that are transmitted by two or more sources. These create a conflict between the sources that requires the conditioning of at least one of them – or the creation of a hierarchy. Consider the following examples:

1. The sense of sight transmits that the paint on the banister is dry; the sense of touch transmits that it's wet.
2. The sense of sight transmits that the paint on the banister is wet; the sense of touch transmits that it's dry.

We can imagine at least five consistent responses to these situations:

a) Believing the data transmitted by the sense of sight in both cases.
b) Believing the data transmitted by the sense of touch in both cases.
c) Believing the more desirable datum (dry paint) in both cases.
d) Believing the less desirable datum (wet paint) in both cases.
e) *Non Liquet*

Options a and b give priority to the chosen datum according to the superior status of its source; options c and d give priority according to content, probably in relation to the agent's predispositions (cautious or nonchalant).

One particular type of compartmentalization is called **external decision**. In this situation, it is established that whenever source α encounters a contradiction between β's data and γ's data, then a fourth source, δ, determines which datum source α will believe. In this sort of situation, δ is called the **deciding source**, and the situation is denoted by two slashes between δ, on the one hand, and β and γ, on the other:

$$\alpha::(\delta//(\beta,\gamma))\equiv\alpha::(((\delta:\varphi\leftrightarrow\alpha/:\beta:\varphi))\wedge(\delta:\neg\varphi\leftrightarrow(\alpha/:\gamma:\neg\varphi))|\delta\neq\alpha,\beta)$$

Note 1: External decision should not be considered a case of hierarchy, in which β and γ are subordinate to δ, since δ's supremacy comes into play only in case of a contradiction between the data of β and γ, while in other cases they may well be superior to δ.

Note 2: There can also be situations in which δ's transmission of a datum is conditioned in various ways.

Note 3: When an adoption restriction sentence states that a datum belongs to a certain set, and this set is empty, the adoption is defeated, and so this situation is one of rejection of the source at issue, as defined above.

Note 4: The concept of a hierarchy helps us explicate the concept of defeasibility more precisely. Defeasibility, which has been proven to be a fruitful concept in contemporary logical and philosophical discussions, is a state in which a datum from a subordinate source is transmitted at first without the transmission of a contradictory datum from a superior source, and so it is worth believing, yet later on a contradictory datum from the superior source is transmitted, which, according to the hierarchy, defeats the previous datum.

All the forms presented so far – ordinary conditions, compartmentalization, hierarchies, external decision and rejection – are specific forms of partial adoption which were developed by substituting certain phrases in the defining formula for partial adoption.

Now we need to distinguish between direct and indirect adoption.

Direct adoption occurs when one source adopts another without the intervention of a third source. For example, a::b represents direct adoption.

Indirect adoption occurs when one source adopts a second one, and the second source adopts a third one. For example, a::b::c represents a situation in which a adopts b directly and b adopts c directly, but a adopts c indirectly. In such a situation we say that a adopts c **by virtue of** b.

Adoption sentences too can be combined with transmission sentences – that is, one source can adopt another source, which transmits a certain datum. This situation is called **transmission by virtue of adoption**. When the adoption is complete, the situation is denoted as a::b:p. This sentences reads, "a transmits that p by virtue of having fully adopted b". Of course, in such a case a also accepts p to be true by virtue of that adoption. If the source is a person, we would say he **believes** in p by virtue of the adoption of b. As with transmission, we call the source that transmits the nuclear datum (here b) the **primary** source, and the source that transmits the primary source's transmission sentence (here a) the **secondary** source. If another source transmits the secondary source's transmission, it is called the **tertiary** source, etc.. Here too the speaking self is never counted in the ordered list of sources.

A source's belief in a datum that it transmitted is called **direct belief,** while belief in virtue of another source is called **indirect belief.**

Now **transmission in virtue of full adoption** will be defined as follows:

$$\alpha::\beta:\varphi \equiv_{def} (\alpha::\beta \wedge \beta:\varphi)$$

But according to the definition of full adoption, using modus ponens, we deduce that $\alpha:\varphi$. We can state this as a theorem:

<u>The indirect adoption theorem</u>
$\alpha::\beta:\varphi \rightarrow \alpha:\varphi$

Proof: By virtue of the definition of full adoption and modus ponens.
This means that, in contrast to transmission, full adoption is transitive.
Note: This implies that direct belief does not have any logical priority over indirect belief.

These situations must be distinguished from that of **mediated adoption.** When a adopts c, but receives c's data from another source, b, we say that a adopts c by virtue of b's mediation. This situation is denoted a::(b:c) and is defined as follows:

$$\alpha::(\beta:\gamma) \equiv_{def} \alpha::(\beta:\gamma:\varphi \to \varphi)$$

In mediated adoption the adoptive source adopts the mediated source not as a source of data about the world, but as a source of data about other data being transmitted from another source. Later we discuss the logical character of this sort of adoption.

Note: Mediated adoption is also a sort of compartmentalization, since the adoptive source accepts the data of the mediating source as true if and only if they belong to a particular set, which is the set of transmission sentences of another source. (To be sure, the adoptive source can also adopt the mediating source for other matters as well, even in direct adoptions, but these additional adoptions are irrelevant for the mediated adoption presently under discussion.)

<u>The self-adoption theorem</u>
$$\alpha::\alpha:\varphi \equiv \alpha:\varphi$$

Proof: By virtue of the self-adoption axiom and the self-credibility axiom.

Note: This means that whenever the expression $\alpha::\alpha:\varphi$ appears it can be abbreviated to $\alpha:\varphi$.

The situation of **transmission in virtue of partial adoption** is denoted $\alpha::(p'/\beta):\varphi$

This means that α transmits sentence φ in virtue of partial adoption, and that p', which is the condition for adopting β, is satisfied. In the abridged form, $\alpha:/\beta:\varphi$, we say that α transmits sentence φ in virtue of partial adoption, and that the unspecified condition for adopting β is satisfied. Here, too, it is obvious that α also accepts φ to be true, or, in a human context, believes it. This situation is defined as follows:

$$\alpha::(p'/\beta):\varphi \equiv_{def} (\alpha::(p'/\beta) \land p \land \beta:\varphi)$$

The conclusion to be drawn from it is that α:φ. The sentence a::(p'/b):p therefore means, "a transmits that p and accepts p as true in virtue of the fact that it has partially adopted b, subject to the condition p'".

There can also be situations such as a:b::c:p (a claims that b adopts c, who claims that p), and so on.

Databases and systems

Database and system have already been defined, but let us recall them:

A **database** is the set of all the data transmitted from a given source or source model.

A **system** is a source or a source model together with the database that was transmitted by it.

The primary sources that transmit the data of the database or the system (and thus serve as their final justification, as explained below) will be called its **basic** sources, and we will say that the database (or the system) is **based** or **founded** on them.

A database is denoted by the letter D, followed by the source on which it is based (in parentheses). If there is one source, the database is denoted D(a); if there are two, D(a,b); and so on. If it is based on a source model m1, we denote it as D(m1).

A system is denoted by the letter S, followed by the source on which it is based (in parentheses). If there is one source, the system is denoted S(a); if there are two, S(a,b); and so on. If it is based on a source model m1, we denote it as S(m1).

The definition of a database is thus similar to the definition of a set of source data:

$$D(\alpha) \equiv_{def} P\alpha \equiv \{\varphi\} | \alpha{:}\varphi, \beta{::}\alpha{:}\varphi, \gamma{::}\beta{::}\alpha{:}\varphi, ...{::}\alpha{:}\varphi$$
$$D(\alpha,\beta) \equiv_{def} P(\alpha,\beta) \equiv \{\varphi\} \cup \{\psi\} | \alpha{:}\varphi, \beta{:}\psi, ...{::}\alpha{:}\varphi, ...{::}\beta{:}\psi$$

Note: The definition of a database as a set should not mislead us. In its pure set-theoretical meaning, a set is an a-temporal entity, and is determined by its members. Consequently, if in t1 the basic sources transmit p1 and p2, these data will constitute one set, i.e. one database, and if in t2 they transmit a third datum p3, they will constitute another database, etc. However, in Source Theory a database is determined not by its data but rather by its sources, and the sources' transmissions take place in time. To bridge this gap, we define a database as the union set of all the data transmitted by the basic sources at all times.

Let's concentrate for the moment on a database based on one source, α. One of the data transmitted by α is the sentence $\alpha{::}\alpha$ (by the self-adoption axiom). According to the notation presented above, this sentence is denoted as $t(\alpha{::}\alpha)$ (t standing here for the adoption sentence). If so, necessarily

$$t(\alpha{::}\alpha) \in P\alpha$$

But if so, then necessarily

$$\beta{:}P\alpha \rightarrow \beta{:}(\alpha{::}\alpha)$$

Of course, this still does not mean that β adopted α; it only reported α's self-adoption. Neither does the fact that β transmits all of Pα entail that it adopted α, since the same set of data could have been transmitted by another source or by multiple sources.

The basic concepts of set theory apply to the relations between databases and data, as well as between databases and databases. Thus, a database α is said to include a database β if all the members of β are also members of α:

$$D(\alpha) \subset D(\beta) \equiv_{def} \forall \alpha, \forall \beta \ (\alpha \in D(\beta) \to \alpha \in D(\beta))$$

In such a case we will say that database $D(\beta)$ is a **subdatabase** of $D(\alpha)$ and that System $S(\beta)$ is a **subsystem** of $S(\alpha)$.

Note: The sources of the subsystem may include only some of the sources of the larger system (see the definition of database above).

Another form of subsystem exists when the sources of one system fully adopt the sources of another. In that case we will say that the former is a subsystem of the latter.

The theorem of the adoption-inclusion relation
$$\alpha::\beta \to D(\alpha) \supseteq D(\beta)$$

Proof: The adoption of a source entails the transmission of the (data in the) database based on it. If $D(\alpha)$ denotes the set of data transmitted by α, then it also includes the data transmitted by α as result of the adoption of β.

This is not a biconditional, since the inclusion of the data of $D(\beta)$ in $D(\alpha)$ may be a result of coincidence, and not necessarily a result of adoption. Consequently, there may be a case in which source α claims that all the data transmitted by source β are also transmitted by itself (namely, by source α), without the adoption of source β. In such a case α's claim will be taken as an ordinary transmission sentence and not an adoption sentence. In view of this, we will say that $D(\beta)$ is an **alleged subdatabase** of $S(\alpha)$, and that $S(\beta)$ is an **alleged subsystem** of $S(\alpha)$.

If α adopted β through compartmentalization, we will say that $D(\beta)$ is a **compartmentalized subdatabase** of $D(\alpha)$ and that $S(\beta)$ is a **compartmentalized subsystem** of $S(\alpha)$. The same is true for all the various types of compartmentalization.

Subordination to logic

In the Source Calculus, the speaking self is subject to the rules of logic (I have used this assumption throughout this chapter, and I formulate it as an axiom below). We cannot define "Logic" with a capital L here, especially nowadays, when a large number of different logics have been proposed. Clearly a "logic" is the most basic collection of the rules of rational thinking, and any attempt to define it in a principled way will bog us down in a comprehensive discussion of the nature of such thinking, which is inappropriate for the present stage of our discussion. However, we actually do not require a principled definition for our present purposes, but need only explain what sense of the term "logic" we are using here. Accordingly, the "rules of logic" I am referring to are the collection of basic inference rules of the classical propositional calculus. I will present this collection of rules here as a sort of dataset, which I call P(L). P(L)={L1...L22}, i.e. D(L) includes the set of sentences L1–L22.

Even though this set of sentences is the collection of basic rules of inference accepted in the propositional calculus, we will restate them for the completeness and clarity of our discussion:

L1: The law of identity
$\varphi \leftrightarrow \varphi$

L2: The law of non-contradiction
$\neg(\varphi \wedge \neg\varphi)$

L3: The law of the excluded middle
$\varphi \vee \neg\varphi$

L4: Modus ponens
$\varphi \rightarrow \psi$
φ
$\therefore \psi$

L5: Modus tollens
$\varphi \rightarrow \psi$
$\neg\psi$
$\therefore \neg\varphi$

L6: Hypothetical syllogism
$\varphi \rightarrow \psi$
$\psi \rightarrow \rho$
$\therefore \varphi \rightarrow \rho$

L7: Disjunctive syllogism
$\varphi \vee \psi$
$\neg\varphi$
$\therefore \psi$

L8: Constructive dilemma
$(\varphi \to \psi) \wedge (\rho \to \sigma)$
$\varphi \vee \rho$
$\therefore \psi \vee \sigma$

L9: Absorption
$\varphi \to \psi$
$\therefore \varphi \to (\varphi \wedge \psi)$

L10: Simplification
$\varphi \wedge \psi$
$\therefore \varphi$

L11: Conjunction
φ
ψ
$\therefore \varphi \wedge \psi$

L12: Addition
φ
$\therefore \varphi \vee \psi$

L13: De Morgan's theorems
$\neg(\varphi \wedge \psi) \equiv (\neg\varphi \vee \neg\psi)$
$\neg(\varphi \vee \psi) \equiv (\neg\varphi \wedge \neg\psi)$

L14: Commutativity
$(\varphi \vee \psi) \equiv (\psi \vee \varphi)$
$(\varphi \wedge \psi) \equiv (\psi \wedge \varphi)$

L15: Associativity
$(\varphi \vee (\psi \vee \rho)) \equiv ((\varphi \vee \psi) \vee \rho)$
$(\varphi \wedge (\psi \wedge \rho)) \equiv ((\varphi \wedge \psi) \wedge \rho)$

L16: Distribution
$(\varphi \wedge (\psi \vee \rho)) \equiv ((\varphi \wedge \psi) \vee (\varphi \wedge \psi))$
$(\varphi \vee (\psi \wedge \rho)) \equiv ((\varphi \vee \psi) \wedge (\varphi \vee \rho))$

L17: Double negation
$\varphi \equiv \neg\neg\varphi$

L18: Transposition
$(\varphi \to \psi) \equiv (\neg\psi \to \neg\varphi)$

L19: Material implication
$(\varphi \to \psi) \equiv (\neg \varphi \vee \psi)$

L20: Material equivalence
$(\varphi \equiv \psi) \equiv ((\varphi \to \psi) \wedge (\psi \to \varphi))$
$(\varphi \equiv \psi) \equiv ((\varphi \wedge \psi) \vee (\neg \varphi \wedge \neg \psi))$

L21: Exportation
$[(\varphi \wedge \psi \to \rho) \equiv [\varphi \to (\psi \to \rho)]]$

L22: Tautology
$\varphi \equiv \varphi \vee \varphi$
$\varphi \equiv \varphi \wedge \varphi$

Now we can establish the axiom regarding the acceptance of these rules by the speaking self.

<u>Axiom 9: The logicality of the speaking self</u>
This axiom consists of three sentences:
(1) $i : P(L)$
(2) $\forall \alpha \neg i :: \alpha$
(3) $\forall \alpha \, (i/:\alpha \leftrightarrow i::(L/\alpha))$

Note 1: This axiom is actually quite problematic, since it is based on the assumption that the speaking self is subordinate to the rules of rational thought, while we can easily imagine a situation in which the speaking self refuses to subordinate himself to them. Nevertheless, we have no choice but to make this assumption, since the basis of our discussion here is the Source Calculus, which is a logical one, and the speaking self is the agent who employs this calculus. The speaking self of a logical calculus must be subordinate to the rules of the logical subsystem. At any rate, as I mentioned in the introduction, the entire Source Calculus, being logical and rational, is like Schopenhauer's ladder, which the climber can throw away once he has reached his goal, but as long as he is using it, he has to use it as it is – that is, as part of logic.

Note 2: The fact that the speaking self is subject to the laws of logic does not mean that the sources whose data he transmits are subject to these laws. If we take the law of contradiction as an example, the speaking self can transmit information about sources that transmit contradictory data, and the like. As long as he himself does not transmit these contradictory data – i.e. claim their truth – there is no problem.

This is analogous to a situation in which a judge writes in an opinion that the witness Tom contradicted himself in his testimony, or that the witnesses Dick and Harry presented contradictory evidence. The judge who presents this situation is not contradicting himself when he reports the contradiction, unless he writes that he believes both versions of Tom's testimony, or that he believes both Dick's and Harry's versions.

Note 3: The fact that the speaking self is subject to the laws of logic makes it impossible for him to completely adopt a source whose data contradict these laws, but it does permit him to adopt it partially, as long as the adoption condition states that those data that contradict the laws of logic cannot be accepted.

Note 4: On the basis of the axiom on the logicality of the speaking self, we can leave out all mention of the speaking self's acceptance of L as a condition for any adoption. Since L is accepted inherently as a set of data prior to any adoption, whenever we mention that a source has been adopted by i, we will read into the text that this adoption is subject to L.

Many theorems can be deduced from this axiom. One example is the following:

<u>The theorem of the consistency of the speaking self's beliefs (for short, the consistency theorem)</u>
$i{:}\varphi \to \neg i{:}\neg \varphi$ (by the logical principle of the speaking self and the law of non-contradiction).

Here another theorem seems appropriate:

<u>The theorem of the hypothetical syllogism of adoption</u>
$\alpha{::}(p'/\beta)$
$\beta{::}(p'/\gamma)$
$\therefore \alpha{::}(p'/\gamma)$

Proof: By the definition of adoption, the axiom of the logicality of the speaking self, modus ponens (L4) and the hypothetical syllogism (L6). This theorem also applies to the speaking self.

I will now elaborate on the issue of avoiding contradictions between different data sources, but the discussion will only be an example, and the law of non-contradiction will serve as a model for all the laws of logic.

Contradictory data

How can the speaking self deal with contradictions among the data that have been transmitted to him? First of all, according to the axiom of the logicality of the speaking self, he clearly cannot believe both of them at the same time. But what other alternatives does he have?

Here it is important to distinguish contradictions between data from a single source from those between data from different sources. (Throughout this chapter, it is given that all the sources are different from i, that is, $\alpha, \beta, \gamma, \delta \neq i$.)

Case 1: A contradiction between data from a single source:

$\alpha{:}\varphi \land \alpha{:}\neg\varphi$

This means

$\alpha{:}(\varphi \land \neg\varphi)$ by the axiom of the distribution of conjunctive transmissions

Since it is impossible to have $i{:}(\varphi \land \neg\varphi)$, from i's point of view there are thus three alternatives:

1) $i{:}\varphi$
2) $i{:}\neg\varphi$
3) $\neg i{:}\varphi \land \neg i{:}\neg\varphi$

Alternatives 1 and 2 can be achieved only by the partial adoption of α (by the adoption axiom, as stated below, ruling out the possibility of full adoption), while alternative 3 means rejecting α, thus creating a state of *non liquet*.

If the speaking self wants to decide on one of the alternatives, he must establish a condition to rule out one of them:

$\alpha{:}(\varphi \land \neg\varphi) \rightarrow i{::}(p'/\alpha)$

where p' leads to the negation of φ or the negation of $\neg\varphi$.

Case 2: A contradiction between the data of two or more sources.
Here I will discuss the case of two sources, but the discussion also applies, *mutatis mutandis*, to more than two.

$\alpha{:}\varphi \land \beta{:}\neg\varphi$

Since it cannot be the case that $i{:}(\varphi \land \neg\varphi)$, from this point of view there are three alternatives:

1) $i{:}\varphi$
2) $i{:}\neg\varphi$
3) $\neg i{:}\varphi \land \neg i{:}\neg\varphi$

Alternatives 1 and 2 can be achieved only by the partial adoption of α and β (by the adoption axiom, as stated below, ruling out the possibility of full adoption), while alternative 3 means rejecting both α and β, at least for the present purposes, thus creating a state of *non liquet*.

The partial adoptions can occur in all the forms detailed above: ordinary adoption conditions for one of the sources, compartmentalization, hierarchy, external decision or rejection. In the present context of a contradiction between the data of different sources, these situations are activated as **consistency mechanisms**, which is what we shall call them.

In light of all this, the possible mechanisms are:

1 Adoption conditions of the regular, basic sort:

$$(\alpha{:}\varphi \wedge \beta{:}\neg\varphi) \rightarrow i{::}(p'/\alpha,\beta)|p' \vdash \neg\alpha{:}\varphi$$

or

$$(\alpha{:}\varphi \wedge \beta{:}\neg\varphi) \rightarrow i{::}(\alpha,q'/\beta)|q' \vdash \neg(\beta{:}\neg\varphi)$$

or

$$(\alpha{:}\varphi \wedge \beta{:}\neg\varphi) \rightarrow i{::}(p'/\alpha,q'/\beta)|(p' \vdash \neg\alpha{:}\varphi \vee q' \vdash \neg\beta{:}\neg\varphi)$$

2 Compartmentalization:

$$(\alpha{:}\varphi \wedge \beta{:}\neg\varphi) \rightarrow i{::}(\in P/\alpha, \in Q/\beta|(Q \cap P = \emptyset))$$

This also includes the possibility of complementary compartmentalization:

$$(\alpha{:}\varphi \wedge \beta{:}\neg\varphi) \rightarrow i{::}(\in P/\alpha, \notin P/\beta)$$

3 Hierarchy:

$$(\alpha{:}\varphi \wedge \beta{:}\neg\varphi) \rightarrow i{::}(\alpha/\beta)$$

or

$$(\alpha{:}\varphi \wedge \beta{:}\neg\varphi) \rightarrow i{::}(\beta/\alpha)$$

4 External decision:

$$(\alpha{:}\varphi \wedge \beta{:}\neg\varphi) \rightarrow i{::}(\delta//(\alpha/\beta)|\delta \neq \alpha,\beta$$

5 Rejection:

$$(\alpha{:}\varphi \wedge \beta{:}\neg\varphi) \rightarrow i{::}\alpha$$

or

$$(\alpha{:}\varphi \wedge \beta{:}\neg\varphi) \rightarrow i{::}\beta$$

Note: As mentioned, a *non liquet* situation is also one of rejection, but it involves the rejection of both of the sources α and β.

Each of these mechanisms can bring about the desired result, namely, either i:φ or i:¬φ.

It is important to remember that the all the consistency mechanisms are particular forms of adoption conditions, and while we could just as well have established only general conditions, it is more convenient to have all the alternatives spelled out.

Moreover, the list of consistency mechanisms is not a closed one, and there can in principle be other mechanisms, but these too are derivable from the basic form of the adoption condition.

Therefore we can establish the following theorem:

<u>The decision theorem</u>
In a case when two different sources transmit contradictory data, then if and only if the speaking self transmits something about these data, he can transmit only one of the contradictory data, through the (partial or full) adoption of the source that has transmitted it.

$$(\alpha{:}\varphi \wedge \beta{:}\neg\varphi) \rightarrow (\neg i{:}(\varphi\backslash\neg\varphi)) \leftrightarrow (i{::}(p'/\alpha,q'/\beta){:}\varphi \vee i{::}(p'/\alpha,q'/\beta){:}\neg\varphi)$$

This is the case when we are given that:

1. The condition sentences p' and q' are adoption restriction sentences of the sort described above;
2. p' and q' can also be tautologies, thus rendering the partial adoption an almost full one (subject only to the rules of logic L), for either of the sources α and β (but not both, due to the theorem on the consistency of the speaking self).
3. p' and q' can also be contradictions, thus leading to the rejection of source α or β (but not both, due to the antecedent that rules out *non liquet* here).

Proof: By the definition of the *non liquet* situation and the argumentation in this section.

Justification

As stated above (Chapter Two), for any source under discussion, writing the adoption sentence together with the transmission sentence not only states the facts of adoption and transmission, but is also the **justification** for the transmitted datum. (In mediated adoption, the mediated source is seen as the source of the justification, rather than the mediating source, which is nothing but a tool for transmitting the data of the mediated source.) For any claim one can ask the transmitting source, "Why should I believe it?" The answer to this question is the justification of the claim. The justification can be either (1) another datum, which supports the one under consideration, or (2) indicating the source of the datum that the speaker had adopted. If the justification is of type (1), then this answer is itself also a claim, and so one can ask the same question about this answer as well, and so on; if the answer is of type (2), we may ask the speaker why he or she adopted that source; and then the answer will be data which support the credibility of that source; but these data will have to face the same question, and so on. The next-to-last "Why?" question is always answered "Because this and that source transmitted it to me", and if this leads to the question, "Why should I believe it?", then this is the last question in the chain, and it must necessarily be answered, "Because I have adopted this source as a source". Since this is the last "Why?" question, it is the **final justification** of the claim. (To repeat, senses, reason and the like are also sources, and therefore justifying data by using them as a final justification is no different from doing so for any other source, from the point of view of Source Calculus.) In any series of adoptions and transmissions, the rightmost adoption (i.e. the closest to the "nuclear" datum) is the final justification, and all the rest are dependent on it.

At this point one may properly ask: Why is the adoption sentence the final justification? Why not data? The choice of the sources also requires justification, and that justification, for its part, is also a datum! However, as we have clearly seen, the corroborating datum too is transmitted by a source, and that source is the justification for the belief in that datum, and so on in an infinite regress (see Chisholm 1964; Armsrtrong 1973; BonJour 1978; Lehrer 1990). However, we must insist that the ultimate point in this line is a source, not a datum. The reason for this is simple: Every datum depends on its source for its very existence, while not every source depends on a datum (even if its status as a source depends on its ability to transmit data).

This description is in the spirit of the foundationalist theory. Another possibility is granting the system justification through a coherentist theory, but this option will be ruled out below. Within the foundationalist framework, then, there are four main approaches to coping with the question of justification (see Chisholm 1964: 264; compare BonJour 1978; Lehrer 1990; Steup 1996).

1) Dismissing the question as based on false assumptions.
2) An infinite line of justification: p1 is justified by p2, which is justified by p3, and so on indefinitely.
3) A circular line of justification: p1 is justified by p2, which is justified by p1.
4) A foundationalist line of justification: p1 is justified by p2, which is accepted as "foundational" because it is one of the following: (4.1) beyond the requirement of justification; (4.2) unjustified; (4.3) self-justified; or (4.4) neither justified nor unjustified.

This list refers to any type of justification, but we need to apply it to the justification of data and adoptions. Here we encounter the infinite regress problem, but in a version peculiar of the source-datum relation. If source a transmits datum p1 and we ask him why he accepts it as true, he would answer that it is because source b transmitted it to him, and he has adopted source b. The adoption of b by a will be denoted as t1. So now we can ask what justifies t1 (namely, the adoption of b by a). Source a would answer that such-and-such data, called in common p2, justify b's credibility; if we, in turn, now ask what makes him accept p2 as true, a can answer, in the spirit of the list above, one of the following:

1) The question is based on false assumptions.
2) p2 is justified by source c, whose adoption is expressed in sentence t2; t2 is justified by data p3; which were transmitted by source d; etc. in an indefinite line.
3) p1 is justified by t1, which is justified by p1.
4) p1 is justified by t1, which is justified by p2; p2, in turn, is accepted as "foundational" because is one of the following: (4.1) beyond the requirement of justification; (4.2) unjustified; (4.3) self-justified; or (4.4) neither justified nor unjustified.
5) p1 is justified by t1, which is accepted as "foundational" because it is one of the following: (4.1) beyond the requirement of justification; (4.2) unjustified; (4.3) self-justified; or (4.4) neither justified nor unjustified.

However, some of these options should be ruled out immediately:

1) There is no evidence that the question is based on false assumptions.
2) There cannot be an indefinite line of justification of sources and data, since the number of sources is finite.
3) Circularity, or self-justification, is an invalid justification (as for coherence theories, see below).
4) Besides the essential difficulties in the four exemptions from ordinary justification, and besides the difficulty of finding data that would qualify for such a foundational character, we cannot accept data as final justifications, as proven above.

We remain, therefore, with option (5). We should now explore which of the alternative options within (5) may serve as an acceptable justification for the final t sentence.

The meaning of final justification is that the adopted source justifies itself. It does not refer to any other source, but "asserts" that it itself is the source by virtue of which the adoption is justified. This is thus a situation of self-justification. A similar situation occurs when source a justifies itself by referring to source b, which it has adopted, while source b in turn justifies itself by referring to source a, which *it* has adopted (this can also be described for a larger number of sources). This is therefore a situation of circular justification, which is only a more complex form of self-justification (compare Stich 1988). These two sorts of justification can be called **internal justification**. In contrast, the ordinary sort of justification, in which a source refers to another source that it has adopted, without the latter referring back to the former, is called **external justification.**

Internal justification can be accepted, if at all, only as part of a coherentist theory, and therefore should be ruled out in a discussion based on foundationalist premises. Thus we can dispense of option (4.3) above. Since option (4.1) is beyond the requirement of justification, (4.2) is unjustified, and (4.4) is neither justified nor unjustified, they themselves require justification. Since in normal cases justification is required, if someone thinks these can be exempted from justification – that exemption itself requires justification; the justification for the exemption will be given by certain adopted source of sources, and this adoption, on its part, also requires justification, and so we return to the infinite regress problem.

We thus remain with the coherentist alternative of self-justification as the only solution to the infinite regress problem, and therefore self-justification (or internal justification) seems to be the only possible means of final justification of a source. For the time being, we will remain with this conclusion, but we will re-examine it later.

In a situation of indirect adoption, the indirect source is externally justified, while the direct source is internally justified; in a situation of direct adoption, the source is always internally justified.

Note: From the standpoint of the Source Calculus, all truth is relative to a source. The truth value of a datum is determined by its being adopted by the speaking self. To illustrate this, let us suppose that there is an unknown source – let us call it g – that transmits absolutely true data about the world, and only such data. Consequently, the definition of truth in the terms of Source Calculus would be: p is true if g:p. However, such a source would be ideal and thus unavailable to us. Hence, from the standpoint of the Source Calculus we could write source g between any source and any data transmitted by it (for example, instead of writing a:p we could write that a:g:p, and so on). This addition, however, would not be helpful and would only complicate the notation, since g itself is unavailable to us. As a result, for our purposes truth is determined not by accord between the data and the "external world", but rather between the data presented at the moment to the agent and the data of the adopted sources of that agent. In other words, as long as we do not have access to the utopian source g, the only "external world" that can make sense to us is the sum total of the data transmitted to us by the sources we have adopted. Indeed, in this sense Source Calculus entails en internalist conception of truth.

When two sources adopt another source as their final justification, whether directly or indirectly, we say that they have a common final justification, or that they are **co-justified** sources. Thus, for example, if a::b::d and c::d, then a, b, c, and d are all co-justified (given that d itself also adopts d, by the self-adoption axiom).

A source model constructed solely by co-justified sources will be called a **co-justified model**.

<u>Axiom 10: The axiom of external adoption (in brief, the adoption axiom)</u>
$\forall \varphi(\varphi \neq \tau) \exists \alpha(\alpha \neq i)(i{:}\varphi \leftrightarrow i/{:}\alpha{:}\varphi)$

That is,

$\forall \varphi(\varphi \neq \tau) \exists \alpha(\alpha \neq i)(i/{:}\alpha{:}\varphi)$

Every sentence that the speaking self accepts as true, and that is not an adoption sentence, is transmitted to him or her by some source that he or she has adopted, either fully or partially.

Note 1: This axiom involves only the speaking self and no other sources, since the speaking self in the Source Calculus is not a source in itself (in virtue of the axiom of the speaking self) but the subject to which the sources offer their data. The speaking self is like a judge, while the sources are like evidence. A judge is not evidence, nor does he present evidence, but only accepts it from witnesses and documents, determines how reliable it is, and uses it to draw conclusions.

Note 2: The restriction $\varphi \neq \tau$ ("which is not an adoption sentence") stems from the fact that an adoption sentence constitutes final justification, as mentioned above. While all other types of sentences require justification through identifying their sources, adoption sentences do not require such justification.

Note 3: Since every sentence transmitted by the speaking self has been transmitted to him by a source, the terminology of direct and indirect belief apply to him differently than to other sources. When the speaking self believes a datum by virtue of the fact that he has directly adopted a particular source (i/:a:p), this belief is called **direct belief** (on the part of the speaking self), but when the speaking self believes a datum by virtue of the fact that he has adopted a source that was adopted by another source (i/:a/:b:p), this belief is called **indirect belief** (on the part of the speaking self).

What happens when the sentence transmitted by the speaking self is *non liquet*? Here too we must assume that there is a source transmitting it:

$i{:}(\varphi \backslash \neg\varphi) \leftrightarrow \exists \alpha \, (i/{:}\alpha{:}(\varphi \backslash \neg\varphi))$

In such a situation we assume that there is a given, fixed source that "decides" between the two possibilities, but that the speaking self does not know what it is. We denote this type of unknown source by g'. We can thus state:

<u>The theorem of the undecidedness of the speaking self</u>
i:(φ\¬φ)↔i:(g':φ∨g':¬φ)

Sometimes the truth source can be **identified** – that is, a constant can be substituted for the variable α – in various ways. Let us illustrate this with a simple, perhaps trivial example:

Given the sentence i:p
∃α(α≠i)(i/:α:p) according to the adoption axiom
Now assume that we have the sentences
a:p
¬∃α(α≠a) α:p
This leads to the conclusion:
∴ i/:a:p

<u>The theorem on the internality of the justification of adoption:</u>
All adoptions by the speaking self are justified internally, whether directly or indirectly.
  Proof:
Assume that the speaking self adopts source a.

1. i/:a
   This adoption has a source, by virtue of the adoption axiom, together with line 1 and modus ponens.
2. i/a→∃α(α≠i)(α/:a)
   ∴ ∃α(α≠i)(α/:a)
3. The adoption of the source can be either direct or indirect.
   ∀α(α=a)i/a/:a:a...∨∃α(α≠a)i/:α:a
4. Direct adoption (the first disjunct) is always internally justified (by definition). In contrast, indirect adoption (the second disjunct) can be justified either internally (i.e. circularly) or externally.
   ∃α(α≠a)i/:α:a→(a/:α:a...∨∃β(β≠α)i/:β/:α/:a)
5. The argumentation begun in lines 3–4 about the relation between α and a also applies, *mutatis mutandis*, to the relation between α and β, and so on.
6. However, the chain of adoptions must come to an end (by virtue of the adoption axiom).
7. Therefore the end of the chain of adoptions has to be an internally justified one, whether ordinary circular adoption or self-adoption.

8. Therefore even an indirect source is internally justified, whether directly or indirectly.

QED

Note: This theorem is true for all adoptions by a source, not only by the speaking self.

If these data are a type of "thoughts" (in the broad, Cartesian sense of the word), then the sources, including the division of labor among them, are the factors that determine which thoughts are created. Thus the differences among thoughts stem from the differences among sources and the division of labor among them. When people are involved, this is the phenomenon we sometimes call differences in "ways of thinking" or "approaches", above and beyond the differences in the thoughts themselves.

Nihilistic absurdities

We have now concluded the presentation of the Source Calculus, including its basic terms: sources, the division of labor among them, data, databases and systems. We shall now present three claims that stem from this calculus, which we call "nihilistic absurdities", and which will serve us in later discussions.

Nihilistic absurdities are similar to paradoxes, although not in the narrow sense of the word. These are three claims stemming from the Source Calculus that lead us to skeptical conclusions and thus require a response. They are called "absurdities" because they are reached through *reductio ad absurdum* and seem to be more unacceptable than ordinary paradoxes; they are called "nihilistic" because they go farther than mere skeptical doubts. While skeptical doubts teach us that no belief is justifiable, the nihilistic absurdities teach us than any belief can be justifiable (and hence, not even one is *truly* justifiable).

The first nihilistic absurdity:

Any sentence that does not contradict the laws of logic and the adoption theorems can be justified.

Proof: Given a sentence r.

Given that r is not an adoption sentence: r≠t.

Assume that the speaking self transmits the sentence r (thus both believing it and claiming that it is true): i:r.

Thus there is a source for this belief that was adopted by i: $\exists\alpha(\alpha\neq i)(i/{:}\alpha{:}r)$, by the adoption axiom.

α was adopted by the speaking self either directly or indirectly. In either case, this adoption is internally justified (by the theorem of the internality of the justification of adoption).

But internal adoption does not require external justification (by definition).

Therefore any sentence that has any source whatsoever can be justified.

QED

Note: A system, as a logical phenomenon, is closed, and so a sentence transmitted in a given system cannot be refuted or verified by the senses or any other source, however intuitive it might be, unless it is one of the sources on which the system is based. The system's sources verify themselves, and so, within the limits of the system, any datum transmitted by its sources is verified and justified.

Thus, as we can see, any coherentist theory is ruled out (this is in addition to the fact that coherentism too seems to suffer from an infinite regress problem; Sosa 1974). When we take our epistemic system as an information system – one of many possible ones, without the mystification we attach to our ordinary rational system – we should understand that all systems, based on any sources, are equally justifiable. Thus, one can invent a system based on one source which can answer only one single question with yes or no, and, in the terms of Source Calculus, it will be acknowledged as a system just as much as the colossal rational system (a similar example is analyzed below, in Chapter Four). In a coherentist test, the former will certainly be seen as more coherent than the latter, and therefore will be better justified. But a very large number of such systems can be invented for any possible question, they can be invented in a manner ensuring that the desired data are provided, and they will be justified to the same degree under the internal justification of the coherentist test.

This leads us directly to the second nihilistic absurdity:

The speaking self's adoption of a given source is no more justifiable than the adoption of any other source.

Proof: Given two sources a and b.

Assume that the speaking self adopts one source a, so that i/:a.

Now this adoption is internally justified (by the theorem of the internality of the justification of adoption).

Now assume that the speaking self adopts the other system: b, so that i\:b.

This adoption too is internally justified (again, by the theorem of the internality of the justification of adoption).

Thus, the justification for the adoption of both sources is internal.

Therefore, the justification for the adoption of either source is no stronger or weaker than the justification for the adoption of the other one.

QED

Note: This absurdity is already present at the basis of the theorem of the internality of the justification of adoption, and is implicit in the first nihilistic absurdity.

The third nihilistic absurdity:
When the speaking self adopts two sources whose data are contradictory, he or she is not obligated to decide between them.

Proof: Assume that a and b transmit contradictory data:

a:p
b:¬p

Now assume that the speaking self adopts both of them: i/:(a,b).
According to the decision theorem (applied to the given sources)

(¬i: (p\¬p))↔(i/:(a,b):p∨i/:(a,b):¬p)

But it is already given that the speaking self does not decide to accept one of these data:

¬i/:(a,b):p
¬i/:(a,b):¬p

Therefore the consequent is negated.
As a result, the antecedent is refuted as well (by the truth table of the biconditional).

Therefore i:(p\¬p)

QED
Note: If this absurdity were the only one, it would not be an absurdity at all. After the two previous absurdities, however, it implies that the speaking self can find his way out of the first two absurdities by refraining from having any beliefs about the world, and this situation may be conceived to be just as acceptable as the adoption of a source that provides data for beliefs about the world. Put bluntly, this absurdity implies that a person who adopts a particular source has no advantage over one who chooses not to think at all.
The nihilistic absurdities stem directly from the Source Calculus. We must therefore try to see how it we can overcome them, if this is at all possible.

CHAPTER FOUR

Cultural Systems – The Pragmatist Line of Argumentation

The nihilistic and absurd character of the nihilistic absurdities

Even though the Source Calculus was constructed properly from a formal, axiomatic standpoint, it has led us to three nihilistic absurdities. The formalist line of argumentation in Source Theory has therefore culminated in these absurdities.

What can we learn from the nihilistic absurdities? If we abandon the technical, formal phrasing of the previous chapter, we can summarize them as follows:

The first nihilistic absurdity shows that almost any sentence can be justified, as soon as it has a source and there is no non-arbitrary way to refute it. Moreover, any particular sentence can be justified by one source and refuted by another.

The second nihilistic absurdity adds that even in the selection of the sources themselves there is no reason for choosing one source rather than another. Any adoption of a source is just as arbitrary as any other.

The third nihilistic absurdity states that it is even possible to avoid choosing a source at all. As mentioned above, given the first two absurdities, this is no less reasonable than attempting to discover the truth about the world through the use of any given sources.

To what can we compare this situation where it is impossible to decide among possible sources? We can say that it is like a computer whose programmers have fed it several different programs. If we choose one of them, we will obtain a certain output; if we choose another, we will get a different output. There is no way of deciding which program is "correct", since such a decision would require a third program (what we have called an external decision), the choice of which is no more "correct" than the choice of any other, including the two existing ones. This is, in fact, a new, radicalized version of the old skepticist challenge.

How to cite this book chapter:
Brown, B 2017 *Thoughts and Ways of Thinking: Source Theory and Its Applications.*
  Pp. 43–72. London: Ubiquity Press. DOI: https://doi.org/10.5334/bbh.e. License: CC-BY 4.0

At first it would seem that the conclusion to be drawn from this line of argumentation is radically relativistic, but it is actually even worse than that – it is nihilistic. If we were faced with only a few sources, and our line of argumentation led us to the conclusion that all of them were equally convincing, then we would be relativists. However, the number of possible truth sources is actually infinite, and for any given sentence it is theoretically possible to match a source by which it can be justified. Therefore, as long as there are no contradictions or other "internal" logical flaws in the speaking self's transmissions, any sentence can be justified.

To show the extreme absurdity of the nihilistic absurdities, I will present an example. Suppose that I build the following system, S(m99).

S(m99) is an isolated system whose only possible output is the weather in Tokyo. Its source model, m99, has only one sensory source, that of smell. This sense can pick only two odors: one of jasmine and one lavender; the other sources are the non-sensory basic cognitive tools and another source, d99, that transmits data as follows: When the agent who uses the system smells jasmine, it indicates that it is raining in Tokyo; while when that agent smells lavender, it indicates that it is now sunny in Tokyo. d99 is the most superior source in the model of S; all the non-sensory basic cognitive tools function only to process the inputs received from the sense of smell and transmit them to d99 to receive its output.

In terms of Source Calculus, S(m99) is a self-sufficient system. There is no way to examine its messages, as the only way to check the weather in Tokyo within that system is by the odor test. The system in itself is perfectly coherent, and any coherentist should approve of it.

Now suppose the agent can choose between S(m99) and the rational system, According to that system he should acquire data about the weather in Tokyo through seeing with his eyes or through secondary sources who transmit data of (reliable) sources who saw Tokyo with their eyes, or tertiary sources, and so on. This system, with its multiple sources, is susceptible to far more contradictions among its data than the simple S(m99). These contradictions, needless to say, may lead to severe incoherencies or uncertainties within it; but even if we solve these problems through hierarchy among the sources of the rational system or some other division of labor, the agent has no stronger justification for choosing the rational system than those that he has for choosing S(m99). Consequently, that agent has no stronger justification to choose the datum about the weather in Tokyo based on the odor in his room rather than the one based on the rational model. He will be equally justified in saying that in view of the impossibility of deciding between the sources, he will refrain altogether from believing anything about the weather in Tokyo.

In short, the nihilistic absurdities completely destroy any attempt to justify a system – *any* system. If we use a foundationalist line, it will lead us to a particularly strong version of the infinite regress problem; if we opt for a coherentist line, it will lead us to the conclusion of justifying almost any possible sentence.

It is obvious that this is an absurd case that we cannot accept. Nevertheless, it arises as the result of rigorous argumentation, as explained above. The question that must be asked, then, is how to avoid such absurd situations, since they imply that one cannot believe anything, and thus one cannot think. Yet we think and believe all the time, and so we have to present a new framework for our discussion that will explain how we manage to do so.

One way that we can do this is to try to dismiss the Source Calculus altogether as flawed; another way is to try to find some sophisticated reasoning within the Source Calculus that will free us of the absurdities without abandoning the calculus itself; yet a third way is to try to limit the adoption of sources by imposing acceptance conditions on them.

I do not believe that we should reject the Source Calculus. On the contrary, I believe that it is useful and can serve us in areas outside of philosophy as well. The calculus works perfectly well insofar as it describes the logic of sources, data and transmission; it fails only at the point where it comes to the nihilistic absurdities, all of which have to do with the unlimited freedom to adopt sources and source-models. Once this flaw is cured or ignored, the calculus can continue working successfully. As I suggested in Chapter One, a flaw in part of a theory should not necessarily impair all of it.

As far as the second alternative is concerned, if others succeed in finding such reasoning, well and good, but I have not been able to do so. This leaves us with the third alternative.

If we want to delineate a formalist line of argumentation that uses the terminology of the Source Calculus to limit the possibilities for adoption through the use of criteria for adoptable sources, then we must admit that we may have to give up our intellectual integrity. It is only too likely that such criteria will create filters that accord with our intuitions – which is merely a euphemism for our prejudices – so that the filter we end up with will "just happen" to produce the systems closest to our hearts, probably beginning with the rational system. This method is untrue to the formalism of logic, and to the most basic tenets of philosophical thinking. It is a foregone conclusion, an artificial way of using a pseudo-formal cover to achieve the results we want in accord with our character.

The obvious conclusion is that we should rather act sincerely, without a formal cover. This means that if we cannot find a way out through a formalist line of argumentation, we should try a pragmatist one instead.

From the formalist line of argumentation to the pragmatist one

What do I mean by a pragmatist line? As I have explained in the Introduction, I do not embrace pragmatism *in toto*, but see it as a plausible outlet for crises of good systems that are under a threat of sweeping dismissal because of a particular flaw that they entail.

The reason that Source Calculus leads to problematic consequences is that it is either too miserly or too generous, i.e., it either allows for no justification (in the foundationalist line) or for a sweeping justification for almost all possible data. The only way out of this entanglement is to find new criteria for the adoption of sources. These criteria cannot be based on purely formalist considerations, as those led us to the entanglement, but should also take the human context into account. In other words, they should not treat data as merely inputs and outputs of an information system, but also as thoughts; not treat source models not only as mechanisms to process data, but also as ways of thinking. This human point of view, which takes psychological and sociological aspects onto account, brings us close to the pragmatist approach.

In the pragmatist approach, a theory is true if it *works*. We will apply this criterion to sources and systems, and will say that sources can be adopted only if there is a system that is based on them and that system is *workable*. A system is workable when it has been shown to be one that can be employed by many people, in a variety of circumstances, for considerable periods of time, and is capable of providing them more or less coherent answers, which, if accepted as true, can serve them in practical life.

The pragmatist line of argumentation has two aspects: the psychological and the sociological. The sociological aspect is the one that deals with systems. While so far we have defined and studied the concept of systems in the logical setting of the Source Calculus, we will now deal with a limited set of systems which actually work among various groups of people, which we call **cultural systems**. The psychological aspect deals only with the connection of the speaking self (or any other subject) to the cultural system. While we have so far assumed that any person can activate any system, we will now investigate the mental conditions that make this possible in real life.

It should be noted that cultural systems are systems in a slightly different sense than logical systems. The differences – most of them in emphasis rather than substance – will be elaborated below. However, at this point I will mention a major difference: The database of a logical system is conveyed only as a set of data, while the database of a cultural system is conveyed as a set of data used by people. People not only "consume" the data offered to them by the system or transmit them to others but also develop them further. Indeed, this development is achieved through the use of the basic sources of the system, and thanks to that the logical sense of system is still pertinent, but the emphasis here is much more on the dynamic character of the system and the role of humans in its development. In the context of cultural systems we will therefore speak about the persons who receive the data of the system and develop it through the use of its basic sources as the **activators** (or **operators** or just **users**) of the system.

Cultural and personal systems; real and ideal systems

We demonstrated above that a system is defined by its sources. The sources we immediately think about are direct ones, which we may regard as the basic cognitive tools. These are functions F1–F8, elaborated above in Chapter One. They include (but are not exhausted by) the four traditional sources: "(1) external perception; (2) memory; (3) self-awareness (reflection, or inner consciousness); (4) reason". These sources will probably be part of every workable system, but they will not receive the same status in the model in every system.

If we wish to maintain the claim that a system is determined by its sources, then each person is a separate system. You (i.e. your mind, or the entirety of your sources and data) can be considered a system whose sources are your senses, your memory, your self-consciousness, your reason, etc., as well as a set of **witnesses** whom you consider reliable: your parents and teachers, some of your friends, some of the books you have read, some media that you trust, and the like. My sources, in contrast, include *my* senses, *my* memory, *my* self-consciousness, *my* reason, etc., as well as a series of witnesses whom *I* consider reliable: *my* parents and teachers, some of *my* friends, some of the books *I* have read, some media that *I* trust, and the like. Since you and I are not the same person, your senses are not my senses, your self-consciousness is not my self-consciousness, your memory is not my memory, your reason is not the same as mine (unless we adopt a strong rationalist approach), your parents are not the same as mine (unless we are siblings), your teachers are most likely not the same as mine, your friends are not my friends, we have not read exactly the same books and the media we trust are not exactly the same ones. According to the nihilistic absurdities, each of us can believe in our data with the same degree of justification. If we are divided on a particular issue, you cannot convince me that your data are true, and I cannot convince you that my data are true. In practice, however, all of us know that this is not the case in real life. In practice, we share a large number of the same sources, which we share with many others as well, and we can argue about many topics. Even if one of us does not always succeed in convincing the other, each of us can understand the other's internal logic. In other words, even if we do not share the same thoughts, we have very similar ways of thinking.

This last point obliges us to make two useful distinctions – one between **personal** (individual) and **cultural systems**; and the other between **real** and **ideal systems**. These distinctions refer to different planes of discussion. The first distinction involves the number of people who have adopted the system, while the second involves the internal stratification of the system itself.

I use the term **personal system** to denote the system used by a person (or any other creature that uses sources to think) which is constructed out of his or her personal truth sources. I use the term **cultural system** to denote a system used by a given community, society, or culture, which is constructed out of the collection of personal systems of the various people who share sources of the same **type**.

"Type" is not a vague word. Two people share the same type of sources when these sources have the same function, but nevertheless have different identities, usually because one belongs to a particular system-activator and the other to another.

Let's continue with the above example. Let us imagine a system based on a model m8, which is comprised of the basic cognitive tools, testimonies of data transmitted by those tools, and, for the limited sphere of social conventions (which I will address below), communities, all arranged in a certain division of labor. In this case, "the basic cognitive tools" are the functions F1–F8 of *any* person. However, I do not have access to your basic cognitive tools, just as you do not have access to mine. When you tell me "I see a tree", my datum is your testimony about the seeing of a tree, not a direct sight of the tree. However, you would be in the same position if I said "I see a tree". I may trust your testimony as reliable under certain conditions (such as being verifiable by others), but you would apply the same conditions, dictated by m8, to my testimony. In such a case, we might well agree that model m8 is a common one: as a system, it accepts your testimony, mine and anybody else's, not as individual persons but as members of the community of the adopters of m8. We can thus define the community as a source in itself. The **community** of the adopters of a model – whom, when dealing with a larger culture, we will call the **cultural community** – will be marked by the letter h, followed by the name of the model in brackets. In principle, the definition of that community should be:

$h(\mu) =def \{\alpha\}| \alpha::\mu$

Which means that

$\alpha::\mu \equiv a \in h(\mu)$

However, for our purposes we will not be so strict as to demand the membership of all the community, and will often make do with a vast majority.

We should note that h(m):p does not imply m:p. For even if all the agents who fully adopted m agree on a certain datum, this does not mean that this datum was transmitted by the sources of m. As long as the adoption is not exclusive, it might well be the case that all of these agents adopted other sources (common or not), and that p was transmitted by one or more of those other sources.

Communities can serve as witnesses, and in that they are not much different from other witnesses; but I mentioned that they may have other roles, as sources for social convention, in the senses attached to this term by Marmor (2005), partly following Lewis (1969), I will refer mostly to conventional practices and languages. Both of these scholars characterize conventions as "arbitrary", meaning that they cannot be rationally justified any more than their opposites. In the terminology of Source Theory we can explicate this "arbitrariness" as a situation in which the community serves not only as a secondary (i.e. mediating) source for other sources (such as reason), but as a final source. If a community transmits, often without any explicit declarations, that a certain behavior is a common practice in it, then it is so not because the testimony is veracious but because the very transmission of such a datum by the community makes it true (in a way, it resembles a performative utterance); and if a community of the speakers of a certain language transmits, again usually without any explicit declarations, that a given word or expression has such-and-such meaning in that language, then this is its meaning in that language (I will elaborate on this issue in Chapter Seven).

Let us continue with the system S(m8), which is founded on the basic cognitive tools, testimonies of agents who share the same model, and, for limited purposes, communities. If we, the adopters of the S(m8) sources, share the same sources, we ought to share the same data as well. Why, then, do we differ on so many issues? The answer to this question makes use of the second of our two distinctions. On the **ideal** level, we think within a system whose sources are our basic cognitive tools, with an intricate division of labor. We all know, however, that in practice, on the **real** level, this is not the case. Sometimes we do not make a full use of the data that the sources of our system transmit to us, and sometimes we do make use of data that are transmitted to us by sources that are not a part of the model we adopted. We therefore have to distinguish between the speaker's **ideal system** – the one he intends or presumes to use – and his **real system**, i.e. the one he uses in practice.

One of the reasons for the gap between the two types of system is that we often do not recognize these divergences and attribute the sources transmitted by alien sources to sources from within the model. This phenomenon will be called **misidentification of the source**. One example of this fallacy is the common phenomenon known as "wishful thinking". In that case, we believe that desired datum is transmitted to us by the basic cognitive tools, while in fact it is transmitted to us by our imagination, which is nourished by our will.

Let us consider the case of a contradiction between a general adoption and a particular transmission. We have three sentences:

(1) a::m8
(2) m8: p
(3) a: ¬p

a transmits a contradiction, and that is permissible in the Source Calculus, as long as a is not i. To be sure, we will judge it as a flaw. Therefore, i will not be able to fully adopt a ("fully" in the sense of subordinate only to logic), and will determine a division of labor that will reject one of the three sentences. From a logical point of view, any one of the three can be chosen for rejection.

This is not so on the socio-cultural level. Here the general adoption seems to take priority. Suppose for a moment that a is a real person. Even though from a logical point of view a cannot keep all the three sentences at the same time, he actually does accept all of them, as many people do in real life. Now suppose we pointed out to a the contradiction between the three. We may assume that in that case we would discover that the significance of (1) transcends its mere logical value: It makes a a part of the community of the adopters of m8. This is even more compelling when m8 is a model on which a whole culture is based. The adoption of m8 expresses the speakers' view that the ideal system is the one based on the general adoption, and the real system that he uses is flawed.

In this case, the gap between the ideal and the real systems overlaps the gap between the cultural and the personal systems. But the same could be true if we put h(m8) instead of a. Indeed, the entire community of the adopters of certain source models do not always, for various reasons, actually follow the models they presume to accept. In other words, there can be a gap between the real system and the ideal system within one cultural system. From a formalist point of view, we can take the real and the ideal systems as two equally full-fledged systems, but from a sociological point of view (which is relevant to the pragmatist line of argumentation) the sharing of the ideal system is what unites the various agents and turns them into a community. Even if their real systems greatly differ from one another, their "official" allegiance to a single ideal system, and their basic willingness to correct their real systems to fit it, serve as a common denominator. The ideal system thus has a symbolic value within the real system, and joins together with other elements of that system which together constitute its **culture** or, when developed and preserved through time, its **tradition**.

The concept of tradition has attracted much scholarly attention in social scientific contexts, especially since the publication of Edward Shils's influential book on the topic (Shils 1980) and the critical response leveled against it by Eric Hobsbawm (Hobsbawm 1983) and others (for example: Heelas 1996). In this context, however, I use the term in a particular sense that relates to Source Theory, tracing the tradition back to its fundamental, epistemic roots.

There are numerous cultures and traditions in the world. In this book I will discuss mainly two: the Western Rational Tradition (**WRS**), and the Monotheist Religious System (**MRS**).

WRS is basically the same as m8 as described above, namely, founded on the basic cognitive tools, testimonies of data transmitted by those tools and, for particular limited purposes, a set of communities, all arranged in a certain division of labor. **MRS** is based on the same sources as WRS, but also on the testimonies of the Holy Scriptures. Indeed, even though the three major monotheist religions differ on the question which Scriptures these are, the source-theoretical statuses of these texts within their system models, as well as the internal disputes about their statuses, are basically very similar. (I must nevertheless add, for the sake of transparency, that the system I have in mind most of the time is that of Judaism, which I know more intimately than Christianity or Islam). We will return to these systems at length in some of the discussions below.

Therefore, when we speak about $h(\mu)$, the community of the adopters of μ, we are not speaking about those who actually accept as true only the data transmitted by μ, but rather those who take μ as their ideal system.

This has important implications. First, all the real systems of a given cultural community are similar to one another, even though they are not identical. Second, but no less important, members of the same cultural community can at least argue with one another and try to persuade one another about various issues, which is not necessarily the case for members of different cultural communities.

We can find a gap between the real system and the ideal one in the personal sphere as well. Take, for instance, a person who consciously adopts sources that are slightly different from those of the cultural system in which he lives, but subconsciously still accepts data from that system. This is an example of "misidentification of the source", and, in practice, opens a gap between the person's ideal system and his real one. Here the gap is not sociological (unless the ideal system is that of a whole community, as described above) but rather psychological.

I would like to expand briefly on this last point. A transmission event can be looked at from either the epistemological or the psychological viewpoint (the latter being relevant to the pragmatist line of argumentation). The epistemological viewpoint looks at the datum as cognitive material "claiming" to be true and therefore considering itself an object for belief. In contrast, the psychological viewpoint looks at the transmission as an event occurring in time and sometimes even in space, under particular external and mental circumstances. One of the psychological aspects is the question of whether the subject is aware of the source that has transmitted the datum to him. To be sure, the speaking self cannot always identify this source, whether because he failed to make note of it at the time when the transmission occurred, or because he forgot it afterwards even though he did identify it at the time of transmission. Nevertheless, we must bear in mind that the identification of a source is also a datum, generally derived through introspection, and so the epistemological discussion is relevant for it as well. And even more importantly, it has far-reaching epistemic implications, especially when the misidentification of the source replaces a source that has been adopted by the speaking self (on the ideal plane) by a source that has not been so adopted. Such misidentification is, as mentioned, one of the main reasons for the gap between an individual's and even a society's ideal and real systems.

This requires a new understanding of the concept of truth. We saw above that truth in Source Theory depends on the source – that is, it is limited to the given system. Any logic-bound system can serve as a criterion for truth, which is what leads to the nihilistic absurdities. In a psychosocial system, however, where ideal systems are distinguished from real ones, the truth of a datum is tested by its fit with an ideal rather than a real system.

On the one hand, there are **real systems** used by actual individuals or societies, in which undesirable sources and limitations are involved in the activation of desirable sources. On the other hand, there are **ideal systems**, which are free of these defects – systems of the logical sort described in the previous chapter. We can imagine such a system by once again using the metaphor of the computer. We imagine a sophisticated computer that knows how to filter the data received from the basic sources of the system, according to the proper division of labor prescribed by the source model of that system, and receives *all* the relevant data from those sources. This is a system in which the sources are activated purely and fully, so its data are unambiguous and absolute by the criteria of that system. We all know that such a system is impossible in practice, especially since our thinking in almost all areas of life occurs without careful attention to sources and the division of labor among them. This creates a gap between the various individuals who belong to the same system in principle. As mentioned, these differences are often described in common parlance as differences in ways of thinking, which lead to differences in the content of thoughts about the world.

We are therefore trying to attain a more exact understanding of the notion of **defeasibility**, which is becoming more and more prominent in modern logic, in particular in nonmonotonic logics. This concept is an outgrowth of the gap between real and ideal systems. Ideal systems work in a utopian situation in which all data included in a system are justified by all the system's model, which on its part operates the system's division of labor and makes use of all the data transmitted by the sources. This is not the case in real systems, either because the sources do not transmit all their data at once, or because the system's activators do not always act according to the rules of ideal systems. The first problem should be called **transmission failure**, while the second might be called **operation failure**. In either case, ordinary systems generally have mechanisms for fixing the problems, which is always done by adding more data – whether new data transmitted by the sources some time later regarding the essential data in question or new data about the way the sources acted in the past (that is, reflective data), which can help us understand the operation failure. In Source Theory terms, we can say that the repair process occurs when new data from sources adopted by the system (or data that seem to be transmitted by such sources) are added, whether they pertain to the issue under discussion or to a faulty use of such sources in the past, from the viewpoint of the requirements of an ideal system. The real system aspires to operate as an ideal system, and the constant repairs that are supposed to advance it toward this goal make it defeasible.

The difference between logical systems and (real) cultural systems

What is the difference between the two types of systems? The ideal system of a community is often very close to a logical system, while real systems are quite different from logical ones. First of all, a real cultural system is a dynamic entity, as opposed to a logical system, which is essentially a-temporal. The dynamism of a real system may be manifested in several aspects, three of which are discussed here: These are the system's **defeasibility, openness** and **detachability**. We will present some examples each of these aspects, which are not meant to be historically exact, but only to illustrate the ideas.

Defeasibility. One of the manifestations of the dynamism of a system is its defeasibility, but this feature can also be part of a logical system, since modern logic has developed a formalism for this phenomenon.

A good example of this process is the development of modern science, which is a subsystem of WRS. The process of self-correction in science stems from the fact that a real scientific system cannot operate according to the requirements of the ideal WRS. Data are received by human beings (that is, by individual system users), who do not have all the relevant data at any given time (due to transmission failures) and sometimes make mistakes in drawing conclusions from the existing data, as they do not always draw their conclusions according to the requirements of the consistency mechanisms of ideal systems (operation failures). But since this system is defeasible, adding new data enables it to correct itself, and it has indeed done so in the historical process of scientific development, even though this process itself is not free of errors.

Openness. Logical systems are basically closed ones. In contrast, real cultural systems are open ones, with windows to the outside. They are influenced by other systems, due to social, cultural or political circumstances. A cultural system (i.e., its activators) may accept *data* from the outside, without adopting the sources that transmitted them, and anchor them in its own sources, while at other times it opens itself up to *sources* that are not part of its ideal system. Its division of labor may change as a result of the penetration of external sources and data.

Now let us consider these two possible situations from the logical point of view. When a subject transmits data transmitted by a source other than its basic sources we would say that, from the pure logical perspective, he actually adopted that alien source without being aware of that adoption. If he was not aware of that source, as often happens, this should be categorized as misidentification of a source. This is even more true if the subject attributed these data to one or more of his basic sources. Basically, all of this is also true in the psychosocial perspective, but with a small difference: The system activator may find a way to anchor the "imported" data in one of the system's basic sources and thus turn them into authentic data of the system. Of course, sometimes this anchoring is artificial and wrong, and then the true source remains the outside source, but sometimes the outside source is only a stimulus that pushes the activator to find a source for a data that could really have been transmitted by the internal sources of the system, and thus bring its transmission from the potential to the actual.

And what about the case of adding a new source to the system? From the pure logical perspective, this would definitely mean creating a new system and discarding the previous one. Systems are defined by their sources, and different sources create a different system. From the psychosocial perspective, however, we recognize from the outset that there is a gap between the ideal system and the real system, and the infiltration of new sources can just as well be a part of this gap. Indeed, from a logical point of view, the ideal and the real systems are two different systems, but from the psychosocial perspective, we cannot ignore the fact that the activators of the real system see the ideal system as their desired objective and wish to bring the real system as close as possible to that objective. Sometimes, though, the infiltration of the new source becomes so prominent that it actually reshapes the whole character of the system. Then we can certainly expect that the change will not stop with the real system, but will also reach the ideal system. In such a case, we will indeed be able to say that the system is altogether a different one, from the psychosocial perspective as well.

There are countless examples of these phenomena, but a particularly radical example is the cultural syncretism that occurred in broad areas of the Roman Empire in its later stages. This syncretism was created in a process by which the dominant, Hellenistic-Roman culture was influenced by the nations conquered by the empire, particularly those to the east. The cultural system that was created in that period was a new one that included not only new data, but also sources that were different from those on which the absorbing culture has been based. These infiltrations certainly changed the real cultural system of the Empire. Did they change its ideal system as well? We cannot tell for sure, and we must leave the question for historians to answer.

Detachability. Sometimes a particular system starts out as a subsystem of a larger one, but after a while it becomes an independent system. This situation should be called the detachment of the system. It often occurs when the activators of the subsystem become aware that the differences between their real system and that of other members of the larger community are too great, or that the differences are not only in their real systems but also in their ideal systems. However, in some cases the activators of the new system are not aware of the detachment, or otherwise deny it, and keep presenting it as a part of the mother system. We can describe it as follows: Suppose we have a system $S(m22)$ whose basic model is $m22$. Now b comes along and says that she adopts $m22$, and that $m22$ transmits, among other data, a set of data P. In this case b believes that P in virtue of $m22$. Now suppose that a adds new data to the system (as part of its defeasibility), and these data are in contradiction with P, or that other activators of $S(m22)$ say that $m22$ does not transmit P. In this case, b may wish to establish

P as a system in and of itself, which we will call S(b), but keep presenting it as part of S(m22), namely, transmitting that S(b)⊆S(m22).

There are several examples of this sort of process. Let us take Frazer's theory about the development of magic, religion and science as a basis for our discussion (without taking a stand regarding its actual veracity). Roughly, according to this theory, in the beginning there was magic. Magic was a pseudo-science, based on a wrong conception of the laws of nature but embracing the essential naturalist idea that the world acts in some fixed physical order. When the wrong conceptions failed, and people were unsuccessful in mastering the world through them, they developed the conception of "superior powers", and hence of deities and religions. In other words, magic was "rational" in the sense of being founded on the basic cognitive tools, but since it failed to work – according to the tests of these sources themselves– it was discarded (a rational move in itself) and people developed the concept of a deity. Deities, however, were not bound to the natural order (Frazer, 1951, Volume 1, Chapter 4). If we continue Frazer's story, we can add that acquiring data about and from these supernatural entities required supernatural capacities (prophecy), and these data were thus transmitted by a supernatural source. The adoption of that source changed the mother system, which from now on was no longer founded on the basic cognitive tools alone, and eventually the new system had to be detached from the old one. The culmination of this process was the medieval recognition of religion's irrational character, embodied in expressions like "*credo quia absurdum est*".

Another example is late Communist thought. The original Marxist theory was considered a subsystem of WRS, and its sources were the basic cognitive tools. However, when the reality perceived by these cognitive tools contradicted the theory, it started using explanations that rejected reality. The theory's basic texts became canons, and Communist scholars claimed that it was not the Marxist theorists who were wrong, but rather reality that needed to be re-explained. Some theorists consider this a process in which Marxism was turned into a religion, but we can use the terminology of Source Theory to describe the process as the detachment of a subsystem from the main system so as to become independent. This process, in contrast to the previous one, was never acknowledged by its bearers, and Communist theoreticians kept seeing their doctrine as perfectly rational and strove to re-explain the reality conceived by the basic cognitive tools as a realization of it.

In fact, religion was not alien to that denial, either. In the Middle Ages, a school of religious rationalism developed, claiming that not only does revelation not contradict reason, but it can even be proven within a rational system. Although these two developments were quite different, we can learn something from both of them. Often, when a new system is detached from the original one, it is still considered as belonging to the original system (in the case of religious rationalism, only a few philosophers were involved, but in the case of late Communism all of them were). This is evidence that people who claim to continue to belong to the old system while being active in the new one continue to consider the original system to be their ideal one, even though their real system has become greatly distanced from it. From this viewpoint, the religious rationalists and the late Communists continued to be part of the same community – the community of the adopters of the basic cognitive tools – since, at least on the surface, they were still able to use purportedly rational means in their arguments.

A third example is the detachment of Christianity from Judaism. Jesus and his Disciples undoubtedly lived within the Jewish religious system. One of their truth sources was the Jewish Bible, and other sources were, at least in some compartmentalized manner, some of the interpretive texts that are called the "Oral Torah" (which had not yet been written down at that time), that later served as the basis for the Talmud. Early Christianity considered itself a subsystem of this Jewish system. Gradually, under the active influence of Paul, the Christian subsystem detached itself from Judaism and became an independent system. Here we see a similar tendency to that discussed in the previous examples: Christian theologians throughout the centuries have tried to show that the Jewish Bible predicts Jesus's advent and even "authorizes" him to spread his new teachings. In parallel, the Rabbinic stream of Judaism searched the Jewish Bible (primarily the Five Books of Moses) for sources that authorized the Oral Torah scholars to re-interpret the Bible and even to issue new commandments. From this standpoint, both Christianity and Judaism see themselves as belonging to the same ideal system. Indeed, during the centuries in which there were religious debates between Jews and Christians, they centered mainly on the question of which interpretation of the Jewish Bible is the correct one. But then do Judaism and Christianity really belong to the same cultural community? It is hard to say that they do, even on the ideal level; although it is accepted nowadays to speak about the "Judeo-Christian tradition", it seems that once the Jews and the Christians each adopted their own canonical texts – the Jews adopting the Talmudic literature and the Christians the New Testament – the two systems became totally detached from each other, even on the level of their ideal systems, and the Jewish Bible was no longer the primary source for either of them. This is the case because each system determines the correct interpretation of the Jewish Bible according to its new truth sources, which the Bible itself is supposed to have authorized. This has created a situation in which the two systems have been constructed on different types of indirect adoption. In both systems, the primary source is the revealed Word of God (some see it as a particular form of "testimony"; Wahlberg 2014), and the secondary source, which transmits the Word of God, is the Jewish Bible, but each of them has a different tertiary source that transmits the content of this Bible. In Judaism this is the Talmud and the literature that has been developed around it, while in Christianity this is the New Testament and the literature that has developed around it. The canonization of the sacred texts has therefore become the crucial point of departure between the two traditions (for a philosophical analysis of canonization in terms of sources – of authority as well as knowledge – see Halbertal 1997, Chapter 1). It would thus seem that the two systems are detached even on the ideal plane, although this is not totally certain.

If we accept the argument that Judaism and Christianity have become detached systems even on the ideal level, what can we say about the relation between the Catholic and Protestant versions of Christianity? Catholicism has developed a system in which there are a number of sources, in addition to the New Testament, that mediate between God, the primary source, and the individual believer: the Church, the Church fathers, the popes, and the ecclesiastical institutions. Protestantism has rejected these intermediate sources, claiming that only the Bible itself – including the Old and the New Testaments – is the source of truth. Does this turn the two forms of Christianity into distinct systems, even on the ideal plane?

At this point a fourth-degree source is added to the controversy. In cases of this sort we can say that the greater the ordinality of the mediating source, the closer the systems are, on an essential plane. Even in this case, however, I believe that historical reality has turned the Catholic and the Protestant traditions into two separate cultural systems, although it seems that on the level of their ideal system they share the same aspiration to achieve the truth through the same sources. Therefore, it seems preferable to see them as opposing subsystems of the same inclusive system, although this too is not totally certain.

Islam presents us with a more complicated challenge. Mohammed declared that his revelation was a continuation of those of Moses and Jesus, but he claimed that the holy scriptures of those revelations were forged by the Jews at later times and that the original version, which had been lost, was revealed to him anew by the angel Gabriel. This seems at first glance to be an attempt to rely on the same ideal system, but in this case it is quite clear that the systems do not actually have much in common, since the ideal source for both Jews and Christians is the Bible, while the Muslims reject this text. If we consider a system's sources to be existing objects that transmit data, then two different texts cannot be seen as different forms of the same source, even if both of them purport to be transmitting the primary source that they have in common – namely, the Word of God as transmitted in a revelation. (One could also discuss the question of whether the God of these systems is the same God, but we will leave this for another occasion.) While Christianity and Judaism are divided on the level of their tertiary source, both of them disagree with Islam on the level of their secondary source. Thus the detachment between them and Islam is more basic than that between the two of them. This is noteworthy because the usual view (from the standpoint of the essential articles of faith and the major commandments) considers Judaism to be more similar to Islam than to

Christianity. While this is indeed true on the level of the data of the cultural systems of Judaism and Islam, it is not true on the level of the sources, which is what determines the identity of a system.

The individual's connection with the system: availability and convertibility

All the aspects discussed in the previous section involve dynamic processes within and among systems, but an equally important issue is the individual's psychological **connection** (or **attachment**) to the system. When we discuss logical systems, we have no expectation that people using a system will have any sort of psychological connection with it. The computer metaphor is useful here: The sources on which the systems are based are impersonal, receiving input and emitting output. Even the speaking self, which is the subject using the system, is nothing but an abstract entity without a history or personal traits, who can change and can actually be just about anyone. In contrast, people's connection with their cultural system is a psychological and social phenomenon involving the people and their culture, the participants in the system under discussion. A person who has a psychological connection to a system not only activates its sources in the technical manner, but also "feels at home" with its data, understands its nuances and implications, and can internalize it as a "way of thinking". In fact, there are different degrees of connection, some stronger and some weaker, which cannot be precisely quantified (although I suggest a way of doing so in the next section). At any rate, people's connection with their system, whether personal or cultural, is an intimate linkage that goes beyond the mere operation of the system. This linkage ensures the **availability** of the system to the adopter, in the sense I will analyze below (note: that availability should not be confused with accessibility, in the sense attached to it in contemporary epistemology).

This point is very important in light of the second nihilistic absurdity, which states that the adoption of any source is arbitrary. If this is the case, then it would seem that any individual could adopt any source she pleases and change it whenever she wants. But in practice this is not the case. First, most people grow up within a particular system, including its basic sources, and only rarely does a person replace it with another one. Second, when people adopt a new model of sources, they also need a long psychological process to acquire the ability to use it, and in general they are not aware of the identity of their sources or the division of labor among them. Therefore it would be difficult for them to make use of a different system, as this requires understanding another culture. Even when a person does decide to replace her original system with a new one, as in the case of religious or secular conversion, she may very often find it difficult to master the newly adopted sources of that system.

The first change of systems we all experience occurs during childhood. When children begin to learn about the world, their main sources are their senses and their parents, where the latter are actually secondary sources transmitted to the child by her senses. However, children gradually detach themselves from these sources and adopt the basic sources of the cultural system in which they live. Although parents, like other reliable witnesses, may continue to serve as sources within the new system, they lose their priority in the hierarchy in favor of other sources, such as the child's own reason, teachers, books and other media. This process is part of children's socialization into their cultural community. Nevertheless, this is not a real change of systems, since both the children and the parents belong to the same cultural community, and thus share the same ideal system. Moreover, normal parents train their children to disconnect themselves from their immature system and adopt the sources of the cultural system for themselves.

This learning process, like others, takes place backwards from a philosophical point of view. Children first receive data as content, and only later become more or less aware of their sources and learn to distinguish among them. This process resembles the acquisition of language: The child first learns to speak, and only later, when he studies grammar, does he become aware of the regularities in language. Similarly, in the context of Source Theory, only people who have studied philosophy or the cognitive sciences are likely to achieve the final stage, in which they perceive these sources as bases of a general system, and even become aware of the division of labor among them within this system. Accordingly, the process of adopting sources also occurs backwards. First the subject believes the data, and only afterwards does she justify her belief by referring to its sources. To be precise, first she accepts the data from the mediating sources, and then she either anchors the same data in the mediated sources, the basic sources of the system, or discards them as contradictory to those sources. When she accepts these data, at least some of them have already been established in her cultural community in the form of tradition. Thus, systems are not "chosen" out of free will, and certainly not in a *tabula rasa* condition. When a person adopts the basic sources of a system consciously, this occurs only after she has already adopted them unconsciously, and, more importantly, after she has already developed a psychological connection to the system.

As mentioned, the change of systems that occurs when children grow up is not a true change, since it merely replaces one real system with another belonging to the same ideal system. However, some people actually do replace their system with a totally different one. *Prima facie*, such a conversion ought to be impossible. When a person begins to criticize his existing system, he still thinks within this very system; and as each system contains a self-adoption axiom with which it confirms its own data, how can anyone manage to escape the internal viewpoint of the system in which he thinks? This question becomes even more interesting when entire cultures disappear as the result of system conversion. How, for example, did millions of people leave the pagan system of the Roman Empire and adopt the sources of the Christian system instead? Nevertheless, we will keep the focus on the individual level, since the really big cultural transformations are made up of a large number of individual ones.

It would seem that people begin to criticize the system they were brought up in when they become aware of the gaps between the ideal and the real system. But since the average person cannot distinguish between the two levels of their cultural system, they see this gap as a problem with the system as a whole, and therefore look for another system to replace it with. Sometimes the crisis does indeed stem from an internal fallacy that lies in the very basis of the ideal system, such as a contradiction between some of its elements. Although it is hard to imagine that anyone has ever abandoned WRS because of the paradoxes that were discovered in modern mathematics or the uncertainty principle in physics, I think it is quite likely that these problems have contributed to the general public impression that the data of this system are not as absolute as they had seemed before, thus making it easier for people to abandon it. Whether or not this is the case, people who replace their system with another one begin the process with data coming from the original system. There simply is no other system they can use, since they have only the data of this system, and it is the one in which they think. For example, if Western youth "search for the truth" in India and convert to Buddhism, they begin their search with ideas they acquired in WRS, such as relativism, the aspiration for "spirituality" as a form of self-realization, openness to the other, and the romanticization of the Orient – all parts of WRS and its internal contradictions.

Often a person who has converted from one system to another tries to explain – that is, justify – his act, and he may even try to convince his interlocutor to follow in his footsteps. At first glance, this request is pointless, since we have seen that the adoption of a system is an arbitrary act that cannot be justified logically. In practice, however, we find that people who have undergone a conversion do indeed try to explain their actions. Here there are a number of possibilities. One is that the person explains his actions in purely subjective, personal terms; however, such an explanation is causal and not justificatory. A second possibility is that the person explains his actions in terms of the system he has abandoned, but this is obviously illogical, since this system includes the self-adoption axiom, which denies any justification for conversion. A third possibility is that the person justifies his conversion with data that are shared by both the system he has abandoned and the new one whose sources he has adopted. In general, data of this sort do indeed exist. Sometimes these data have been transmitted by different sources that attain a coincidental accord, and sometimes by sources common to the two systems. Moreover, sometimes a commonality of this sort (whether of the data or of the sources) stems from the influence of one of the systems on the other. In any case, the commonality of the data is a reasonable basis for a justification of this sort. Nevertheless, the commonality of the data is coincidental. As we have seen, the essential identity of the system, and therefore its essential degree of closeness to other systems, is determined by the degree of commonality of the sources rather than that of the data. An attempt at persuasion which is based on data and ignores the sources on which the different systems are constructed cannot succeed without making the mistake of equating the sources, whether or not this is done intentionally.

Another important point is that almost all the cultural systems in existence today are basically quite similar to one another. All of them seem to give a major role to the basic cognitive tools (the senses, introspection, abstraction, reason, the understanding and the like) as their fundamental sources of truth. The division of labor among them is often different, but at times even that is quite similar. This commonality, which might seem strange if we consider the great differences and disputes among the various systems, undoubtedly stems from the fact that these are, after all, the basic human cognitive tools, so we could expect that many human beings would tend to use all of them.

The main difference among the systems is generally their other sources, especially of the type known as testimony. There are some systems that rely on a particular text and its accepted commentators, while others rely on a different text and/or different commentators, and yet others do not rely on texts at all but only on other people. Since such testimony is a mediating source, as explained above, it too is received through the basic cognitive tools (this, however, does not give the basic cognitive tools any supremacy over the witnesses themselves, because the *justification* of the former is not prior to that of the latter, as demonstrated in Chapter Three). An imaginary system of the sort I described above – like the one that finds out about the weather in Tokyo by assessing the odors I detect where I live – does not exist, although there are indeed systems with magical elements that come somewhat close to it. To be sure, experience shows that people usually convert to a system that is similar to their original one. It would be extremely unlikely to find a person in our times who had, for example, converted from WRS to a magical pagan system of the sort that can still be found among some African native tribes or a person who converted from Jewish or Christian faith to that of the Australian aboriginals. Indeed, there have been quite a few Western anthropologists who tried to get inside the heads of the members of these cultures, but this was not because they wanted to personally adopt these cultures' sources, but only to be able to describe them properly for the purposes of their research, which was done with the tools of WRS. The lack of conversions of this sort does not stem only from the psychological difficulty they would pose, but also from the logical difficulty due to the great gap between the cultures in the identity of their sources and the division of labor among them. The essential logical difficulty is the same, however, even when the cultures involved are apparently much closer, and only the large amount of common data, together with the fallacy of equating the sources, enables the convert to ignore the distance involved in the transition from one system to another.

Moreover, any system that will ever be created has its source in human beings. I am not speaking only about existing systems, but also about possible ones, if they are to be workable. If we consider, for example, the possibility that I will develop an imaginary system in which my kitchen table tells me everything I need to know about the world, I am the one who will develop it and I am the one who will receive its data, using my basic cognitive tools. But even if I develop a system that is closer to a pure logical one, whose data are provided by computers and received by computers, and for which computers are the "speaking selves", it will still be a human being who builds the computers and programs their software, since the system represents a way of thinking, which is created (whether intentionally or not) by people who think with that system. And even if they are searching for alternatives to the way they think, they construct these alternatives as changes in the way they think. This shows that there cannot be a system that is entirely detached from human beings or from the culture in which it is constructed and the people who feel a psychological attachment to it.

The psychological connection between a person and a system is not necessarily exclusive. One can have such a connection to two systems, and perhaps even three or more. Sometimes this stems from changes in an individual's life. We can imagine a person who grew up in a traditional Muslim society and immigrated to a Western country, where he discovered Western culture and adopted it without detaching himself from his original one. We can imagine more than this. Within Western culture itself there are quite a few cultural enclaves of minority groups that could not or would not assimilate within the majority culture. These minorities are undoubtedly aware of the majority culture; they take part in it and are influenced by it to one degree or another. Nevertheless, most people in these groups do not cross the line by converting to the majority culture, but continue to maintain their connection with the minority's cultural system. Such people are capable of conversing with members of the majority culture and carrying on a dialogue in the terms of that cultural system. These people are thus using two systems, both of which they adopt with some degree of psychological attachment. This situation can clearly lead to internal conflicts, which I discuss below.

As mentioned, people can have different degrees of psychological attachment to their systems, which cannot be precisely quantified. This is important when a person's connection to two or more systems is involved. The person can have a weaker attachment to one system and a stronger attachment to the other one. Does this difference affect her ability to utilize the two systems? Since we have stated that it is the psychological attachment that makes it possible to use a system, the answer to this question must be affirmative. The difference, however, is only one of degree. In general, the determining criterion is the strength of the attachment. If we assume that there is a minimum degree of attachment required to use a system, then the determining factor is whether the individual's attachment is at or above this minimum. If the person's attachment is above the minimum in both systems, then she can, in principle, use both of them with a reasonable degree of proficiency.

While the greatest degree of psychological attachment is complete psychological adoption of a system, the lowest degree is unrealized availability. A cultural system is available to anyone in close proximity to it (geographically or sometimes even culturally), and this availability is considered unrealized if this person does not adopt the sources of the system at all or adopts them in a partial way that emits only a very limited set of its data. Although such people have not adopted the sources that are available to them, they are nevertheless aware of them and are therefore more able to adopt them than they are able to adopt the sources of some distant cultural system. Moreover, even within their own culture, if people adopt the sources of a close culture, they are considered to have undergone a conversion of some sort, while if they adopt the sources of a very distant system (for example, if people in contemporary Western culture adopt the sources of a pagan system) they are considered mentally ill (indeed, some mental illnesses are nothing but individual systems that are defined as illnesses because they are so distant from the general cultural system). Psychologically, the availability of a system makes it easier to convert to that system than to an alien one to which the individual does not have any psychological connection whatsoever. This is why such a weak connection nevertheless deserves to be considered a type of psychological connection, albeit of the lowest degree.

The individual's connection with the data: technical belief and vivid belief

People's psychological connection to a system is not restricted to their attitude towards the sources of the system or the system as a whole, but also includes their attitude towards particular data within the system. In the epistemic realm, this is the phenomenon of **belief** in data.

A person believes the data that are transmitted to him by sources he has adopted. However, he may have different types of psychological attitudes to different data. There are some data that he believes only because they have been justified in virtue of having been transmitted by one or some of the system's sources, while there are others that he believes almost instinctively. The data of the first sort are acquired through the (more or less) conscious operation of the system sources, while the data of the second sort are perceived as inherent within the subject, and thus as obviously true. Thus various degrees of **belief strength** are involved here. The first type of psychological attitude to data will be called **technical belief**, while the second type will be called **vivid belief**. To be sure, this is not a sharp dichotomy, since the distinction is unquantifiable and there is a whole range of intermediate degrees of belief between the two poles.

Consider an example from WRS. People believe in what *they* have seen themselves, and they believe *their* parents' reports about what *they* have seen. It is clear, however, that the strength of their belief in the former type of data is stronger than that of their belief in the latter type. In such a case, the difference in strength can be attributed to the hierarchy of truth sources in the cultural system, but there are other causes of such differences. Clearly people using this system believe that 2+2 = 4, and they also believe that 2,354+2,453 = 4,807. However, their belief in the first datum is stronger than their belief in the second. They automatically accept that the first one is true, while the latter requires a conscious act of calculation. This is no longer a matter of placement in the hierarchy of a cultural system; at most it may be considered placement in a personal hierarchy.

The strength of a person's belief is determined largely by habit, conventions, emotions and the like. These function to save the person the need to actively employ sources as they provide the data immediately, directly, and intuitively. This makes the data very powerful in the individual's personal world, even though the requirements of the cultural system – certainly the ideal one, but also the real one – do not give them any advantage over weaker data. The issue of the strength of data is thus purely psychological, having nothing to do with the system's function as a tool for finding the truth. Nevertheless, it is important to discover the strength of data so as to understand this phenomenon and try to prevent it from influencing the functioning of the system itself.

This issue is also important for people's psychological connection to their system. Even though the degree of this connection cannot be quantified, the strength of people's beliefs can nevertheless give us some quantitative indication of it. This can be described as follows: The degree of a person's psychological connection to a system is determined by the ratio between the amount of data in the system in which the person has a vivid belief and the entire amount of data that the system has provided him. This criterion is especially important when the person has a psychological attachment to two or more systems. If the ratio of the person's vivid beliefs in one system is greater than that in the other(s), then the person's psychological attachment to the first system is greater than his attachment to the other(s).

To be sure, a person can make use of a system (or subsystem) even with only minimal psychological attachment to it, but this use is limited in both scope and strength. The best example of this is a work of literature. Logicians have sometimes discussed this issue using the term "domain", which is explained by Source Theory as a sort of subsystem (or maybe even a system) distinguished from a larger system to isolate the discussion about it from other issues within that system. The text of a literary work is a subsystem that transmits data and can therefore be defined as a source of the testimony type. That is, the data are transmitted to us through mediated "adoption" in which our basic cognitive tools transmit what the text says. To get into the frame of mind of the story, we have to read it as if we believe what it says, and this enables us to create a type of psychological connection with the text. Sometimes this connection is quite strong, especially when we identify with the hero, "hate" the anti-hero, and the like, but we are always aware, at some level of consciousness, that the story is not true and does not even purport to be true. "The suspension of disbelief" – i.e., the temporary subordination of the person's generally adopted sources to that of the literary work – is only "for the moment", as Coleridge noted (Coleridge 1939, II: 5–6; compare Frege 1979:129–130). Even though there is a psychological connection in such cases, it is only *ad hoc*, and is of limited strength. Its range is also limited, since it involves only the data transmitted by the text itself. Generally we are not interested in knowing more about the characters than what the text provides us with, and even professional commentators do not attempt to use the text to find out things about the world, but at most to discover something about the text's (or its author's) view of the world. To be sure, covert assumptions about the world in which the plot unfolds do often appear in the text. For example, readers of Greek mythology have to take on a worldview in which miracles are possible, while readers of Orwell's *1984* are presented with a world in which miracles do not occur because everything is supposed to take place according to the laws of modern physics. If, however, Orwell had surprised us by introducing a miracle into the novel, we could not refute this datum, because the book is a subsystem in which the text is the supreme source in the hierarchy, while our cognitive tools are being used only as mediating sources for understanding the text. At most, we could express our reservations about the author's distasteful choice, but this has nothing to do with the truth value we ascribe to what we read.

In the margins of this discussion we can address a question that has disturbed modern literary scholars, which can be rephrased in terms of Source Theory: What is the source of a literary work, the author or the text? We cannot decide this question unambiguously, but we can explicate the arguments of the two sides more precisely. On the one hand, it is obvious that the text is the source. If we want to know what happened in Orwell's *1984*, we read the book rather than ask Orwell. Moreover, *1984* and *Animal Farm* do not share the same general system, even though they were written by the same author. For example, pigs can talk in *Animal Farm*, while this would be impossible in *1984*. Since every system (or subsystem) is determined by its sources, we must conclude that each of these books is an independent subsystem, detached from the author. These observations support the stand of those scholars who believe that literary works should be detached from their authors. However, it is also clear that we cannot understand such works without interpretive tools. It is hard, for example, to see how to understand the intent of *Animal Farm* without knowing its historical context. The book's anti-Communist message is the author's message, which can be understood even better if it is combined with the similar message of *1984* as well as Orwell's own experience as a disappointed Communist. It seems to me that most of the literary scholars involved in the dispute would agree to this. Thus it is now possible to reduce the controversy between the two sides to a question of the hierarchy of the sources: What should be the division of labor between the sources of the text itself and the sources that help us interpret it (on the basis of background data connected with the author and his other essays)? Once again, my purpose is not to decide this dilemma but rather to explicate it.

Pragmatic guidelines: the adoption of a system as a practical issue

We have discovered that workable systems are those that exist as cultural systems, so that the people who use them have a psychological attachment to them. Logical systems exist only on a theoretical plane. Although they do have considerable importance, especially since the ideal system of a culture is fairly close to a logical system, their importance is not in the realm of practice. In the latter realm, every system depends on the people who create and develop it. After all, each system represents a human way of thinking.

People do not operate in a vacuum. There are no human beings who were born and grew up outside of any cultural system, and who were allowed to choose some system when they were old enough. Each person is born into and grows up in a particular cultural system, which she adopts by virtue of the circumstances of her birth and upbringing, without conscious choice. We will call this system the person's **native system**. A person's connection to her native system is a fact of life; the most she can have is the opportunity to convert to another system if she is unsatisfied with the first one. Conversion as well cannot be justified in a non-arbitrary manner, and it too can be explained only by psychosocial causes, not logical justifications. A person's ability to justify her attachment to a particular cultural system rather than another one is logically no different from the ability of any other person, who was born into a different system, to justify his own attachment to that system.

From a broader perspective, we can say that our formalist line of argumentation has led us to a situation in which we are faced with an infinite number of systems, each of which can be justified equally. The pragmatist line of argumentation limits the variety of systems to a finite number, by basing them only on existing cultural systems, but it does not affect our ability to justify any one of them more than any other.

These observations inevitably lead to a relativistic conclusion. I do not deny this, despite the unfavorable connation the term "relativistic" has in many circles. I merely insist that without the pragmatist argument we would be left with the logical one, whose conclusions are not merely relativistic but actually nihilistic. Relativism is still much better than nihilism. Nihilism leads to a situation in which any datum can be justified, meaning that no datum can be justified. In such a case we cannot believe anything, and so it is impossible to think at all. Relativism, in contrast, leads us to a situation in which belief is at least possible, even if it impossible to justify belief in a specific datum coming from one cultural system more than a contradictory datum taken from another one. Relativism thus allows us to think, even if it requires us to be aware of the conditional validity of our thoughts.

I do not consider it necessary to search for a way to overcome or "refute" relativism at any cost. Such a search, which first shoots the arrow and then draws the target, does not demonstrate intellectual honesty. Instead of trying to refute relativism we should elucidate it and explain how to find our way within it. Here too, since we cannot adopt a logical method of doing this, we have to look for a pragmatic method. Such a method will not have the crushing conviction of logical argumentation, but I think it will make sense. We will do it in the form of guidelines for the adoption of a system.

Before presenting these pragmatic guidelines, let us remind ourselves of the point I made earlier, that the adoption of sources is not necessarily a voluntary act, and sometimes it is not even conscious, but even in such cases it is still an **act**. Therefore it can be investigated as part of normative discourse (compare Pollock 1986, Chapter 5; Armstrong 1973: 166). The list of pragmatic guidelines I present below belongs to this sort of discourse. Indeed, since this discourse itself can only be held within a given system, it involves the same problem of circularity and arbitrariness discussed above. However, this normative discourse is not meant to determine fixed truths (in this context, normative truths), but only to make it possible to offer tentative suggestions based on ways of behaving that are common to most of us in most of the systems that are available to us. Following Schopenhauer and Wittgenstein, I have compared the formalist line of argumentation to a ladder which allows us to raise ourselves above the system in which the discussion is being held and see the various systems as if from above, and which we can throw away after we have used it. Here, in contrast, I am suggesting that we take the ladder back and use it to come down again, even if it is no longer standing on firm ground. After all, the refusal to adopt sources is also an act, and every act that involves the adoption of sources – whether we adopt basic sources of one system or another, or refuse to adopt any of them at all – is still an act, and so is subject to normative judgment. Thus, in no case can we escape the need to act. In light of this, it is best that we should at least be aware of the way we adopt sources and try to do so according to the most prudent considerations, even if they are drawn from a given system or systems and are therefore true only in these systems. The pragmatic guidelines are thus a collection of good recommendations, and are worth listening to even if they cannot be justified in all possible systems.

The essence of the pragmatic guidelines can be summarized in the following principle, which we shall call **the principle of the purest utilization**: A person should utilize all the systems he is capable of utilizing, and only those systems. This principle is not equivalent to the basic tenet of pragmatism, "True is what works", but is a derivative of that tenet or, in fact, its application to the particular question of choosing a truth system. This principle leads to more concrete guidelines, which I call the conservative rule, the separation rule and the exhaustiveness rule.

The conservative rule: A person should stay with his native system unless he can no longer maintain it. Although the particular culture that people are born into and raised in is arbitrary, it is a given fact, and since converting to a different system is no more justifiable than remaining in one's present system, the pragmatic line of thought implies that people should stay in the system they are already in, for two reasons: (1) *Semper necessitas probandi incumbit ei qui agit* ("The necessity of proof always lies with the person who lays charges", i.e., who seeks to change the existing situation); (2) it is hard to develop an attachment to a new system, and even with a great deal of effort it is not always successful.

This rule does not apply when a person feels that she can no longer employ her native system. Such a situation can occur for either logical reasons or personal reasons, or both. Logical problems may arise when a flaw is discovered in the system or when the self-adoption axiom of that system does not hold, i.e., when the system itself does not claim that all its data are true. Personal alienation from a system may occur when an individual, for whatever reason, no longer feels a real psychological attachment to it. The conservative rule is not meant for such cases; it applies mainly to people who are considering converting to a new system only for reasons of relativism, curiosity, adventure, and the like. The rule does not apply to people who want to add another system that is available to them without abandoning their native system. This leads us to the second rule.

The separation rule: A person who has two or more native systems should keep them all without trying to combine them. It is indeed possible for a person to be raised within two or more systems. People have a psychological tendency to try to combine the two systems into one, to avoid compartmentalization. This tendency is legitimate on the level of one's own personal system, but it is not justified by any existing cultural system. According to the pragmatist line of argumentation we are using, such a combination is flawed, as one should adopt only existing cultural systems in their entirety (since, as shown above, only existing cultural systems are workable). Moreover, such a dual personal system would not have a counterpart ideal system, creating a situation in which the first nihilistic absurdity is even stronger.

The best way out of this dilemma is for people to hold their two native systems in parallel. This means that they should think according to the two systems at the same time, but separately. If they have a question for which they need an answer, they can use both systems separately as if they were two different computer programs. At the end of the process they can say that system A provides one answer and system B provides another. There is no need to decide between them (according to the theorem of the undecidedness of the speaking self). This way they can be loyal to both systems.

This rule seems to create several problems. First, there is the problem of the person's "inner consistency". People generally feel uncomfortable in a state where they are "of two minds". Their natural tendency is to try to overcome this duality and achieve "inner consistency". All these terms, however, are purely psychological and are irrelevant to epistemology. From the epistemological viewpoint, the only relevant question is which system can help us know the world better, or at least have a greater probability of achieving this goal. Since there are an infinite number of systems on the logical level, with no way of deciding among them, and there are a very large number of such systems on the sociological level as well, the individual is left with only those systems that are available to him because he has some psychological attachment to them. However, the existence of this psychological attachment is also an epistemological consideration, as it is one of the conditions for making the system workable for the individual. In the case described here, even the psychological plane does not satisfy the individual completely, since he has two parallel systems at his disposal, but this limits his possibilities considerably. From this point on, choosing one system over the other would be totally arbitrary. If the individual feels a psychological need to make this sort of choice for the sake of "psychological consonance", he can do so, but he should know that this choice has nothing to do with his ability to discover the truth. Thus even if he does make a choice for this reason, he should continue to think in the other system in parallel, for the sake of his epistemic and intellectual consonance.

Second, there is a problem from the aspect of the systems themselves. Each system is total, due to the self-adoption principle, which means not only the system's affirmation of itself but also the negation of opposing ones. Even though the real systems are open, the ideal systems are not. The fact that the speaking self has parallel psychological attachments to two or more systems is thus a flaw from the standpoint of each of these systems.

However, this is not a real problem either. On the contrary, it is precisely the separation rule that provides an appropriate solution to the problem of totality. After all, the individual who maintains a parallel but separate psychological attachment to each of his native systems preserves the totality of each one – even if separately and in parallel. Although each system demands total control over the individual's mind, it is precisely the rival solution – merging the two systems – that threatens this totality, much more than does the solution of separation, since the merging of the systems requires a mechanism of hierarchy or compartmentalization between their sources within the combined system, whereas separation makes it possible to preserve each system in a pure state. In the case of separation, the totality of the two systems is only minimally affected.

Complete totality is impossible anyway, since the totality of one system requires the rejection of all competing systems, and the individual under consideration has no non-arbitrary justification for rejecting one system rather than the other.

Finally, there is the problem of deciding normative practical issues. While people can use both their systems in parallel when dealing with data from the descriptive sphere, they have to choose one or the other in the sphere of normative data needed for practical decisions. Since the discussion so far has not dealt systematically with normative data, the problem is quite acute and demands a solution. Indeed, this issue requires an extensive, systematic discussion, which cannot be provided here, so I will merely outline it.

From the logical standpoint, there are two major normative categories: obligations and permissions. Both are divided into two qualities: positive and negative. Thus, there are positive obligations (one must perform act A) and positive permissions (one may perform act A). The positive obligations stand in opposition to the negative obligations, or prohibitions (one must not perform act A), while the positive permissions stand in opposition to the negative permissions (it is permissible not to perform act A). There is no contradiction between the two permissive categories, because permission to perform act A includes permission not to perform it, and vice versa. There is no necessary contradiction between the two negative categories either, since the prohibition on performing act A includes the permission not to perform it. Thus the only necessary contradiction among the normative categories is that that between positive obligations and negative obligations.

In light of these observations we can say that in cases when both systems transmit data referring to the same normative question one should act in the following ways:

> When both systems transmit a positive obligation, one should act accordingly.
> When both systems transmit a negative obligation, one should act accordingly.
> When both systems transmit permissions, one may do as one wishes.
> When system A transmits a positive or negative obligation and system B transmits a permission, one should act according to system A.
> When system B transmits a positive or negative obligation and system A transmits a permission, one should act according to system B.

Thus a problems arises only in the following cases:

> System A transmits a positive obligation and system B transmits a negative obligation.
> System B transmits a positive obligation and system A transmits a negative obligation.

These are indeed hard cases, since whatever the individual does, he will necessarily be violating the rules of one of the systems to which he feels a psychological attachment. This dilemma can be solved in one of the following ways: (a) the conservative solution – "when in doubt, do nothing" (based on BT Eruvin 100b) – that is, keep the negative obligation; (b) the libertarian solution – "when in doubt, do what you want" – i.e., the decision returns to the individual's judgment, so he can decide according to his vivid beliefs or emotional tendencies, or in any other arbitrary way; (c) the subjective solution – "when in doubt, act according to the obligation to which you feel more attached", even if you cannot justify it any more than the opposite obligation.

Indeed, anyone who was raised within two cultural systems is liable to incur such problems from time to time. The psychological difficulty of thinking in two separate systems in parallel poses a challenge, which is all the greater when there is a normative dilemma in everyday life. But the person who faces this challenge does not have to feel unfortunate. On the contrary, he has the great good fortune of living in two worlds, which provide two potential parallel opportunities for achieving the truth, while people who were raised within only one system do not have such opportunities.

The exhaustiveness rule: A person should be as knowledgeable as possible about his/her adopted system, its basic sources and the division of labor between them, and should try to receive the maximum amount of data that the system can provide him/her. The same is true in the case when one has more than one adopted system.

This rule seems to be ethical rather than epistemic, akin to the ancient Greeks' "Know thyself". However, in light of what has been said above, it also has epistemic value.

On the ethical plane, people are obligated to their adopted system and its cultural community. Since it is people who operate the systems, the data that are received within them are transmitted to all the people who belong to the cultural community. Thus, every activation of the system helps use its sources to the maximum extent and constitutes a contribution to the cultural system as a whole. Every system aspires to totality, however, and consequently it can be realized fully only when external sources are not involved, i.e. on the utopian level of the ideal system. Indeed, all real systems, including personal ones, fail to meet the standards of the ideal systems to which they aspire. To make the fullest possible use of the sources in the ideal system, people need to distinguish between data that are transmitted as part of the system and data from outside sources that have become intermingled with it. A full and pure operation of the ideal system can be achieved only when all the data are drawn exclusively from its own sources, without the intervention of any external source. Unattainable as this goal may be in real life, it can still mark the end of the road.

On the epistemic plane, this rule is a condition for discovering the truth according to the requirements of the system that the individual activates. Since even a personal system considers the ideal system as the object of its aspiration, every deviation from an ideal system, even on the part of a personal system, leads to missing the opportunity to discover the truth in the given cultural system. To approach the ideal system to the maximum possible degree, however, one must make sure that the data actually fit the system.

I believe that the pragmatic principle and the rules derived from it are based on rational considerations, and so they are valid only for WRS. As hinted at above, even arguments presuming to have a "neutral" perspective on all the systems can only be made within a particular system. Still, the purpose of this argumentation is only to explicate the process of adopting sources, and once this has been done, there is no longer any need for it.

The result of the principle of making the purest use of a system and the rules derived from it is clear. People who have a psychological attachment to two or more systems are, practically speaking, in a permanent state of *non liquet* with regard to these systems. With regard to the data, such people are in a state of *non liquet* only when there is a contradiction between the systems. Only in a utopian situation in which the truth is fully known in such a way that it is agreed upon by all viable systems would people be able to know which system is better than the others.

CHAPTER FIVE

Source Theory and the Philosophy of Religion

WRS and MRS as systems

We now consider the applicability of Source Theory and its basic concepts to other fields of philosophy. Since we deal with data and data processing in most spheres of life, it seems that we can apply Source Theory to a wide range of disciplines. For the present discussion, I will use only three examples, as stated in the introduction.

One of the most appropriate applications of Source Theory is in the philosophy of religion. We have already discussed the Western Rational System (WRS) and the Monotheist Religious System (MRS), presented in Chapter Four, as examples of two different cultural systems. These two systems can provide us with an excellent test case for applying Source Theory since each one represents an important, centuries-old tradition of thought, and they have considered each other as rivals for much of this time. We will therefore use them in this chapter as a concrete example of the application of Source Theory to the philosophy of religion.

For our purposes, WRS is the philosophical and scientific system that has been dominant in Western civilization at least since the nineteenth century, but its origins can be traced back to Greek philosophy. This system, in its mature form, evolved primarily in Christian cultures, and therefore still contains some religious remnants, but for our purposes we can consider these negligible, and see the entire system – at least as far as the ideal system is concerned – as secular. We have already called it S(m8).

The model of MRS that I will use here is roughly pertinent to Judaism, Christianity and Islam (or at least the more traditionalist and anti-modernist movements in these religions), with greater emphasis on Judaism. Indeed, it is likely to fit many of the non-monotheist religions as well, but since I cannot discuss

How to cite this book chapter:
Brown, B 2017 *Thoughts and Ways of Thinking: Source Theory and Its Applications.* Pp. 73–102. London: Ubiquity Press. DOI: https://doi.org/10.5334/bbh.f. License: CC-BY 4.0

all of them here, I will confine myself to these three. These three traditions all accept the basic cognitive tools as truth sources, but add some testimonies: a text and its authorized interpreters. The adoption of the text and its authorized interpreters thus becomes a first principle of any religious tradition, and entails the belief in all its dogmas (See Sofer 1841–1912, Volume 2: 356). In this respect, even if the text and its interpreters vary from one tradition to another, they all share the same *type* of model, and in this sense we can treat them as one for our purposes. This is what justifies talking about MRS as one system, even though in reality there has never been a single unified system including all three monotheist religions. A discussion with higher "resolution" would therefore require a distinction between the three – MRS1, MRS2 and MRS3 – but for our discussion we will make do with MRS. We will denote its model as m7, and the system will therefore be denoted as S(m7).

My main interest in this chapter is in the conflict between the reason-based and the religious systems (in this context I use the term reason in its broader sense, as representing rationality, i.e., the source model founded on the basic cognitive tools, and not the specific function mentioned in Chapter One). In its medieval version, this discord was known as the "reason-revelation conflict"; in its modern version, it has taken the form of the science-religion conflict; here we will consider both of them under the general title of the reason-religion conflict. When dealing with practical reason in particular, we may also call it the morality-religion conflict (with morality, in this context, referring to secular-humanist morality).

Indeed, even in antiquity there was tension between religion and philosophy, but it emerged sharply only during the Middle Ages, when it became one of the major topics of philosophy and religious rationalism. The main discord was in the descriptive realm, that is, on the issue of the conflict between the data about the world transmitted by the religious traditions and their canonical texts on the one hand, and the data transmitted by the basic cognitive tools on the other. One major question that occupied the medieval thinkers was whether the world is eternal or created. The religious traditions claimed that the world was created *ex nihilo* at a particular point in time, while the Aristotelian philosophers, who reigned in the field at that time, claimed that the world is eternal and has always been in existence. At present, the conflict centers around the question of creation versus evolution, as well as the issue of the age of the universe. The conflicts in the normative realm have become most intense in the modern age. Among these are the debates over euthanasia and abortion, as well as the status of women, members of other religions, and heretics.

MRS and WRS are two great, wide-ranging systems with rich histories and glorious traditions. They differ from each other on a list of fundamental issues, but they also represent different ways of thinking. This insight is not only based on a source-theoretical analysis, but also accords with our empirically-based intuitions. We can often sense that purely religious people (if they exist at all nowadays) "think differently" from purely rationalist people (if there have ever been any). Thus the root of the great differences between them is their sources or the division of labor among them.

Here I will survey various approaches that have been put forward for dealing with these conflicts, and formulate them in terms of Source Theory. The various approaches include the rejection of religion, the rejection of reason, the double-faith theory with religious supremacy, the double-faith theory with rationalist supremacy, the separation theory with religious supremacy in the descriptive realm, the separation theory with religious supremacy in the normative realm ("orthopraxy"), and the double-truth theory (as distinguished from the "double-faith" theory).

All these approaches are largely "ideal types". In practice, people are more complex, with more contradictions and arbitrariness than the theoretical types. I will therefore change my method of presentation and cite a list of quotations from thinkers representing each of these approaches. These thinkers come from different periods and cultures, and each of them dealt differently with the reason-religion conflict. As we shall see, hardly any of these thinkers belongs purely to the type of theory he is supposed to represent, so I will allow myself to slightly simplify their ideas from time to time so as to sharpen them. At any rate, the discussion does not revolve around the views of the thinkers themselves, but rather the ideal types that we will delineate with their assistance, even if some modifications are required.

The adoption of reason and the rejection of religion

The rejection of religion has been the approach of radical secular thinkers of all ages These thinkers adopt only the basic cognitive tools in the WRS model. If we call a typical member of this group a1, we can therefore say that a1 X::m8, i.e. that a1 exclusively adopts m8. Typical representatives of this approach are Baron d'Holbach and Bertrand Russell, who asserted that religion is based mainly on fear, while science liberates us from it. D'Holbach wrote:

> Savage and furious nations, perpetually at war, adore, under divers names, some God, conformable to their ideas, that is to say, cruel, carnivorous, selfish, blood-thirsty. We find, in all the religions, "a God of armies," a "jealous God," an "avenging God," a "destroying God," a God who is pleased with carnage, and whom his worshippers consider it a duty to serve. Lambs, bulls, children, men, and women, are sacrificed to him. Zealous servants of this barbarous God think themselves obliged even to offer up themselves as a sacrifice to him. Madmen may everywhere be seen, who, after meditating upon their terrible God, imagine that to please him they must inflict on themselves the most exquisite

torments. The gloomy ideas formed of the deity, far from consoling them, have every where disquieted their minds, and prejudiced follies destructive to happiness.

How could the human mind progress, while tormented with frightful phantoms, and guided by men interested in perpetuating its ignorance and fears? Man has been forced to vegetate in his primitive stupidity: he has been taught stories about invisible powers upon whom his happiness was supposed to depend. Occupied solely by his fears, and by unintelligible reveries, he has always been at the mercy of priests, who have reserved to themselves the right of thinking for him, and of directing his actions. Thus, man has remained a slave without courage, fearing to reason, and unable to extricate himself from the labyrinth in which he has been wandering. He believes himself forced under the yoke of his gods, known to him only by the fabulous accounts given by his ministers, who, after binding each unhappy mortal in the chains of prejudice, remain his masters, or else abandon him defenceless to the absolute power of tyrants, no less terrible than the gods, of whom they are the representatives.

Oppressed by the double yoke of spiritual and temporal power, it has been impossible for the people to be happy. Religion became sacred, and men have had no other Morality, than what their legislators and priests brought from the unknown regions of heaven. The human mind, confused by theological opinions, ceased to know its own powers, mistrusted experience, feared truth and disdained reason, in order to follow authority. Man has been a mere machine in the hands of tyrants and priests. Always treated as a slave, man has contracted the vices of slavery.

Such are the true causes of the corruption of morals. Ignorance and servitude are calculated to make men wicked and unhappy. Knowledge, Reason, and Liberty can alone reform and make men happier. But every thing conspires to blind them, and to confirm their errors. Priests cheat them, tyrants corrupt and enslave them. Tyranny ever was, and ever will be, the true cause of man's depravity, and also of his calamities. Almost always fascinated by religious fiction, poor mortals turn not their eyes to the natural and obvious causes of their misery; but attribute their vices to the imperfection of their natures, and their unhappiness to the anger of the gods. They offer to heaven vows, sacrifices, and presents, to obtain the end of sufferings, which in reality are attributable only to the negligence, ignorance, and perversity of their guides, to the folly of their customs, and above all, to the general want of knowledge. Let men's minds be filled with true ideas; let their reason be cultivated; and there will be no need of opposing to the passions, such a feeble barrier, as the fear of gods (Holbach 1900, preface).

Russell clearly follows the same idea, and points to science as a better source:

> Religion is based, I think, primarily and mainly upon fear. It is partly the terror of the unknown and partly, as I have said, the wish to feel that you have a kind of elder brother who will stand by you in all your troubles and disputes. Fear is the basis of the whole thing — fear of the mysterious, fear of defeat, fear of death. Fear is the parent of cruelty, and therefore it is no wonder if cruelty and religion have gone hand in hand. It is because fear is at the basis of those two things. In this world we can now begin a little to understand things, and a little to master them by help of science, which has forced its way step by step against the Christian religion, against the churches, and against the opposition of all the old precepts. Science can help us to get over this craven fear in which mankind has lived for so many generations. Science can teach us, and I think our own hearts can teach us, no longer to look around for imaginary supports, no longer to invent allies in the sky, but rather to look to our own efforts here below to make this world a better place to live in, instead of the sort of place that the churches in all these centuries have made it (Russell 1967: 26).

The expected conclusion is that religion should be completely rejected in favor of science, based on the basic cognitive tools, which Russell calls "intelligence":

> We want to stand upon our own feet and look fair and square at the world – its good facts, its bad facts, its beauties, and its ugliness; see the world as it is and be not afraid of it. Conquer the world by intelligence and not merely by being slavishly subdued by the terror that comes from it. The whole conception of God is a conception derived from the ancient Oriental despotisms. It is a conception quite unworthy of free men. When you hear people in church debasing themselves and saying that they are miserable sinners, and all the rest of it, it seems contemptible and not worthy of self-respecting human beings. We ought to stand up and look the world frankly in the face. We ought to make the best we can of the world, and if it is not so good as we wish, after all it will still be better than what these others have made of it in all these ages. A good world needs knowledge, kindliness, and courage; it does not need a regretful hankering after the past or a fettering of the free intelligence by the words uttered long ago by ignorant men. It needs a fearless outlook and a free intelligence. It needs hope for the future, not looking back all the time toward a past that is dead, which we trust will be far surpassed by the future that our intelligence can create (ibid.: 26–27).

When Russell uses the word "intelligence", he is speaking about the basic cognitive tools. When he claims that intelligence is free, he means that it should apprehend the world directly, without the mediation of any sort of accepted texts. When he says that "we want to stand upon our own feet", he means that we are not interested in any sort of intermediaries to whose authority we are subjected. All this implies the absolute rejection of traditional religion in favor of "intelligence" as a source of directly apprehending the world.

Later versions of atheism flourished in the 20th century and the list is too long for even a short survey. Antony Flew (1923–2010) attacked religious belief on the grounds of the "falsification argument" (Flew et al. 1964), was subject to many rebuttals and turned to a form of deism at an advanced age. Richard Dawkins (born 1941) famously attacked religion on the basis of its contrast with science (for example: Dawkins 2006). Kai Nielsen based his atheism on skepticism and naturalism (1995, 2001, 2005 and more) and was engaged in a deep debate with D.Z. Phillips and his Wittgensteinian fideism (see further below in this chapter; Nielsen and Phillips 2005; analysis in Carroll 2010). Indeed, continuing corroborations of reasons for disbelief, as well as responses by proponents of belief, are still enthusiastically discussed to this day (Peterson and VanArragon 2007; Taliaferro et al. 2010, Part VI). All these discussions of atheism are clearly part of a WRS discourse.

In my opinion, the complete, consistent adoption of WRS does indeed lead to atheism. No attempt to prove the existence of God using the sources of this system has ever succeeded. From the viewpoint of this system, when Napoleon asked Laplace what place God had in the cosmic system he described in his book, and Laplace replied, "Sir, I have no need of that hypothesis", Laplace was correct.

The adoption of religion and the rejection of reason

The polar opposite of this approach is the rejection of the basic cognitive tools and the exclusive adoption of a model based on other, non-rational sources. However, such a polar opposite has never existed and probably will never exist. Everyone, including the staunchest anti-rationalist, needs senses to perceive the world, memory to preserve the data he has perceived and reason to analyze those data. He needs those capacities even to understand the non-rational sources he had adopted as testimonies and to read the irrationalist texts in which he believes. The religious system is therefore a system that embraces the rational system together with non-rational sources, usually texts, and their authoritative interpreters. I will now try to schematize this symbolically.

Let us call the non-rational model (or sub-model) m7.
m7: $(\forall x,y...\alpha,\beta...((x1,x2,x3... \in A) \land (\alpha,\beta... \in H)) \leftrightarrow ((m8(\alpha,\beta....):\varphi \to \varphi) \land ((m8:x1:(\alpha,\beta...):\varphi \to \varphi) \land (m8:x1:x2:(\alpha,\beta...):\varphi \to \varphi) \land (m8:x1:x2:x3...))))$

where A denotes the set of authoritative interpreters of the holy texts and H denotes the set of those holy texts themselves. To be sure, we need the basic cognitive tools to understand of the words of the authoritative interpreters, but in m7 these tools do not serve any role other than that of transmitting the words of the holy texts and their interpreters. The members of H differ from one monotheist religion to the other, and so we can speak about h1, h2, and h3, which are the bases of the models m7.1, m7.2, and m7.3. respectively. These differences, however, do not change the basic structure of m7, which we call MRS in general.

m7 refers only to the model of the non-rational sources of MRS, but these do not exhaust the full model of its *real* system. This latter model consists of both m7 and m8; namely, it may adopt the basic cognitive tools for purposes other than understanding the holy texts and their authoritative interpreters. That model, which we may call m9, will therefore be defined as follows:

m9::(m7, m8)

where the division of labor between m7 and m8 is not specified. In principle, the comma in the formula serves us only when that specification is not important, while in the case of m7 and m8 it would be very important to specify the division of labor among the different sources. The problem is that there is not one single model in any of the three traditions, and this issue was subject to fierce debates within each of them. In this case, therefore, we will leave the definition of the model with commas instead of elaborating their division of labor not because the elaboration is not important (as is the case in most of the instances in which we use commas) but because it simply does not exist, not even on the ideal level. Thus we may ask whether different schools or thinkers are actually parts of the same tradition if they do not have even an ideal system in common. The answer must be yes. Although they do not share the same division of labor among the sources, they do share the same sources.

Even though the basic cognitive tools are part and parcel of MRS, there still are eminent anti-rationalist schools and thinkers within this system. These are often referred to as fideists (for the history of the doctrine and the uses of the term see Carroll 2008). As we noted, the fideist thinkers do not and cannot reject the basic cognitive tools altogether, but they do subordinate them completely to the holy texts. These schools generally call the systems constructed out of the basic cognitive tools "reason", "understanding", "investigation", or "philosophy".

Among the Church Fathers the best-known representative of this anti-rationalist approach is Tertullian, but in fact the famous saying attributed to him – "Credo quia absurdum est" – was never really written by him. However, the fideist stance was well represented in later generations by quite a few important thinkers.

In Islamic theology Taqi Ad-Din Ahmed Ibn Taymiyyah (1263–1328) is known as a staunch representative of anti-philosophical (and anti-mystical) orthodoxy. To be sure, he is not one of the most radical fideists, but he is undoubtedly one of the most influential. Ibn Taymiyyah distinguished among the various areas of rational thought. While he acknowledged its credibility in secular fields, in which the religious sources have no claim, he adamantly preached rejecting in favor of any data transmitted by the Qur'an and its authoritative interpreters. Thus, while criticizing the Sufi (mystical) and illuminationist schools, who preached suppressing one's rational faculties to achieve a mystical experience, he equally criticized the rationalist schools, especially the Mu'atazila, who subordinated the revelation to reason:

> Many theologians base their idea simply on reason, and rely exclusively on it. ... Knowledge is derived from general principles of reason, sufficient in themselves without a resource to faith on the Qur'an.
>
> Most Sufis, on the other hand, condemn reason and find fault with it. They assert that sublime states and higher spiritual stages are never attained without negating reason. They expound ideas which contradict reason and lead to rapture, ecstasy and intoxication. They believe in truths and experiences which, as they claim, accrue only when reason is completely suppressed; they also believe in things that are clearly denied by reason or are not attested by it.
>
> Both these sources are wrong. To be sure, reason is prerequisite to all knowledge, as it is the prerequisite of virtue and good life. With it we acquire knowledge and virtue, but it is not sufficient by itself. It is only a faculty of the soul, a power like the power of vision in the eye. It works only when it receives light from faith and the Qur'an, as the eye sees only when it receives light from the sun or a fire.
>
> Left to itself, reason cannot know things which it is not equipped to know by itself. On the other hand, when it is completely suppressed, the ideas that one receives and the acts that one performs may be things such as happen to the animals. One may have love and ecstasy and other experiences, but they will not be different from what the animals get. Hence the states that one attains by negating reason are defective, and the ideas that one receives contrary to reason are false.
>
> Prophets came with knowledge which reason could not attain in and of itself; never did they come with what reason considers to be impossible. People who place unjustified faith in reason make statements regarding the necessity, possibility or impossibility of things purely on the basis of reason; they work all the while under the impression that their views are correct, whereas they are false; they are even audacious enough to oppose the views which the prophets taught. On the other hand, those who decry reason and affirm things that are false, revel in

> satanic states and evil practices, and cross the boundaries which the sense of discrimination (between good and evil) draws, with which God has endowed man and elevated him above other creatures (Ibn Taymiyyah 2000: 5–6).

He further states:

> Knowledge is what is demonstrable, and of that what is useful has been conveyed by the prophets. However, there is a part of knowledge which we get from other sources. This concerns the matters of the world, such as the objects of medicine, mathematics, agriculture and commerce. But so far as divine things and religious truths are concerned, the only source of their knowledge is the Prophet. He knows them best, is most eager to preach them to the masses and most competent to formulate and expound them. He is above everyone in knowledge, will and competence – things which are required to accomplish his mission perfectly (ibid.: 16).

In terms of Source Theory, Ibn Taymiyyah's model is based on compartmentalization. If P denotes all the data pertaining to religious matters, we can describe his model as m9.1, according to the following formula:

$$m9.1: \forall \varphi ((m7:\varphi \rightarrow \varphi) \wedge ((\psi \notin P) \leftrightarrow (m8:\psi \rightarrow \psi)))$$

A similar position, though less sharply phrased, is taken by AlGhazali, who is usually considered as a more mainstream thinker than Ibn Taymiyyah (Al-Ghazali 1980:63–64; *idem* 2000, Introduction). This seems to be the position of other Ash'arite thinkers as well.

Similar ideas appear, though quite sparsely, in medieval Jewish thought. The sharpest representative of the fideist approach was apparently R. Joseph Yabetz (? – c.1505), who has become particularly influential in Orthodox Judaism in modern times:

> [It should be] explained that we have been commanded not to follow logical deductions. You must know, my son, that just as we have been commanded not to follow our desires, because it is an important principle in performing God's commandments, so we have been commanded not to follow the deductions made by our reason. For just as the nature of our desires is to love to do sins and despise observing prohibitions … , so it is the nature of human reason to mislead people to love the intelligibles that they can apprehend, and despise the true opinions of the Torah, such as the belief in reward and punishment, the divine provenance of the Torah, the resurrection of the dead and the great Day of

Judgment, which are all opposed to rational deduction. Therefore people must become accustomed to remember the commandments, which are the Divine intelligibles, so as to be saved from human reason which lies in wait for people at every time (Yabetz 1554, Chapter 8).

In the Catholic Church, the marked influence of Thomas Aquinas usually led to a rejection of fideism (also, recently, see John Paul II 1998, esp. article 53). It is in the early Protestant Church that we encounter the most flamboyant anti-rationalist statements. Luther's famous words against reason, even if they do not represent the more complex stance that scholars find in his entire work, are good examples of this. I will quote from his last sermon in Wittenberg (1546):

> [Reason] is the foremost whore the devil has; the other gross sins can be seen, but nobody can control reason. ... [R]eason mocks and affronts God in spiritual things and has in it more hideous harlotry than any harlot. ... As a young man must resist lust and an old man avarice, so reason is by nature a harmful whore, ... Therefore, see to it that you hold reason in check and do not follow her beautiful cogitations. Throw dirt in her face and make her ugly. ... Reason is and should be drowned in baptism, and this foolish wisdom will not harm you, if you hear the beloved son of God saying, "Take, eat; this is my body, which is given for you; this bread which is administered to you, I say, is my body", If you hear and accept this, then I trample reason and its wisdom under foot and say, "You cursed whore, shut up! Are you trying to seduce me into committing fornication with the devil?" That's the way reason is purged and made free through the Word of the Son of God (Luther 1959, Volume 51: 374–377).

Luther sees people's attraction to reason as a result of their pride and self-satisfaction:

> When whoredom invades you, strike it dead, but do this far more when spiritual whoredom tempts you. Nothing pleases a man so much as self-love, when he has a passion for his own wisdom. The cupidity of a greedy man is nothing compared with a man's hearty pleasure in his own ideas, ...
>
> Therefore I exhort you, says Paul, by the grace God has given me, not to think of yourselves more highly than you ought to think [cf. Rom 12:3]. What he is saying is: You still have your own proud ideas, as well as other gross sins; therefore take heed of yourselves. Hitherto you have heard the real, true Word, now beware of your own thoughts and your own wisdom. The devil will kindle the light of reason and rob you of your faith (ibid.: 377).

And again elsewhere:

> Reason is the Devil's greatest whore; by nature and manner of being she is a noxious whore; she is a prostitute, the Devil's appointed whore; whore eaten by scab and leprosy who ought to be trodden under foot and destroyed, she and her wisdom ... Throw dung in her face to make her ugly. She is and she ought to be drowned in baptism... She would deserve, the wretch, to be banished to the filthiest place in the house, to the closets (Luther 1959/73, Volume 16: 142–148).

Luther believed that reason is nothing but a tool for man's evil inclinations and corrupt morals, and thus he saw it as the messenger of Satan. In his commentary on Paul's Epistle to the Galateans he states:

> [W]e, excluding all works, do go to the very head of this beast, which is called Reason, which is the fountain and headspring of all mischiefs. For reason feareth not God, it loveth not God, it trusteth not in God, but proudly condemneth him. It is not moved either with his threatenings or his promises. It is not delighted with his words or works, but it murmureth against him, it is angry with him, judgeth and hateth him: to be short, 'it is an enemy to God' Rom. 8 [:7], not giving him his glory. This pestilent beast (reason I say) being once slain, all outward and gross sins should be nothing.
>
> Wherefore we must first and before all things go about by faith, to kill infidelity, the contempt and hating of God, murmuring against his judgment, his wrath and all his words and works; for then do we kill reason, which can be killed by none other means but faith, which in believing in God giveth unto him his glory, notwithstanding that he speaketh those things which seem both foolish, absurd and impossible to reason (Luther 1833: 172–173).

But even in the Catholic Church we find expressions of fideism. The most famous version is the ideal of *sacrificium intellectus*, sharply presented by the great persecutor of the Protestants, Ignatius Loyola. In his 1553 letter to the Jesuits of Portugal he first preaches to sacrifice one's will, and then turns to the sacrifice of the "understanding". This, Loyola states, is the utmost expression of obedience to God:

> [H]e who aims at making an entire and perfect oblation of himself, in addition to his will, must offer his understanding, which is a further and the highest degree of obedience. He must not only will, but he must think the same as the superior, submitting his own judgment to that of the superior, so far as a devout will can bend the understanding.

For although this faculty has not the freedom of the will, and naturally gives its assent to what is presented to it as true, there are, however, many instances where the evidence of the known truth is not coercive and it can, with the help of the will, favor one side or the other. When this happens every truly obedient man should conform his thought to the thought of the superior.

And this is certain, since obedience is a holocaust in which the whole man without the slightest reserve is offered in the fire of charity to his Creator and Lord through the hands of His ministers. And since it is a complete surrender of himself by which a man dispossesses himself to be possessed and governed by Divine Providence through his superiors, it cannot be held that obedience consists merely in the execution, by carrying the command into effect and in the will's acquiescence, but also in the judgment, which must approve the superior's command, insofar, as has been said, as it can, through the energy of the will bring itself to this.

Would to God that this obedience of the understanding were as much understood and practiced as it is necessary to anyone living in religion, and acceptable to God our Lord. I say necessary, for as in the celestial bodies, if the lower is to receive movement and influence from the higher it must be subject and subordinate, the one body being ordered and adjusted to the other, so when one rational creature is moved by another, as takes place in obedience, the one that is moved must be subject and subordinated to the one by which he is moved, if he is to receive influence and energy from him. And, this subjection and subordination cannot be had unless the understanding and the will of the inferior is in conformity with that of the superior.

Now, if we regard the end of obedience, as our will so our understanding may be mistaken as to what is good for us. Therefore, we think it expedient to conform our will with that of the superior to keep it from going astray, so also the understanding ought to be conformed with his to keep it from going astray. ...

[H]ow perfect it is in itself, and how pleasing to God, can be seen from the value of this most noble offering which is made of the most worthy part of man; in this way the obedient man becomes a living holocaust most pleasing to His Divine Majesty, keeping nothing whatever to himself, and also because of the difficulty overcome for love of Him in going against the natural inclination which all men have of following their own judgment. It follows that obedience, though it is a perfection proper to the will (which it makes ready to fulfill the will of the superior), yet, it must also, as has been said, extend to the understanding, inclining it to agree with the thought of the superior, for it is thus that we proceed with the full strength of the soul—of will and understanding—to a prompt and perfect execution (Loyola 1959: 290–293).

One of the famous rabbis of the eighteenth century, R. Eliyahu ben Shlomo Zalman, known as the Gaon of Vilna (HaGra; 1720–1797), expressed opinions that may remind us of Ibn Taymiyyah. He too supported the study of sciences, but mainly in order to help us understand the Torah. On the other hand, he abhorred philosophy, mainly for because it presumed to discuss metaphysical questions. The only source of true data, he believed, is the Torah. And its written text of itself can provide answers to all possible questions:

> The principle is that whatever has been, is now and will be forever and ever is all included in the Torah, from "In the beginning" (Genesis 1:1) to "before all Israel" (Deuteronomy 34:10). And not only the general concepts [are there], but even the details of every species and every person in particular, and everything that has happened to him from the day he was born until his end, and all his reincarnations (*gilgulim*) and all his subtlest details, as well as those of every … creature in the world and every plant and inanimate substance, and all their details … And also, all that was said of our forefathers and Moses and Israel reappears in every generation, since their [Holy] Sparks [i.e. souls] are reincarnated in every generation, as is well-known. And all their actions from Adam to the end of the Torah exist in every generation, as is known to those who understand (HaGra 1820, Chapter 5).

The Torah text is apparently autarchic, and can serve as an exclusive source. It is clear, however, that this does not refer to the overt meaning of the text but rather its "inner" notions, which must be deciphered through proper interpretation. Here too, then, the text itself cannot serve as the sole source, as intermediary sources are required to access it.

Another Jewish thinker, R. Nahman of Breslav (1772–1810), belonged to the hasidic movement, which the Gaon harshly opposed, but he embraced a similar anti-rationalism. He claimed that one should not rely on the basic cognitive tools because people are not capable of freeing themselves of the unfavorable influences of the unwanted sources – "desire and emotion". The Jewish tradition, in contrast, has been transmitted by people who raised themselves above these limitations:

> [In contrast to what some philosophers suggested], there are no biblical verses that teach us to know God through human speculation built on confused sophistry. Heaven forbid! The only way to know God is in the way taught by our holy forefathers, who struggled all their lives for Him. They divested themselves of all worldly matters, totally subjugating all desire and emotion. Above all, they achieved total mastery of their sexual drives, releasing themselves from the bondage of the universal root of evil. They were consequently able to perfect their intellect and truly

recognize their Creator. This is the heritage they bequeathed us. It is our duty to accept this heritage with joy. Thus we say in our prayers: "Happy are we! How good is our portion! How pleasant is our lot! How beautiful is our heritage!" – The main lesson of these verses is that we take this holy knowledge into our minds, bring it into our hearts and bind it there constantly, "that His fear be on our faces that we sin not" (R. Nahman of Breslav 1973: 217).

The intended conclusion is that one should adopt the sacred texts as one's sole source. The source of these texts is God, but the intermediary sources are the holy individuals (*Tzadikim*) who transmitted the word of God to the people over the centuries:

> You must carefully remove all speculation from your heart. Cast it away and do not think about it at all. All you need is pure faith in God and in the true *Tzadikim*. [For w]e have received the Torah through Moses our Teacher, and it has been transmitted to us by the awesome *Tzadikim* of each generation. There is no question as to their integrity and they can be relied upon without question. All one must do is follow in their footsteps, believing in God with innocent simplicity and keep the commandments of the Torah as taught by our holy ancestors (ibid.: 32).

Kierkegaard (1813–1855) typically presents the "ridiculous" – i.e., irrational – character of religious belief and sees it as the believer's main test:

> The antinomy must now be resolved: that one *shall* believe that which derision can render ridiculous, which one can see done in a secular and earthly way. This is an even higher accentuation than *credo quia absurdum*. To the simple man it simply says: All you have to do is believe. To the comprehending understanding it says: It is diametrically opposed to the understanding, but you *shall* believe. Here the *shall* is stronger just because it is in opposition to something. In relation to the most caustic mockery of intellectuality it says: Well now, seen from your point of view it is ridiculous, extremely ridiculous, the most ridiculous of all — but you *shall* believe; it is a matter of heaven or hell, you *shall*. This is a frightful *shall* precisely because it makes such a great concession to the opposition.
>
> I now understand better and better the original and profound relationship I have to the comic, and this will be useful to me in illuminating Christianity.
>
> For this reason it is appropriate for my own fragment of life to express this dialectic: that I have allowed myself to be laughed at – but what I say is true.

> When no concession at all is made to the opposition, then the *shall* related to it is not nearly so strong. The greater the concession, the more frightful this *shall*. The concession is, so to speak, the height of the shower bath.
>
> Therefore the one who is to present Christianity must eminently have what the most caustic scoffer has at his disposal – precisely in order to pose this: *shall* (Kierkegaard 1967–78, VI, article 6373:133).

But even he, the great paragon of fideism in the modern era, does not reject the "understanding" altogether. He continues:

> [T]he believing Christian both has and uses his understanding, respects the universally human, does not explain someone's not becoming a Christian as a lack of understanding, but believes Christianity against the understanding and here uses the understanding—in order to see to it that he believes against the understanding. Therefore he cannot believe nonsense against the understanding, which one might fear, because the understanding will penetratingly perceive that it is nonsense and hinder him in believing it, but he uses the understanding so much that through it he becomes aware of the incomprehensible, and now, believing, he relates himself to it against the understanding (Kierkegaard 1982, I: 568).

Fideistic approaches also exist among contemporary thinkers. Fideism is often attributed to the theology of Karl Barth (1886–1968), and, following Wittgenstein's later philosophy, a philosophical stream of "Wittgensteinian fideism" has emerged recently (Nielsen and Phillips 2005; Carroll 2010). Philosophers such as Norman Malcolm (1911–1990), Dewi Z. Phillips (1934–2006) and Peter Winch (1926–1997) consider religion as a "language game" of its own, different from that of science and other reason-based fields. As a result, they contend that religion is not expected to comply with science, nor should religion be confronted with science (See: Malcolm 1995; Phillips 1976, 1986, 1993; Winch 1995). Even if these thinkers are inclined to the currently fashionable reliance on linguistic rather than epistemological models, their theories in fact have epistemological meaning and fit well into the formula presented above. (This book does not reduce aspects of epistemology to language, but rather reduces some aspects of language to epistemology, as we shall see below in Chapter Seven.)

Each of the thinkers presented in this section is saying that only one system, namely his own, should be adopted, and that its rival should be rejected. The same is true for the radical secular approach presented in the previous section. In spite of the apparent symmetry between the two exclusivist approaches, there is a difference as well. The radical secular approach absolutely rejects the religious sources, while the radical religious (fideist) approach – even though it sometimes seems to completely reject "reason" and "investigation" on the declarative level – actually means that these should be rejected only on issues that are liable to clash with the data of the religious tradition, since it is unlikely that even anti-rationalist religious thinkers would insist that the basic cognitive tools should not be used for everyday issues. Moreover, they too accept the fact that in order to understand the data transmitted to us by the holy texts, we need to use our basic cognitive tools. Thus it would seem that there is no system that completely rejects the basic cognitive tools. We can therefore say that the symmetry between the approaches is not total, since the radical secular approach does not consider religion to be a source at all, while the radical religious approach considers the basic cognitive tools to be sources subordinate to the supreme source, which is the holy text. It seems that this is the case for most of the systems whose models apparently reject the basic cognitive tools. Nevertheless, we can say that once the fideist MRS model is established and the basic cognitive tools are given their (humble) place in it, they become part and parcel of it, and from now on there is a symmetry: Each of the exclusivist approaches vocally rejects the rival one. The issue becomes more complex among the religious thinkers who make an attempt to adopt the basic sources of both systems.

The double-faith theory

The medieval religious rationalist tradition is dominated by the double-faith theory. This theory claims that there are two parallel roads to religious belief – through the religious tradition and through "Reason" (that is, the basic cognitive tools) – and that both lead to the same data. This basic idea is expressed by Saadia Gaon, Ibn Rushd (Averroes), Thomas Aquinas, and many other thinkers.

This claim is obviously a dogmatic one. Clearly, even the promulgators of this theory were well aware that the data of MRS and WRS are sometimes contradictory, but they thought that such contradictions stem from the improper operation of one of the two systems and that it is necessary to put in the effort to resolve the contradictions. This implies that in cases of this sort, the proponents of this approach think that the contradiction is merely an apparent one and that the data of either WRS or MRS must be reinterpreted so as to eliminate it. However, these two potential ways of resolving the contradiction are very different. One method is to consider the data of MRS superior and try to interpret the data of WRS accordingly, while the other is to do exactly the opposite. The first method can be formulated as follows:

M10.1: $((m7{:}\varphi \rightarrow (\varphi \wedge m8{:}\varphi))$

while the other can be formulated as follows:

M10.2: $((m8{:}\varphi \rightarrow (\varphi \wedge m7{:}\varphi))$

The first method (m10.1) is represented by Saadia Gaon (c.882–942), Ibn Rushd (Averroes; 1126–1198) and Thomas Aquinas (1225–1274). In Saadia's opinion, if people come to have doubts about their religious faith due to rationalist inquiry, they must have fallen into one of seven fallacies in the rationalist method of thinking:

> Should, therefore, someone come to us with an allegation in the realm of inferential knowledge, we would test his thesis by means of these seven criteria. If, upon being rubbed by their touchstone and weighed by their balance, it turns out to be correct as well as acceptable, we shall make use of it. Similarly also must we proceed with the subject matters of authentic tradition – I mean the books of prophecy (Saadia 1948, *Introductory Treatise*, Section v: 26) .

God is the one who implanted the capacity of rational thinking within us, and therefore it cannot contradict His Word. According to Saadia, God assures the believer:

> There is no wise or distinguished man that I do not know. Hence it is impossible that he should be able to produce an argument against you in the matter of your religion or do injury to your creed, because my knowledge is all-embracing and I have imparted it to you (ibid., Section vi: 30–31).

A similar view is presented by Ibn Rushd. He claims, however, that there is a religious obligation to attain the shared truth through reason as well, and that the data transmitted by the Qur'an are not sufficient:

> We maintain that the business of philosophy is nothing other than to look into creation and to ponder over it in order to be guided to the Creator – in other words, to look into the meaning of existence. For the knowledge of creation leads to the cognizance of the Creator, through the knowledge of the created. The more perfect becomes the knowledge of creation, the more perfect becomes the knowledge of the Creator. The Law encourages and exhorts us to observe creation. Thus, it is clear that this is to be taken either as a religious injunction or as something approved by the Law. But the Law urges us to observe creation by means of reason and demands the knowledge thereof through reason. This is evident from different verses of the Qur'an. For example, the Qur'an says: "Wherefore take example from them, you who have eyes" [Qur'an 49.2]. That is a clear indication of the necessity of using the reasoning faculty, or rather both reason and religion, in the interpretation of things (Ibn Rushd 1961: 1)

Thomas Aquinas expresses a similar opinion in his introduction to *Summa Theologica*. First he states that human reason does not exhaust all the truth and therefore divine revelation is needed. However, he insists, it would be better if that truth could be obtained from another source:

> Sciences are differentiated according to the various means through which knowledge is obtained. For the astronomer and the physicist both may prove the same conclusion: that the earth, for instance, is round: the astronomer by means of mathematics (i.e. abstracting from matter), but the physicist by means of matter itself. Hence there is no reason why those things which may be learned from philosophical science, so far as they can be known by natural reason, may not also be taught us by another science so far as they fall within revelation. Hence theology included in sacred doctrine differs in kind from that theology which is part of philosophy (Aquinas1920, Introduction).

If human understanding can grasp metaphysical truth by its own power, why was it given to us in the sacred writings? According to these three thinkers, metaphysical truth was transmitted in the sacred writings in laymen's terms, so that even the masses who are not capable of grasping the truth with their intellect could at least obtain it in a simple form, but a complete understanding of this truth through reason would be preferable.

These three religious rationalists thus claim that the two systems cannot lead to a contradiction, and if this seems to occur, then the only explanation is that the individual using WRS has failed in one of methods of using the system. This implies that in such a case he must reconsider the matter until he reaches the right conclusion – that of MRS – and if he cannot do so, then he must subordinate his own opinion to "authentic tradition – … [namely], the books of prophecy" (in the words of Saadia Gaon). Aquinas too claims that the "sacred doctrine" is a type of science, based on reason, but subordinate to the "principles" transmitted by the sacred writings:

> Sacred doctrine is a science. We must bear in mind that there are two kinds of sciences. There are some which proceed from a principle known by the natural light of intelligence, such as arithmetic and geometry and the like. There are some which proceed from principles known by the light of a higher science: thus the science of perspective proceeds from principles established by geometry, and music from principles established by arithmetic. So it is that sacred doctrine is a science because it proceeds from principles established by the light of a higher science, namely, the science of God and the blessed. Hence, just as the musician accepts on authority the principles taught him by the mathematician, so sacred science is established on principles revealed by God … The

principles of any science are either in themselves self-evident, or reducible to the conclusions of a higher science; and such, as we have said, are the principles of sacred doctrine (ibid).

In terms of Source Theory, these three thinkers are trying to construct a combined system out of two different systems – WRS and MRS – by establishing a clear hierarchy in which MRS is superior and WRS is subordinate to it. This subordination is supposed to be achieved by re-interpretation of the philosophical (that is, rational) truths in a way that will make them comply with the "principles" of the sacred writings. Indeed, in practice all three thinkers are not always faithful to this method, and in many cases they re-interpret the religious texts so that they fit the data of WRS, but their declared method is the one that allegedly gives supremacy to MRS.

The opposite method, which subordinates MRS to WRS, is represented by Maimonides, at least in one of his famous arguments. When he discusses the idea that God is not material and is not a power within the material, he devotes the whole first part of his *Guide of the Perplexed* to a re-interpretation of the Biblical verses which present anthropomorphical formulations. When he discusses the issue of whether the world is created or eternal, he comes to the conclusion that this is an antinomy for the basic cognitive tools (which he calls "demonstration") – that is, it is possible to argue that the world is eternal as persuasively as to argue that it is created. He therefore claims that the latter view should be accepted because it is the one that is found in the Biblical text. He adds, however:

> Know that our shunning the affirmation of the eternity of the world is not due to a text figuring in the Torah according to which the world has been produced in time. For the texts indicating that the world has been produced in time are not more numerous than those indicating that the deity is a body. Nor are the gates of figurative interpretation shut in our faces or impossible of access to us regarding the subject of the creation of the world in time. For we could interpret them as figurative, as we have done when denying His corporeality. Perhaps this would even be much easier to do: we should be very well able to give a figurative interpretation of those texts and to affirm as true the eternity of the world, just as we have given a figurative interpretation of those other texts and have denied that He, may He be exalted, is a body.
>
> Two causes are responsible for our not doing this or believing it. One of them is as follows. That the deity is not a body has been demonstrated; from this it follows necessarily that everything that in its external [=literal] meaning disagrees with this demonstration must be interpreted figuratively, for it is known that such texts are of necessity fit for figurative interpretation. However, the eternity of the world has not been

demonstrated. Consequently in this case the texts ought not be rejected and figuratively interpreted in order to make prevail an opinion whose contrary can be made to prevail by means of various sorts of arguments. This is one cause.

The second cause is as follows. Our belief that the deity is not a body destroys for us none of the foundations of the Law and does not give the lie to the claims of any prophet. The only objection to it is constituted by the fact that the ignorant think that this belief is contrary to the text; yet it is not contrary to it, as we have explained, but is intended by the text. On the other hand, the belief in eternity the way Aristotle sees it – that is, the belief according to which the world exists in virtue of necessity, that no nature changes at all, and that the customary course of events cannot be modified with regard to anything – destroys the Law in its principle, necessarily gives the lie to every miracle, and reduces to inanity all the hopes and threats that the Law has held out, unless – by God! – one interprets the miracles figuratively also, as was done by Islamic internalists; this, however, would result in some sort of crazy imaginings.

If, however, one believed the eternity according to the second opinion we have explained – which is the opinion of Plato – according to which the heavens too are subject to generation and corruption, this opinion would not destroy the foundations of the Law and would be followed not by the lie being given to the miracles, but by their becoming admissible. It would also be possible to interpret figuratively the texts in accordance with this opinion. And many obscure passages can be found in the texts of the Torah and others with which this opinion could be connected or rather by means of which it could be proved. However, no necessity could impel us to do this unless this opinion were demonstrated. In view of the fact that it has not been demonstrated, we shall not favor this opinion, nor shall we at all heed that other opinion, but rather shall take the texts according to their external sense and shall say: The Law has given us knowledge of a matter the grasp of which is not within our power, and the miracle attests to the correctness of our claims (Maimonides 1963, II, Chapter 25: 327–329).

In this case Maimonides does indeed give priority to the data of MRS, but only because WRS did not provide enough clear, unambiguous data. Here too the important thing is his general credo, which states that whenever WRS provides us with clear, unambiguous data we have to accept them and reinterpret the religious sources accordingly. Thus Maimonides has also created a combined hierarchical system, except that in his case the WRS sources have priority and the MRS sources are subordinate to them. He himself indicates an example of his use of this method – his willingness to reinterpret the Biblical verses whose surface meaning is that God has a body, so as to accord with rationalist philosophy, which claims that He does not.

Incidentally, Maimonides's method, involving a change in the concept of the Deity, is also a good example of what I discussed in Chapter Four above, about changing the boundaries of a concept. At first glance it would seem appropriate to ask whether Maimonides's God is actually the Biblical God. Doesn't the change in the concept of God lead to a situation in which the two texts – the Bible and Maimonides – are actually talking about different objects? The answer to this is not unequivocal. Let's take it as a premise that the author of the Biblical text meant the literal ("external") sense of its words, as understood by the common people. Now, if Maimonides and the common people shared the same system, we could say that Maimonides had taken an accepted datum from his cultural community and attempted to change it out of a new understanding drawn from the sources of that system. But since Maimonides actually tried to subordinate this system to another one, which is not shared by the common people, it is very likely that he was trying to introduce a new term in place of the old one, taking advantage of the old term's prestige within the cultural community (in the way that Spinoza's use of the word "God" should be understood). However, the fact that Maimonides seems to truly and sincerely consider his concept of "God" to be the same one that is transmitted by the Bible shows that he considers himself as drawing from the same religious system as the community he belongs to, and is merely trying to "amend" this concept from within, as it were.

It should be added, that the basic idea of the "double-faith" theory is shared by some of the contemporary philosophers of religion. Most notable is Alvin Plantinga (born 1934), whose theory attempts to meet the challenges of evidentialist criticism and prove that religion is rational (Plantinga 2006 and other works). William Alston (1921–2009) contended that religious experience is not significantly different from sensual perception, and therefore should be admitted as one of the sources of WRS (Alston 1991). Theories of "religious epistemology" suggest that we can offer rational justification to religious truths if we only recognize that slightly different rational standards than the ones that apply to philosophical and scientific knowledge should apply to religious knowledge. One of the most intriguing theories in this field, and one that speaks in a language quite close to Source Theory, is Zagzebski's theory of "epistemic authority" (Zagzebski 2013). Zagzebski claims that there are moral as well as epistemic good reasons to trust not only our own capacities, but also that of others. This, she continues, may give epistemic justification to religious beliefs. We can easily identify Zagzebsi's concept of "trust" as a form of "source adoption", in our terminology. If so, in Zagzabski's theory the religious sources are not adopted as superior sources but only authorized by virtue of arguments in WRS, and thus adopted only as subordinate sources of that system. Thus, MRS becomes a subsystem within WRS. In this way a full compatibility between the two is achieved (at least in principle), in the spirit of the "double-faith" theory.

The separationist approach

This is actually a family of approaches, which claim that the sources of one system should be adopted for some particular purposes and the sources of another system for other purposes. In terms of Source Theory, these approaches suggest compartmentalizing mechanisms. There can clearly be many different ways of compartmentalizing, but for our purposes we will concentrate on the approaches that separate descriptive data (called "beliefs" in MRS) from normative data (called "commandments" in this system). I will call this family of approaches "separationist" (following Rosenberg 1988), but two the specific forms I will discuss here, both relating to the Jewish context, is the one known as "orthopraxy" and the one I will call "Orthopistism".

"Orthopraxy" is the name often used to describe the approach that attempts to draw only normative data from MRS and disregard it descriptive data. If N denotes the set of normative data, this approach can be formalized as follows:

$$m11.1: (((\varphi \in N) \leftrightarrow (m7:\varphi \rightarrow \varphi)) \wedge ((\varphi \notin N) \leftrightarrow (m8:\varphi \rightarrow \varphi)))$$

or, in short:

$$m11.1::((\in N/m7), (\notin N/m8))$$

The most radical proponent of this approach in modern Jewish thought is Yeshayahu Leibowitz (1903-1994). He claims that any attempt to draw descriptive data from the Bible is an attempt to make use of it to satisfy human needs. He considers this an inferior religious commitment. In contrast, his religious ideal is that the Bible should not serve as a means for satisfying human needs, not even the need for "scientific information", but only for religious imperatives to serve God – that is, the practical commandments. He puts it this way:

> Does religion provide information? This was considered obvious in the Middle Ages, when thinkers did not distinguish between information and meaning. The meaning they attributed to reality was embodied in the information they had, or thought they had, about the world. ... But now we draw information without any meaning from science, and we are not obligated to attribute any informative content to religious thought.
>
> We have a source of information, which is science, and from a psychological standpoint the information it provides imposes itself on the mind of anyone who understands it, since no one is capable of not knowing what he knows. The basic, determining factor of religious feeling and

awareness is not the information that can, or cannot, be extracted from religion; rather, it is the fact that the essence of religion is **a demand presented to the individual: to worship God.** This aspect of religious belief has, of course, always been the essence of Judaism, although nowadays it is likely to be more salient than it was in the Middle Ages, when people attributed informative meaning to religion as well.

If we derive our information from science, which is independent of beliefs and values, then the world of people with the awareness that they are standing before God is not the same world that they grasp through the information they receive; rather, their religious awareness is concentrated on the point of obedience to the demands that this stance implies: accepting the burden of the Torah and the commandments. The essence of religious belief is not the **knowledge** that something is a fact; it is what the religious person **determines** and **decides** (1992, Chapter 13; emphasis in original).

Thus Leibowitz sees the Bible as the source of normative, but not descriptive, data. He claims that descriptive data should be drawn from WRS, which relies on the basic cognitive tools, and especially from science, which is a subsystem of WRS. He does not, however, consider this system to be a source of normative data.

The opposite separatist approach can be called "orthopistism".. This approach sees the holy texts of MRS as sources of only descriptive statements (beliefs), while it considers the basic cognitive tools as the source of normative statements. In the Jewish context discussed here this approach can be described as non-halakhic. If D denotes the set of descriptive, this approach can be formalized as follows:

m11.2: $(((\varphi \in D) \leftrightarrow (m7:\varphi \rightarrow \varphi)) \wedge ((\varphi \notin D) \leftrightarrow (m8:\varphi \rightarrow \varphi)))$

or, in short:

m11.1::$((\in D/m7), (\notin D/m8))$

As far as I know, no Jewish thinker has ever made such a radical statement. The closest position to this approach in the Jewish world is that of some early thinkers in the Reform movement. One of the pioneers of this movement, Saul Ascher (1767-1822), expresses this view as follows:

It seems, as will be explained later, that at first the Eternal God did not plan to give the Jewish people laws in the full sense of the word. If He had chained the weak powers of the nation with laws, He would have tested their tolerance too severely and caused them to sin without reason (Ascher 1792, Volume 2, Chapter1).

In Ascher's view, the Torah is not a source of laws, but mainly of beliefs:

> If we carefully consider what we have deduced and developed from the Torah, we will find proven what we proposed at first – that belief is the prior condition for any revealed religion.
>
> We see that faith was in decline from the time of Noah until a certain generation of his descendants. The Torah describes Noah in only one way – as a person who walked in the way of God. Nature had thus granted him a stronger faith than was common among other people. This faith was the condition for the Divine revelations he received, and he never refused, even for a moment, to act according to the command of the revelation.
>
> Second, what we have discussed so far shows that religion lies at the basis of Judaism. This means that Judaism includes a method by which a particular human society becomes accustomed to defined concepts, and all its members are required to understand these concepts the same way. The true, sublime goal of every religion is to provide people with certain truths and describe them in a way that is more understandable than they could grasp as children.
>
> Third, we see that God chose revelation because human beings cannot understand the truths with their own understanding, without any intermediary. Revelation created more interest in these truths and caused people to adhere to them more strongly.
>
> Fourth, at the time in Jewish history that we have been discussing, we have seen that faith was merely regulative as a condition for revelation ... All people had the same traits – they only knew one way to go. Therefore God did not need to use threats to compel the people to hold their faith. He merely gave them signs. A particular event or vision was enough to strengthen their faith. This was the case with the crossing of the Red Sea; when the Israelites saw the doomed Egyptians behind them, in the words of the Bible, "They believed in God and in Moses His servant" [Exodus 14:31].
>
> All this makes it clear that Judaism is a revealed religion. That is, God chose Judaism as a means of teaching some people to think in a different way. This is how the concept of "revealed religion" should be understood (ibid., Chapter 2).

A first glance, it seems that Ascher is saying that the Torah is also a source of norms, but that these are not "laws" (influenced by Kant, he vehemently opposes the "statutory" character of traditional Judaism), but rather abstract values. However, a deeper look shows that these values are moral ones, which he (and his contemporaries) considered to be deduced from universal reason. Thus, in the realm of norms, Ascher is not using MRS but rather WRS.

According to his declared compartmentalization, MRS is purely a source of beliefs, while the "commandments" are drawn from WRS.

Here we can ask if Ascher was really loyal to MRS in the realm of beliefs. If he had been faced with the more modern problems of the conflict between science and religion that came up some decades after his time, would he have adhered to the Torah as the sole source of beliefs and rejected science? It would not be prudent for me to speculate about this, but it does seem probable that in such a case Ascher would have rejected the beliefs provided by MRS in favor of those provided by the scientific subsystem of WRS, as did most Reform thinkers in the following generations, whether by rejecting the religious beliefs explicitly or by reinterpreting them according to the prevailing scientific beliefs. If so, Ascher's compartmentalization is not absolute; however, it is not the specific individual that we are focusing on here, but rather the ideal type that we can delineate through Ascher's writings.

In sum, both methods of compartmentalization – the orthopraxic and the orthopististic – represent attempts to preserve the two systems in parallel, even if they actually do both systems a disservice, since each system considers itself a total one, and such a separation cannot be justified. Even though two of the thinkers cited here tried to justify their methods within MRS, it seems to me that they used a manipulative interpretation of the system's data in a way that was dictated by the sources of another system – that is, WRS.

The double-truth theory

Finally, we will consider the double-truth theory, which was developed in medieval philosophy, but did not acquire many supporters. Siger de Brabant (c.1240–c.1284) and Boethius of Dacia (13th century) were accused of accepting it, but probably did not really embrace it. One of the very few who openly held this theory was Isaac Albalag (13th century), who was one of the most impressive Jewish thinkers of the Middle Ages (even though he has not been given much scholarly attention). In a certain sense, he developed the initial nucleus of Source Theory, which was one of the inspirations for the theory presented here, and he did this clearly and systematically. His book, *The Emendation of Opinions*, which was written as a commentary on Al-Ghazali's book, *The Opinions of the Philosophers*, deals with the two systems, MRS and WRS. He calls rationally-attained knowledge "demonstration" or "the natural way of thinking" and knowledge drawn from Scripture the "prophetic or miraculous way of thinking". As with most medieval philosophers, the main issue he discusses is whether the world is created *ex nihilo* or is eternal. On the philosophical, rational level, he suggests his own solution, which he calls "the perfect creation *ex nihilo*" – a clearly manipulative extension of the term "creation *ex nihilo*". This solution is that the world is contingent, and therefore depends on

God at every moment, but in actuality it has always existed without any starting point in time. He is aware that this idea is closer to the idea of the eternity of the world than to the simple Biblical notion that the world was created at a point in time. He claims that he could reinterpret the Bible allegorically to fit his notion, and he even provides an example as a sort of intellectual exercise, but he insists that this is not the proper way to deal with the issue. Instead he presents a different way of treating the two systems, which was called, centuries later, the "double-truth theory" (as distinct from the double-faith theory discussed above). This theory states that we should hold both systems in parallel and take a *non liquet* approach to them. In the language of Source Theory we could formulate it as:

$$m12: m8/m9,$$

which means:

$$m12:(m12:m8 \vee m12:m9)$$

Albalag describes this theory as follows:

> One should learn truth from demonstration, and then consult the Torah. Now, if its words are in conformity with the demonstrated doctrine, we shall admit it into our belief both in virtue of demonstration and in virtue of faith. If no scriptural text can be found to support the demonstrated doctrine, we shall believe it in virtue of speculation alone. Finally, if a scriptural text is found to contradict this doctrine, we shall similarly believe the literal sense of the text in the miraculous way [of thinking], while bearing in mind that the doctrine of the scriptural text in question is alien to our [rational] knowledge only because it is one of those divine doctrines reserved for the prophets to understand, and depends on a supernatural capacity. It is in this way that you shall find my rational opinion contrary to my faith in many points, for I know by demonstration that such a thing is true by the natural way [of thinking] and I know at the same time by the words of the prophets that the contrary is true by the miraculous way [of thinking].
>
> Moreover, even if I confirm that the demonstrable doctrine is compatible with a scriptural text, I am not certain that this is the veritable intention of the text, and not another. Therefore I do not claim to believe in the truth of the biblical exegeses that I have been able to provide here, nor to teach them as a belief that I transmit to you. Rather, I meant to show you that the speculative doctrines are reliable, and that scripture can accord with them just as much as it accords with their contrary, and perhaps even more.

The reason I did this is that you should not be one of those who rush to deny speculative doctrines because of what seems to them at first glance to be the opinion of Scripture, since they try to corroborate this opinion by arguments that they believe to be stronger than those of the philosophers' ... and think their own arguments to be demonstrative, although they are definitely not. There are many people who follow this path in every nation, even in ours, and even our master Moses [Maimonides] is one of them. These people failed twice: once by denying the speculation and claiming that it was non-demonstrative; and secondly by claiming that their own idea was what the prophet meant. I mentioned at the beginning of the book that the our understanding cannot grasp the intentions of the Torah beyond any doubt, for just as only a philosopher can grasp the intent of [another] philosopher, so only a prophet can grasp the intent of [another] prophet. The reason [for this] is that their ways of understanding are different from one another – indeed, opposite to one another, since the latter conceives the intelligible through the senses while the former conceives the sensual through the intellect.

Undoubtedly, just as their ways of understanding are very different, so the contents of their understandings are very remote from one another, so much so that one may conceive from below the very opposite of what the other conceives from above. Therefore we should not question one from the viewpoint of the other; rather, the wise man should believe the one when his argument is based on demonstration and accept the words of the other in the way of simple faith. And even if the statements of the one contradict those of the other, one should not reject these in favor of those, for one of the virtues of religious belief is that even if it is refuted by [rational] demonstration it is not denied the possibility of being true, since what is [conceived as] impossible under the laws of nature from the standpoint of logical investigation may be affirmed as a part of the Lord's powers by prophetic understanding ... Therefore there are numerous things that are conceived as impossible by the speculative knowledge, yet are conceived as possible by Torah knowledge. Moreover, there are things that the philosopher can grasp in his investigations that cannot be grasped by the prophet through prophecy, but only insofar as he is engaged in rational investigation. And this is not because prophecy is deficient [in comparison to rational thinking], but rather because it transcends it. (Albalag 1973, Chapter 30; translation based partly on Sirat 1985: 241).

When Albalag claims that prophecy should be given priority over rational thinking, he is merely paying lip service to the concept. He actually believes that those who are not prophets, and therefore cannot clearly understand what the prophets are saying, should not give the words of the prophets any supremacy over the data transmitted by rational inquiry. Rather, they should continue to make use of both systems in parallel. Moreover, he insinuates that if the common people thought rationally, they would come to the same conclusions that he himself reached through the use of WRS, and then it would be clear that "their [rational] opinion is undoubtedly my opinion and the belief of the Torah is my belief, the one according to the natural way and the other according to the miraculous one. And if you understand what I am saying, then you will know that my opinion is true and my belief is true".

Albalag seems to be discussing only the descriptive data of the two systems, but he does not say this explicitly, so I will take the liberty – at least for the purposes of our theoretic discussion - of interpreting his comments as referring to all aspects of the systems – their descriptive data, their normative data, and any other data they may transmit. Under this interpretation, Albalag is presenting a method that clearly adheres to the principle of the purest utilization, which was presented above (Chapter Four) as the recommended method for people who are looking to adopt a source model. This principle stated that every person must utilize all of the systems he is capable of utilizing, and only those systems. To remind ourselves, the following secondary principles were derived from it:

> The conservative rule: A person should stay with his native system unless he can no longer maintain his adoption of it.
> The separation rule: A person who has two or more native systems should keep them all without trying to combine them.

The exhaustiveness rule: A person should be maximally knowledgeable about his or her native system, its basic sources, and the division of labor among them, and should try to receive the maximum amount of data that the system can provide him. The same is true in the case when a person has more than one native system.

As I deduced above, the result of this principle and the rules derived from it is that people who have a psychological attachment to two or more systems are in a permanent state of *non liquet* with regard to these systems.

Albalag seems to systematically hold this principle and the rules derived from it. It would seem that he was fully and deeply acquainted with both MRS and WRS, and that he had formed a psychological attachment to each of them. He felt a deep identification with each system, understanding its internal logic and self-justification, and he considered it unfair to distort either system or reject parts of it in favor of the other in an attempt to achieve a forced harmony between them. He therefore held each one separately, acting as if each one were a different computer program. He would input a question into each of the programs to see what answer it would provide on the basis of its sources. He would then compare the outputs, but would not attempt to decide between them, since he had no non-arbitrary way to make such a decision. He therefore chose to keep each one separately, in a state of *non liquet*.

Some people feel uncomfortable with this approach, considering it a form of intellectual split or compartmentalization. After all, the critics say, Albalag was a human being who was unlikely to be able to maintain absolute neutrality between the two systems. Thus, whenever their basic sources would have provided him with conflicting data, he would probably have felt a greater psychological attachment to the data of one system than to those of the other. However, on this issue Albalag, fortunately enough, was not a modern thinker. He was not interested in the existential question of whether the self identifies with "its truth", but rather with what the truth itself is. Indeed, he would have been willing to sacrifice his psychological needs and intellectual comfort for that "truth". Moreover, he would even have been willing to sacrifice his own sense of psychological integrity for the sake of preserving the integrity of the systems that aspire to provide that truth. From his standpoint, even if he felt a greater psychological closeness to the data of one system than to the contradictory data of the other, this sense of closeness is not evidence that these data are more true, but only of the subjective psychological state of the system user.

However, even if it was not Albalag's main intent, his approach paradoxically also satisfies some deep existential sentiments, maybe even deeper than the need for harmony between sources. Anyone who has become deeply acquainted with both WRS and MRS, as Albalag was, is aware of the immense cultural and intellectual forces that they contain. Anyone who fully and sincerely allows himself to absorb these forces will find it difficult to identify with radical secular messages of the sort proposed by d'Holbach and Russell or radical anti-rationalist messages of the sort proposed by Loyola, Luther, Rabbi Nahman, and the like. Anyone who is truly familiar with a religious tradition and is acquainted with modern believers can no longer say that such traditions are based solely on fear, just as anyone who is familiar with WRS can no longer say that its only purpose is to release people's "desires" and evil inclinations. The roots of the two systems are different. WRS maintains a cautious trust in the basic cognitive tools, under the assumption that these sources are after all more reliable than authorities who presume to transcend them, while MRS maintains a great deal of distrust for these cognitive tools, both in view of their limited capacity and in fear of the influence that undesired sources may exercise upon them. Rather, MRS favors the data transmitted by sources that are considered reliable, having passed the test of time, and are said to be traced back to a supernatural source, which is free of the limitations and weaknesses of human nature. Now, since the adoption of a source model is to a great extent a function of psychological attachment, the question of trust is a crucial factor in it, as every individual adopts a source model according to the trust that he has in it. However, when a person is closely acquainted with both of the systems to more or less the same degree, he can understand the internal logic of both of them and can develop a psychological attachment to both.

Indeed, the model presented here for the philosophy of religion, which was illustrated for two particular systems, is equally applicable to the relations between any two systems that a person becomes deeply acquainted with and with which he identifies. Source Theory makes it possible for people to live in two worlds, as it were, on the condition that they become accustomed to replacing the Kantian question "What can I know?" with the question "What can I know within each of the systems that I am able to operate?"

CHAPTER SIX

Source Theory and the Philosophy of Law

The law as a subsystem

The law is a compartmentalized subsystem within every developed culture. In most (if not all) of those cultures we can find a definite, separate set of data that are known as laws. These data are transmitted by unique sources – the legislature, the courts and the like – that are not identical to those of the larger system, though not completely detached from them. These sources not only transmit the data, but also determine their being laws (the rules of recognition, in H. L. A. Hart's terms). In jurisprudence they have for ages been termed "sources of law", a terminology that anticipated that of Source Theory, and so it almost invites an analysis in terms of Source Theory.

Indeed, problems in the philosophy of law too can be expressed, and perhaps even solved, in terms of Source Theory. Since I cannot discuss all possible legal systems here, I will choose for my test case the modern legal system – the rational, Western one, a subsystem of WRS – which most of philosophers of law have considered. Here, too, I will not discuss a specific legal system but will take an ideal type as an object for analysis. This can be called the Western Rational Legal Subsystem. Nevertheless, at least some of the arguments I present here are true, *mutatis mutandis*, of more traditional legal systems as well.

Even though in every culture the law is a subsystem of the general cultural system, it does not always have the same degree of attachment to the parent system. Max Weber (1978, Volume II: 656) distinguished between formal (or formalistic) and non-formal systems. He defined a formal system as one that does not decide the law "upon an ethical, emotional or political basis" (ibid). To formulate Weber's stand more sharply and more radically (even if Weber himself would probably disapprove of this alteration), we could say that the Weberian ideal is that of an autarchic subsystem detached from the parent

---

How to cite this book chapter:
Brown, B 2017 *Thoughts and Ways of Thinking: Source Theory and Its Applications.*
　Pp. 103–117. London: Ubiquity Press. DOI: https://doi.org/10.5334/bbh.g. License:
　CC-BY 4.0

system, which is supposed to provide data from within itself. At first it would seem that it is supposed to provide an answer for every legal question without using any additional sources; and, indeed, Weber defines the formal system as "gapless" (ibid.: 657–658); However, as we shall see, such complete detachment is impossible, and the most that one can consider is the maximal degree of detachment.

We begin the discussion with the fundamental question of all political or legal philosophy, the question of authority. Afterwards we will discuss the sources of judgment and the application of judgment to facts.

Authority and its justification

The problem of authority is one of the oldest and most important in political philosophy and the philosophy of law. For the purposes of the present discussion we will define authority as one person's right to obligate another individual to obey his orders. This person could be a king, a legislator or any other person who claims to have legal authority. (Actually this applies, *mutatis mutandis*, to ethics as well, even though it was not legislated by any particular person, but for this reason we will leave it out of the discussion, to avoid complications). The question it raises is thus what gives the former person this right. The answer to this question, insofar as the responder affirms that this person actually has such authority, is that he has gained it by virtue of principle p. p is a sentence, and therefore it is transmitted by a source – let's call it d. The real authority behind p is therefore d. If d is a person, we can ask further who or what gives him/her that authority, and so on. In terms of Source Theory, a person with authority is nothing but a source (of orders), while the people who obey him have adopted this source (whether by choice or coercion). Thus the problem of justifying authority is parallel to the problem of justifying adoption in Source Theory. Both involve an infinite regress in a peculiar version stemming from the source-datum relation (See Raz 1970: 102). The principle p can therefore be considered the **authority justification principle**. (In philosophical discourse, the term "legitimation" is generally used to denote the justification of authority, so I will use it occasionally in place of "justification").

The legal philosophy that seems most suitable to Source Theory is Hans Kelsen's Pure Theory of Law (Kelsen 1965; see also Kelsen 1961, Chapter 10). Kelsen described law as a hierarchic structure of norms often equated to a pyramid. In this structure, most of the norms attain their validity from "higher" norms. Thus, municipal enactments attain their validity from the law of the state and the law of the state attains its validity from the constitution. At the top of every such system there is a basic norm of "You must obey x" that gives validity to the entire system. In a monarchy, for example, x is the king, but if some rebel topples that king, that basic norm will soon be changed. The basic norm itself is not justified by anything further; otherwise it would not be basic. As the ultimate justification for all the norms in the system, the basic norm cannot itself be subject to justification. It has been rightfully contended that Kelsen's theory is one of legal-theoretic foundationalism. It has received numerous critiques, many of them attacking it exactly for its foundationalist character. Source Theory can provide some defense for Kelsen's theory, but not in its entirety, as will be discussed below. The basic norm can be described as none but an adoption sentence, and the x of the basic norm is none but a superior source in the source model of the legal system. There is, however, one important distinction: in Kelsen's theory, law is a system, while in Source Theory, law is a subsystem. This is not just a matter of labeling. Kelsen is completely indifferent to the cultural environment in which law is established and of which law is a part. Being a staunch positivist, he is eager to detach law from morality, viewing the basic norm as not a moral norm but a "pure" legal one. He therefore also detaches law from the normative conventions of the society in which law works. These norms, however, are those that give the basic norm, and therefore the whole legal system, its legitimacy. Legitimacy is the sociopolitical twin of the epistemological "justification". As a result, these legitimizing norms prove superior to the basic legal norm. This point will be addressed further below in this chapter.

But the applicability of Source Theory to law does not necessitate a full commitment to the Pure Theory of Law over other theories. Kelsen's idea of a basic norm is not very far from H. L. A. Hart's "rule of recognition" (Hart 1961, Chapter 6; see the analysis in Marmor 2011, Chapters 1–3). Although Hart himself alluded to differences between the two concepts (Hart 1961: 105), it is quite clear that both of the rules serve as foundational elements of the legal system and can be considered adoption sentences. The claim of Bentham (1945, 1960) and Austin (1995) that the sovereign is that foundational element can also be reformulated in the terms of Source Theory, i.e. that the sovereign is a superior source in the model. Raz (1970), who coined the term "chain of validity" to describe the order of authorization in a way quite similar to our "chain of adoptions", claims that usually legal systems are defined by more than one source of authority (see Raz 1970, 1986, 1990), and so his theory calls for its reformulation in terms of "source model". In light of the insight I presented in Chapter Three, which claims that the issue of adopting a source or a system is essentially normative, we can say that the issue of the justification (legitimation) of authority is almost fully parallel to the issue of the justification of adoption.

In modern political philosophy, several principles have been suggested for justifying authority. Each of theories that have been presented in the history of political philosophy, such as those that determine the justification principles by "natural law", "social rules", "the social contract", or "the divine right of kings", assumes that its particular principle is self-evident. There is, however, reason to ask what the source of this principle is and what justification there is for its authority. To be precise, the source of this justification is not merely a truth source, but also an authority source, since it demands obedience, and, in this case, obedience to its command to grant authority to the authoritative body it "chose" by virtue of the principle it transmitted. As in epistemology, there is no escape here from the claim that the last justification is always internal – that is, arbitrary.

An especially interesting theory on this issue is offered by Joseph de Maistre, according to Owen Bradley's interpretation (1999, Chapter 5; its grains can be found in Huber 1958 and Lebrun 1965). Although this interpretation does not seem to be perfectly faithful to the French philosopher's thought, it is too brilliant and challenging to be abandoned; for precision's sake we will therefore call it the "Maistre-Bradley theory". To sum up the theory simply and briefly, it claims that all authority was originally acquired by force – that is, by violence (a similar theory was previously suggest by Paine 1792, who used it to mock the traditional authority, and later by Freud,1933). When this authority is maintained over time, it acquires legitimacy, which makes violence unnecessary. On the contrary, this legitimation is intended to deprive others of the right to use violence so as to obtain the authority. For this authority to become established, it must hide its historical roots. Therefore real authority can never be based on a particular event or document, but rather on a hidden, unrecognizable source. This provides the authority with a mysterious aura of "holiness" or "divinity", which makes it self-evident and allows it to be accepted. To quote Bradley:

> [L]egitimacy does not derive from "birth" but from simple longevity: "Everyone knows that there are fortunate revolutions and usurpations very criminal in their beginnings, to which, however, it pleases Providence to affix the seal of legitimacy by a long position". Maistre indeed expresses the suspicion that no great power has origins as "humble" as they might appear: "At the present day, with our philosophy, all our civilization, all our fine books, there is not, perhaps, one European power in a position to justify all its possessions in the face of God and Reason". ...
>
> Maistre presents this same general claim in an even more provocative form. In the early history of constitutions, "everything reduces to what I have called *legitimate usurpation*; the sovereign acts, obedience is general, tranquil, and constant; the option, if there is one, is particular, turbulent and temporary; finally, the sovereign sits down, and on his throne is written: I possess because I possess". This is legitimacy!
>
> For Maistre the beginnings of sovereignty, its "birth", if not its acquired name, are always illegitimate: hybrid, puny, inglorious, vague, and bloody (Bradley 1999: 112–113).

Despite this theory's cynical charm, however, it does not provide a solution for the essential problem. In effect, it gives up on the possibility of justifying authority. If violence is the justifying principle, then we can ask what justifies this very principle. One may suggest that the justifying source is some "unknown source", but this does not advance us any further. Its invisibility may make it an effective practical instrument on the level of the Machiavellian enterprise (which the Maistre-Bradley theory discusses), but it does not provide any answer on the level of philosophical justification. On this level, an unidentified source not only fails to serve as a good justification for an argument, but may even weaken it.

We therefore come to the same conclusion here about the concept of authority as we did in the epistemic arena about the concept of truth. This concept is meaningful only within a particular system whose basic sources are the ones that transmit the justification principle. The basic sources themselves do not need to be justified, since their justification is necessarily internal, that is, arbitrary. This characterization, which is pertinent for logical systems, is also correct, *mutatis mutandis*, for the social arena, where a cultural system is involved, and consequently for its normative subsystems. All of the "truths" in the system are those that it transmits and endorses, including normative truths. One of these truths is authority. This is the root of the centralized authority of the state (which is sometimes called "sovereignty"), including the authority of its various powers, one of which is the law. Since the law is also a system, it should be seen as a subsystem of the cultural one (see Mautner 2011, and the different approaches and rich references presented there).

Since the law's authority is derived from that of the cultural system, a situation in which the legislature enacts norms that are at odds with values accepted in the cultural system is quite problematic. Such a situation can be defined as a contradiction between two norms within the same cultural system: a substantive norm, which in this case is a value accepted by the cultural system; and an "empowering" norm, which is the one that authorizes the legislature to enact laws. As in cases where there are contradictions among the data in the epistemic arena, the source model is called upon to solve the problem through the division of labor, particularly through the hierarchy. The nature of the hierarchy that can accomplish this is the subject of the controversy in the philosophy of law between the naturalists (who advocate the theory of natural law) and the positivists. The former place the substantive norms higher on the hierarchy, with the empowering norms subordinate to them, while the latter advocate the opposite order.

How laws are made

The legal process is one in which the law is applied to the facts. There are thus two levels of discussion, that of the law and that of fact. The faculty of judgment is apparently the sole factor in this process, since the legal process connects general norms to individual cases through *modus ponens*: All those who steal things are liable to three years' imprisonment; John stole something; therefore John is liable to three years' imprisonment. This is the traditional conception of the legal process. Although Hage (1996) suggested a different calculus, based on a nonmonotonic logic, which claims that judgment is defeasible, for the purposes of our discussion I will ignore this novel idea and merely note that the essence of what I have to say here can be applied, *mutatis mutandis*, to this new logical conception of the legal process as well. I will therefore base my discussion on the conception of the legal process as the application of *modus ponens*. However, we must first understand how this is done, by analyzing the way the courts determine each of the levels, that of the law and that of the facts.

Judgments are determined by their sources. As I mentioned above, the term "source", which we have been using throughout all our discussions in this book, was developed mainly for the theory of law, and the term "sources of the law" was probably used in jurisprudence much before the term "sources of knowledge" was commonly accepted in epistemology. The classic theory of law recognizes various sources of law: written law, which is enacted by a legislative body; precedent, which is determined by the courts; custom, which is generally decided by the community, or at least by parts of it; and the like. The two great traditions of Western culture – the Continental and the Anglo-American – have been divided on the issue of the hierarchy of these sources. However, in most modern law systems the written law has the highest status in the hierarchy, while precedent and custom are valid only through its force. In any case, this will be the starting point of our discussion here, if only for the purpose of simplification.

Since the law is a general norm, from the standpoint of Source Theory it is a general datum. Underlying the laws are values, or principles, which the legislators seek to protect. In the simplest cases, each law embodies one value, but cases of this sort are actually very rare. In general each law embodies a number of values, as well as the balance among them as determined by the legislature. Since a logical analysis of the layers of such laws would be very complex, we will consider a very simple example here. With such an example, where the legislators are defending only one value, the defense is categorical. Thus the defense of this value takes the form, "Any action that is contrary to value v is prohibited", or, in more extreme and very rare cases, "Any action that promotes the value v is obligatory". Nowadays legislators generally do not express their orders in terms of prohibitions or obligations, but rather in terms of the sanctions to be imposed on anyone who acts in contradiction with the stated order. This is quite clear in criminal law, but it is also true of civil law, in which the protected value is generally private property and the sanctions are generally of the civil sort. As a result, prohibitions are now expressed in the form, "Those who perform act w will be sanctioned in the following way", while obligations are expressed in the form, "Those who do not perform act w will be sanctioned in the following way". However, this change of form should not divert us from the true normative content of the law, which is a prohibition or an obligation.

Consider, for example, the law that prohibits discrimination in hiring. The value that the law is protecting is equality. We can therefore analyze the layers of the law as an argument with this structure:

Acts that are opposed to the value of equality are prohibited.
<u>Discrimination in hiring is an act opposed to the value of equality.</u>
Conclusion: Discrimination in hiring is prohibited.

Let us analyze this argument with the classical distinction between normative and descriptive statements (ignoring its philosophical difficulties for the moment). In this example, both the major premise and the conclusion are normative statements, while the minor premise is a descriptive one. This is the case because it states that the concept "discrimination in hiring" is included in the concept "an act opposed to the value of equality". Even though this statement refers to normative concepts, it expresses the relationship between the concepts, which is a descriptive one. We can therefore say that the analysis of the law has the following layers: a normative major premise, which determines the higher norm, or the value; a descriptive minor premise; and a normative conclusion. Thus the justification of the law requires the following sources: one that justifies the higher norm; one that justifies the description; and one that justifies the logical deduction, that is, the conclusion.

Now consider the following example:

Acts that are opposed to the value of not risking human life are prohibited.
<u>Driving at more than 70 mph is an act that is opposed the value of not risking human life</u>.
Conclusion: Driving at more than 70 mph is prohibited.

In this example, too, the major premise and the conclusion are normative statements, while the minor premise is a descriptive one. However, the minor premise is not transmitted by the analysis of concepts but rather by experience – that is, the senses, with the aid of abstraction, which tell us that driving at more than 70 mph risks human life.

In ordinary legal proceedings, the major premise is a general datum, i.e., a sentence with the universal quantifier, while the minor premise applies it to a particular person. For example:

All those who steal are liable to three years' imprisonment.
<u>John stole something</u>.
Conclusion: John is liable to three years' imprisonment.

However, we can also imagine a case in which the minor premise is also general:

All those who steal are liable to three years' imprisonment.
<u>All politicians steal</u>.
All politicians are liable to three years' imprisonment.

In a case of this sort, the conclusion, too, is a general datum, and therefore a law. This allows it to appear as the major premise of yet another syllogism – for example:

All politicians are liable to three years' imprisonment.
<u>John is a politician</u>.
Conclusion: John is liable to three years' imprisonment.

However, we must now ask what status a general datum has when it becomes a law. The answer depends, as usual, on the source. If the sources of the law in the system decide that this datum is a law, then it has the status of a law; if not, it has the status of a fact, which must be proven by evidence for each case separately. Law courts also recognize another situation, in which the datum can be a **presumption**. A presumption of fact is a descriptive datum about which one of the sources of the law – generally the legislature – rules that it should be considered like a proven fact. However, most legal systems distinguish between a conclusive (or irrebuttable) presumption and a rebuttable one. If the presumption is conclusive, then it is just as valid as any other law, since the conclusions drawn from it are also conclusive. In contrast, if the presumption is rebuttable, then its main force is that it transfers the burden of proof to those who are trying to defeat it.

Consider another example:

All citizens who are responsible for their actions have legal capacity.
<u>All citizens over the age of 18 are responsible for their actions</u>.
Conclusion: All citizens over the age of 18 have legal capacity.

The minor (factual) premise is clearly arbitrary. We all know citizens under the age of 18 who are more responsible for their actions than some citizens over the age of 18, and citizens over the age of 18 who are not particularly responsible for their actions. The presumption that the legislature asserts here is conclusive, and they do not even bother to formulate it as a presumption, but draw the conclusion directly and formulate it as a law.

We can therefore state in summary that almost all laws are constructed out of several hidden layers. The datum that appears as the law itself is the "lower" datum in the pyramid of the syllogism, called "the legal rule" in the theory of law. The higher data are the **considerations** that led the legislature to enact the law. These data generally consist of two layers: the major premise, which is normative, and the minor premise, which is factual. At the top of the pyramid are the principles, which are normative data out of which the entire legal system is built.

This brings us to the questions of where the supreme principles of the legal subsystem are drawn from, and what is the origin of the factual data that serve as premises for its "lower" norms, As for the supreme principles, two alternatives are possible: Either they are principles of the cultural system in which the legal subsystem operates, or they are not. If the first alternative is correct, then the principles of the legal subsystem are justified by the principles of the cultural system. If the second alternative is correct, then they have no external justification – in other words, they are arbitrary. However, since the legal subsystem is generally a social phenomenon, such a situation hardly ever occurs, and when it does, it is considered problematic. Thus the supreme principles of the legal subsystem are generally drawn from the values of the broader cultural system. If the cultural system is WRS or one of its branches, then these values are moral ones (I mean moral in the secular-humanistic sense of the word). If the cultural system is a religious one, then these values are religious as well. As a result, in normal situations, the legal subsystem is not and cannot be autarchic, in contrast to Max Weber's postulation.

This is also true for the factual premises upon which laws are based. In the vast majority of cases these factual premises are not determined by the judge as "trier of fact" through a proceeding subject to evidence law, but are accepted by the lawmakers (legislators, judges, commentators) as true on the basis of common conventions. These conventions are accepted not by virtue of the legal subsystem, which does not deal with things of this sort, but because they are data within the general cultural system. As in the case of the principles, this case demonstrates the legal subsystem's dependence on the cultural system to which it belongs. Moreover, even if the legal system can be autarchic in the realm of principles, although this is not a healthy situation, in the realm of factual premises such autarchy is simply impossible. We need to keep this in mind for the next section of this chapter.

From a broader perspective, it would seem that Source Theory leads to normative relativism. A norm that is accepted within a particular system is justified by the basic sources of that system, and no source of any other system can validate or invalidate it. According to these claims, we cannot denounce cannibalism or murder based on "family honor" in cultures where they are accepted.

To be sure, this conclusion is derived from Source Theory in a purely formalist line of argumentation, and can therefore be considered as a normative version of the nihilistic absurdities, which are also derived directly in a similar line of argumentation. The way out of this relativism is likewise similar to the one we used in the case of the nihilistic absurdities – namely, the transition from a formalist to a pragmatist line of argumentation. At first glance it would seem that this does not solve our current problem, since even in the sociological arena, there are ancient cultural systems in which cannibalism and "family honor" murders are valid norms. Indeed, we cannot invalidate the internal justification of these norms within their systems. However, just as we used the **conservative rule** for individuals in our discussion of the absurdities, we can use it here for the society as a whole. The conclusion is not that we should rid ourselves of any basic sources we have because they are particularistic, since such a move would make it impossible for individuals to think at all. Instead, the legal subsystem should stick to its "native" sources, the ones that are at the basis of its cultural system. This system is the one in which it developed historically and in which it can be justified. In contrast to the individual, who may sometimes take a stand of a *non liquet* (and even that is not so appropriate in the normative realm), the society cannot afford a condition of a normative vacuum or undecidedness. Therefore the state, which is the body within which the legal subsystem exists, is not value-neutral, and it is pointless for it to aspire to be so. On the contrary, a state adopts the sources of a particular cultural system with all of its values, and one of its roles is to embody these values in its laws. Consequently, it should not allow other cultural systems that exist within it the freedom to act as they please, unless their values are not opposed to the fundamental values of the state. This does not mean that it should prevent any other system from existing, but it can, and perhaps even should, prevent an alien system that exists within its borders from damaging its most fundamental values. This means that it is the right of a legal system which embraces cannibalism to suppress a legal system that opposes it, if the latter exists within the political borders of the former, and that the people who do not embrace cannibalism should subordinate their norms to it. It is the right of the people who adopt the humanist legal system, which opposes cannibalism, to try to escape the one which embraces it, or even oppose it within the constraints of that system, but as long as they live within the state (or culture) which embraces it, they should accept its authority.

How judgments are made

Our discussion of the structure of legal norms also has some ramifications for the distinction between formalistic and non-formalistic (or value-oriented) legal systems (I am now using the term "formalism" in a legal-theoretic sense, in contrast to the way I used it above, which was in contrast to pragmatism). This is not a dichotomy but rather a continuum that can be formulated as follows: The more the legislators try to formulate the rules in more general terms, the less formalistic they are, and vice versa (Brown 2008).

It has been claimed that, in general, traditional normative systems tend to be more formalistic, while modern legal systems tend to be less so (Wigmore

1981, Volume IX, §2405; Barak 2005, 30). To paraphrase Hobsbawm (1989: 4), the increase of non-formalistic interpretations of traditional formalistic norms demonstrates that they have become weaker. This is true only for traditional systems because formalism is one of the typical features of such systems, at least in their external appearance.

Law theorists have pointed out that the justifications for the formalistic approach are the law's certainty and predictability. However, the formalistic approach in traditional systems actually has quite a different origin. In the non-formalistic approach it is necessary to make a deduction from a major and a minor premise to obtain a normative conclusion. This procedure is carried out by human beings – commentators or judges. The traditional approach places less trust in human beings in general, and their individual sources in particular. It embodies the tacit assumption that it is better for the system's basic sources to carry out the deductive procedure themselves, and not leave it to the people who happen to be around at some particular time. Traditional systems therefore tend to use presumptions extensively, and this is what actually leads to their formalistic character.

As we concluded, the principles of a legal system are those of the cultural system in which it developed. Consequently, a radical non-formalistic approach cannot merely use the principles of the legal subsystem itself, but must attempt to go beyond them to the principles of the larger cultural system. Thus, although a Weberian separation between the legal subsystem and the cultural system does indeed reflect the formalist approach to legislation, it does not necessarily guarantee that the legal subsystem has no gaps. On the contrary, sometimes a legal system that tries to detach itself from the larger cultural system is less successful in coping with gaps, as it has abandoned a source that might have filled them in, while a non-formalist system might be more successful in that regard (as will be discussed further below). Actually, it is the formalist systems that have greater difficulty in removing their gaps. We may conclude, then, that the undetachable link between the values of the legal subsystem and those of the larger cultural system supports the non-formalist tendency to make use of the latter, at least in cases of normative gaps.

Part of the judicial process is the determination of the minor premise – the facts. The legal branch that determines how facts are decided in the legal process is evidence law. The laws of evidence determine which data should be considered "facts" and be presented in the legal proceedings, and which should not. From the viewpoint of Source Theory, the laws of evidence are a prototypical model of compartmentalization, as they are used to determine which of the existing data are admissible or inadmissible by the law, which is a source in the legal subsystem. Other sources are then applied to the admissible data – mainly the basic cognitive tools of the presiding judges.

The rejection of inadmissible data is a prototypical example of compartmentalization that is not based on a contradiction between data from different sources. The presentation of contradictory data, such as contrasting testimonies, is not prohibited. On the contrary, such data are often an important layer in the construction of the decision about the facts. The reasons for rejecting evidence are generally flaws in the way the evidence was gathered, such as "fruit of the poisonous tree" (in legal systems in which this rule prevails) or fact-based presumptions about the unreliability of the sources from which they were transmitted, as in the rule against hearsay.

Incidentally, in most legal systems, when a judge is faced with a question involving a law from a foreign legal system – especially if this law applies to the litigated case in virtue of the rules of private international law – the content of the law is considered a question of fact. It is decided according to the testimony of an expert witness, whose opinion is considered evidence of fact. Such witnesses are examined and cross-examined about their testimony in the same way as any other witnesses. This rule of evidence, although reasonable in and of itself, raises serious philosophical questions about the very distinction between law and fact. When a judge decides a case within her legal subsystem, isn't she determining a fact about the legal situation of this subsystem, just as the expert witness does in connection with a foreign legal system? It seems to me that this might actually be a correct description of the matter.

To return to the main issue, as soon as a judge is presented with an assortment of admissible data, she is faced with the problem that some of these data may be contradictory. Since all of them are admissible, they all belong to the system, and so her job is to decide among them. Most legal systems have few if any decision rules, so the decision must be made with the judge's discretion, which means her own sources. Since the legal subsystem does not provide any sources of this type, the judge's sources should be, once again, the basic sources of the cultural system to which she belongs, which the legal subsystem is also part of. This sort of decision, which is critical for the results of the proceedings, is thus based on the sources of the cultural system rather than any "autarchic" sources of the legal subsystem. Once the judge has come to a decision on the basis of these sources, the facts that were determined according to them are considered to have been proven.

At this stage we come to an issue that philosophers of law have dealt with more than any other – the application of the law to these proven facts. The legal-theoretic literature generally distinguishes between "easy cases" and "hard cases" in this regard. In terms of Source Theory, one could say that easy cases are those where the connection between the factual data and the legal data is established by the simple application of the power of judgment (*Urteilskraft*), using *modus ponens* – that is, when the facts clearly establish a special case of the antecedent of the general rule. In contrast, hard cases are those where there is no such match, and applying the rule to the facts requires interpretation, so that the judge or the commentator has to use additional sources and a more complex process of deduction. According to Hart (1961, Chapter 7), at this stage the judge is faced with an "open texture" where she has to use her judicial discretion. Since this discretion is free, whatever decision the judge makes is valid, and as soon as she makes the decision it becomes part of the law. According to Dworkin (1978, Chapter 2; 1985, Chapter 5), at this stage the judge must consider the principles of the legal system, which are an inseparable part of it, and try to find the proper balance among them. Dworkin claims that there is only one balance that is correct within the system, and if the judge fails to find it, her decision does not become part of the law.

We can reformulate this controversy in terms of Source Theory. Hart claims that judicial discretion is virtually free, but since "no man is an island", and even judges are part of the cultural system in which the law operates, judges normally make use of considerations that are derived from sources in this cultural system. Dworkin claims that judges must remain within the limits of the legal subsystem, but even he admits that its principles are those of "morality" (Dworkin 1978, Chapter 2) – that is, the principles are drawn from the cultural system (he uses the term "morality" because he is referring to WRS). Moreover, since, as we have seen, the legal subsystem's principles are almost always based on the values of the cultural system to which it belongs, there is practically no difference between them on the issue of the sources used by the judges. This lack of difference is extended to other areas by some of Hart's followers, who explicitly claim that even the judicial discretion have "sources" – such as the system's fundamental moral values, public opinion, and the judges' personal tendencies, all closely linked to the judge's cultural system – so that they are not absolutely free, as Hart seems to be claiming. In light of this analysis, the Hart-Dworkin controversy seems to be greatly diminished.

However, we still need to consider one aspect of this controversy that has remained open – whether every legal question has only one right answer (as the question is often formulated in the literature). Here, too, it seems that Source Theory can help us by greatly simplifying the discussion. Since we have concluded that judges must consider their cultural system's sources, we must distinguish between two levels of this system – the real one and the ideal one. We have shown above that the sources of the ideal system transmit data that are necessarily compatible (though not always accessible). Thus there cannot be two incompatible right answers to the same question within one ideal system. The real system, in contrast, is much less perfect. It embodies the aspiration to attain the purity of the ideal system, but the full achievement of this aspiration is utopian, and even its partial achievement is at best occasional. Therefore, Dworkin, who claims that there is one right answer to any legal question, is right on the ideal plane, but on the real plane it is not always possible to achieve one such answer, and so the law must recognize a range of possible answers as long as all of them are within the "zone of legitimacy" of the system (in the formulation of Barak 1989: 12).

Dworkin himself seems to admit the ideal of nature of his "one right answer". Even if that answer remains unattainable, its existence is important to him as a tool for criticizing judicial decisions in "hard cases". In Hart's theory, where such cases create an "open texture", the judge seems to be free to decide, and any decision he makes will become the law, and will thus become "right". Thus, while in Dworkin's theory the existence of "one right answer" allows for criticism of the judge's decision, in Hart's theory its absence prevents any such criticism. This, indeed, is one of the arguments raised against Hart's theory. We can now support this argument by Source Theory. Only in a situation where there is a fixed system with agreed-upon basic sources can there be criticism or debate about judicial discretion (or anything else), since, as we have seen above, there can only be debates on the basis of common sources.

In many ways, the relation between law and morality in the normative sphere is quite similar to the relation between science and metaphysics in the descriptive sphere. On the ideal, utopian plane, in both disciplines, data should go from the basic to the derivative, or (to use Hegel's terms) from the abstract to the concrete. On the utopian plane, we know the basic moral principles, we know the correct formulae for how they should be balanced, and from those we safely derive the rules of law. Similarly, in the descriptive realm, we know the principles of reality, and they form the basis of any particular science that covers this or another part of reality. However, neither moral philosophers nor metaphysicians have reached the evident truths, and, given the society's urgent need for more everyday truths, the law has given up the quest for the solid rock for the norms and science has given up the quest for the solid rock for the facts. Neither lawyers nor scientists seek absolute truths, but rather something that will work. They have thus ignored the basic questions, taken some less basic premises for granted (usually without much awareness), and built their disciplines upon them. Indeed, in this sense both law and science are disciplines of despair.

To be sure, this despair has never occurred in reality, because in the development of human cultures, people did not even try to go from the abstract to the concrete but rather the other way around. The persons who established the law or the sciences took their underlying principles for granted, usually without even being aware of them. Only after concrete norms or facts were established did philosophers come and try to uncover the principles underlying them, whether in order to reaffirm them or in order to re-examine them. These lawyers and scientists often showed little interest in the discussions of those intellectuals who tried to explain the foundations of their daily work. However, the more their disciplines developed, the more they returned to the basic questions that they had originally sought to avoid. And so, from time to time they have had to deal with the principles that underlie their disciplines. They had to cope with philosophical questions, often without philosophers' professional tools

We can now return to the discussion we started previously, where we defined "formalism" and "non-formalism" in legislation, and discuss the two concepts as they relate to judicial decisions and legal interpretation. Hart defined "formalism" according to his theoretical model, as a situation in which a judge does not recognize the existence of a "penumbra" and decides according to the existing rules, even if they do not really apply to the facts at hand. He defined the opposite approach, which he called "rule-skepticism", as a situation in which the judge does not recognize the rules and decides according to his own discretion, even when the rules fully apply to the facts at hand (Hart 1961, Chapter 7). In terms of Source Theory, Hart's model can be reformulated as follows: The formalist uses only the lower sources of the legal subsystem, while the rule-skeptic uses the basic sources of his own personal system and, to an even greater extent, those of his cultural system, which overlap with the higher sources of the legal subsystem (these seem to be the main sources of his discretion). This model is quite similar to our distinction between the formalist and non-formalist approaches to the nature of the legal subsystem itself, as discussed above. In the spirit of that discussion, we might say that formalism and non-formalism are not necessarily connected with the issue of the core versus the penumbra. Rather, we can now return, with greater support, to the model we suggested instead. Formalism is an approach that tends to use mainly the less general norms, while non-formalism tends to use the "higher" factual and normative layers they reflect, especially those of the legal subsystem itself, but also those of the cultural system as a whole. The distinction between the two approaches is not dichotomous, but rather ranges over a continuum.

In the epistemological realm, we argued that difference in the identity of the sources or the division of labor between them is not only a difference in *thoughts* but also a more fundamental difference in *ways of thinking*. Now we can similarly say that in the legal realm, the difference between the formalists and the non-formalists is not only in their substantive thoughts about the law and the facts, but is also a difference between two distinct legal ways of thinking (which Source Theory calls sources or source models). Indeed, it seems to me that this insight also agrees with the intuitions of experienced jurists.

We have so far examined the relations between two systems (Chapter Five) and the relations between a subsystem and a mother system (Chapter Six). We will now examine the functioning of another type of subsystem within the larger system, i.e. language (Chapter Seven).

CHAPTER SEVEN

Source Theory and the Philosophy of Language

Language as a subsystem

Language is a compartmentalized subsystem within every culture. Large traditions may often include a few or even many languages as subsystems. It should be noted, however, that language is a peculiar type of subsystem. In the previous chapter we examined law, which is a typical subsystem: Western legal systems are transmitted by the sources of WRS, Jewish law by the sources of the system of Judaism, Christian law from those of Christianity, Muslim law from those of Islam, etc. Not so is the case with language. The sources of languages are neither the basic cognitive tools nor any holy scripture. Consequently, Western languages are not particularly more rational than others, and the languages used by the monotheist religions are not particularly "religious". In this sense, the characterization of language as subsystem is rather problematic, and I definitely do not wish to cover up this difficulty. The reason for which I still consider language as a type of subsystem is because it develops within a **culture**, and cultures, at least in some aspect of their existence, can be described as **cultural systems** in the sense attached to this term in this book. In this context, the languages are built through data transmitted by the agents who operate those cultural systems.

In all the natural languages, the primary source of this subsystem is the cumulative factor which we called "the cultural community" and named h. By saying this, I am not necessarily committing myself to Wittgenstein's private language argument (Wittgenstein 1953, §§244–271), which argues that such a language is impossible. Rather, I am contending that if such a language is possible, it requires a separate and different analysis. The following analysis relates to natural languages which clearly all exist as subsystems within multi-personal

---

How to cite this book chapter:
Brown, B 2017 *Thoughts and Ways of Thinking: Source Theory and Its Applications.*
  Pp. 119–136. London: Ubiquity Press. DOI: https://doi.org/10.5334/bbh.h. License: CC-BY 4.0

cultures. The subsystem of language should be considered as a compartmentalized one because it has a very limited role of determining the **meaning** relations among different types of data, usually auditory or visual, in the larger system. The former are words or collections of words ("expressions") and the latter are objects or designata. The relation between them – meaning – has been the focus of many debates, some stressing its representational function, and others its emotive and activating one. Some philosophers have claimed that a word has a meaning only if it denotes a particular object in the "external" world, while others contend that some words (e.g. prepositions) do not have such referents, and acquire their meaning only through use, often in the context of larger units such as sentences. Some claim that a word's context is often crucial for understanding its meaning. In any case, meaning is a relation in which verbal objects (words, expressions, sentences) are attached to objects in the world ("things", "states of things"), and – which is more important for us – it is source h that almost always determines which words will mean what. Source h is also responsible for any changes in this linkage.

In this process, source h works almost completely independently of all the other sources of the system. This is clear because the great majority of links between words and the world are arbitrary. There is nothing "doggish" in the sound of the syllable "dog" or in the view of the three letters d-o-g. This arbitrariness applies to all of the systems: there is nothing "rational" in this link in WRS, just as there is nothing "religious" in this link in MRS. Even onomatopoeias – rare phenomena anyway – do not provide sufficient reasons for the naming of their objects, both because different sounds could be attached to those objects with equally convincing "reasons" and because they do not work in the case of written words. There might be some rationality in the rule that an adjective related to a noun appears in proximity to that noun, but there is no particular rationale in putting it right after the noun, as in Latin, or right before it, as in English, or sometimes before and sometimes after, as in French. These three languages are all subsystems within cultures that all heavily contributed to the development of WRS. In short, languages are based on arbitrary rules embraced by the community. This makes language a form of convention, in the sense attached to this term by Lewis (1969) and Marmor (2009). The subsystem of language therefore works independently of the other sources of the system and is compartmentalized to its limited role. The fulfillment of this role, however, is crucial for the proper functioning of the cultural system as a living system, since any living system consists of testimonies, which are transmitted in a language.

The fact that a certain word has a meaning relation to a certain object, or the fact that a certain expression (or sentence) means that such and such action is required or expected of the listener will be called **meaning data**. Except for very rare cases, meaning data reflect the meaning relations determined by h. Meaning data are usually transmitted by secondary sources: In early childhood, our parents teach us the meanings of words, and in later stages our teachers and books assume this function. The media and other means of public communication also play a role in this process.

There is something unique in the subsystem of language: Most of our secondary sources use language to transmit the data of the primary sources. In the earliest stages of language learning, this cannot work, since the child does not have even the most basic vocabulary. "One needs pincers to make pincers" (*Tzevat bitzevat 'asuyah*), as the Mishnah says (M. Avot 5, 6). The exact way in which this process takes place is the business of developmental psychologists, who indeed give it much attention, and will not be addressed here. What is important for our discussion is the fact that such non-linguistic testimony data can and do exist.

The philosophy of language has become one of the major areas of modern philosophy. I intend to discuss only a few of the issues that have been raised in this area. I claim that philosophers of language have created an atmosphere of mystification about the relation between words and the objects they denote. I believe that Source Theory can help eliminate this mystification with its claim that objects, as well as the words denoting them and the sentences referring to them, are all the results of the same act: transmission of data by sources. Different sources transmit the data, while witnesses – generally from the system user's community – transmit the words that refer to them. Since language is part of every cultural system, the fact that a certain word pertains to a certain object is a datum about the way the cultural community uses the word.

On the basis of these claims I intend to propose a semantic theory for words and sentences, but I begin the discussion with the issue of naming individual objects, partly because I want to start out with an existing theory that is somewhat similar to Source Theory. This is Kripke's naming theory, which I use as a basis for discussing other aspects of language.

Naming individual objects

The issue of how to determine the identity of objects was raised by some important philosophers, but was brought to attention of many mainly by Saul Kripke in his lectures, which later became his book, *Naming and Necessity*. Kripke discusses only the identity of individual objects, but his theory is applicable, *mutatis mutandis*, to general terms as well (Kripke also expanded his theory to "natural kinds"). Kripke presents two main theories. The first one, whose ancestors are Frege (1952a, b) and Russell (1956), considers names a shortened form of definite descriptions – that is, the collection of general properties attributed to an object. If these properties change (which raises the question of what properties are at issue), then the object loses its identity. Kripke presents the theory's problems at length, finally rejecting it. Instead he proposes another theory, which was originated by Mill but developed mainly by Kripke himself, and has come to be known as the "causal-historical theory". He formulates the essential points of his theory as follows:

> Someone, let's say, a baby, is born; his parents call him by a certain name. They talk about him to their friends. Other people meet him. Through various sorts of talk the name is spread from link to link as if by a chain. A speaker who is on the far end of this chain, who has heard about, say, Richard Feynman, in the marketplace or elsewhere, may be referring to Richard Feynman even though he can't remember from whom he first heard of Feynman or from whom he ever heard of Feynman. He knows that Feynman was a famous physicist. A certain passage of communication reaching ultimately to the man himself does reach the speaker. He then is referring to Feynman even though he can't identify him uniquely. He doesn't know what a Feynman diagram is, he doesn't know what the Feynman theory of pair production and annihilation is. Not only that: he'd have trouble distinguishing between Gell-Mann and Feynman. So he doesn't have to know these things, but, instead, a chain of communication going back to Feynman himself has been established by virtue of his membership in a community which passed the name on from link to link, not by a ceremony that he makes in private in his study: "By 'Feynman' I shall mean the man who did such and such and such and such."
>
> … A rough statement of a theory might be the following: An initial "baptism" takes place. Here the object may be named by ostension, or the reference of the name may be fixed by a description. When the name is "passed from link to link," the receiver of the name must, I think, intend when he learns it to use it with the same reference as the man from whom he heard it (Kripke 1980: 91–92, 96).

Kripke does not offer a theoretical or symbolic development of this "chain of communication", but it is clear that Source Theory, as well as the Source Calculus underlying it, fits Kripke's theory very closely. In source-theoretic terms, each of the "links" Kripke mentions is a source of the testimony type, which is adopted, like all testimony, in a mediated manner (that is, the basic cognitive tools transmit the property, in this case of being named so-and-so). The "community" that Kripke mentions, of which the individual under discussion is a member, is precisely our cultural community, which we denote by h. The source model of this subsystem also includes a hierarchy rule, which states that if the datum at stake is of the type of naming datum (that is, data transmitting the name attached to an object), then h has supremacy over all other sources in the system. Thus system users believe that the name of any object is the one that was transmitted to them by their cultural community.

However, Kripke comes to some very far-reaching conclusions – namely, that the name of an object is its rigid designator, which fixes its identity in all possible worlds. It seems to me that Kripke is mistaken here, and I will try to show why. To make the ideas concrete, I will present a simple, prosaic episode based on Kripke's description, and then try to deduce its implications.

A baby is born. His parents have not yet named him. Actually, they are not sure about the name they want to give him. In the meantime, they call him "the baby" – a "name" given to billions of newborns in similar conditions. They can recognize him easily in the hospital and can recount quite a few facts about him: when he was born, to whom, at what weight, how he looks ("just like his grandmother!" of course), what his health condition is, and the like. Furthermore, they can report these data for each and every day of "the baby"'s young life. A week passes and they decide to call the baby "David".

Now let's analyze what has happened here. In Kripke's terms the "baptism" stage occurred when the young parents decided on the baby's name. At this point, David acquired a name and this name, according to Kripke, is his rigid designator in all possible worlds. In terms of Source Theory, on the other hand, there were several stages to this process. At the first stage, right after the baby's birth, the new parents' senses (together with some other basic cognitive tools) transmitted data about the baby: the fact that he was born to this particular woman, the time and place of that birth, his weight at birth, his external properties, his health condition (as reported by the doctors and nurses), and the like. They also identified him as their first/second/third… child. In the following days, they received more data about his development and other data that could help them recognize him. Only at a later stage did they give him an official name.

Now suppose that the young parents had not given him his name a week after he was born, but had kept learning more and more data about him. In this case, all these data would be ascribed to "the baby". His identity as the person initially recognized through such-and-such features could therefore be fixed without naming him (in fact, Kripke himself gave an excellent example of this sort of case, as "the man who corrupted Hadleyburg" [ibid, p. 24], but did not confront it with the theory he himself presented later on). Even when they would eventually give him his name, this datum would not be different in its logical status from all the other data that they had accumulated along the way. Even if, for some reason, they one day decided to change his name and call him Jonathan, the fact that he was named David a week after his birth would remain one of the data in his biography. This would not change anything about the identity of the child, because it was fixed before any name was given to him, and without any connection to it.

According to a story that I once heard (I cannot vouch for its truth, but even if it's imaginary it could well have happened), Yemenite Jews used to believe that when the Angel of Death goes out on his lethal journey, he identifies intended victims by their name (apparently they had read *Naming and Necessity*...). Therefore a family which had suffered several cases of infant deaths would avoid giving the newborn a name, calling him simply "Al-Walad" ("the boy"), so that the Angel of Death would have trouble identifying him. When the boy was eight days old, he had to be circumcised according to Jewish law, and the circumcision is customarily accompanied by naming the child (this is the Jewish equivalent of baptism). When the ritual circumcisor asked the parents what to name the child, they said "Al-Walad", and this became his name. In such a case, does the child not have an identity? If we say that the circumcision ceremony established that his name was Al-Walad, then we can ask what his status was until the eighth day. Did he not have an identity before that? During that first week, would it not have been possible to ask what would have happened to him in other possible worlds? Would a definite description such as "the youngest son of the Tzan'ani family" not have established his identity sufficiently? Kripke's theory seems too rigid in light of these questions. All this shows us that there are two different types of "baptism". The first one is the person's first acquaintance with the object, when the latter is transmitted to the former as a datum and becomes a part of his/her individual system. The second is the one that Kripke discussed, that is, the data that transmits the name of the object, which represents its identity from the standpoint of the cultural system.

In this way, the problem of identity is solved almost automatically. The philosophical literature is full of sentences of the sort of "Samuel Clemens is Mark Twain". In general, such sentences are presented to demonstrate the impossibility of substituting identical objects for one another, since the sentence in the example is different from the sentence "Mark Twain is Mark Twain". While the first sentence tells us something new, the second one is a mere tautology. One of the solutions suggested for this problem makes use of Frege's distinction between sense and reference, claiming that the identity is one of reference but not of sense. Although Frege's distinction is indeed an important one, Source Theory eliminates the problem from the outset. In Source Theory the name "Samuel Clemens" is essentially an abbreviation of "the object that sources a, b, and c (his parents, the registrar of births, and his early acquaintances, for example) called 'Samuel Clemens'", while "Mark Twain" is an abbreviation of "the object that sources d, e, and f (he himself, his publisher and the community of bibliophiles, for example) called 'Mark Twain'". The identity sentence thus tells us something new because it does not involve two identical data. Moreover, even when the identifications come from the same sources, as is the case with Frege's famous sentence "The morning star is the evening star", different transmissions are involved.

Let us take one step further. Although naming an object is an accepted social practice in all the societies we know about, it is definitely a culture-dependent pattern and not a necessity. We can imagine another possible world, or even merely another society, in which people do not have names but are identified by their occupations and places of residence, and are enumerated in order of age if there is more than one person with the same occupation in the same place. For example, one person might be the oldest carpenter in Pinsk, while another might be the second oldest shoemaker in Minsk. Children who have not yet acquired an occupation are identified in this world according to their parents and their order of birth, so that one child might be the oldest son of the oldest carpenter in Pinsk, while another might be the youngest daughter of the school principal in Minsk. Even if this system is more complicated than giving a person a short, simple name, it is still possible.

How would questions of the sort posed by Kripke be answered in this world? We could ask whether the oldest carpenter in Pinsk would be the same person if he had not been a carpenter, or whether he would be the same person if he was the youngest carpenter in Pinsk. The answer to these questions would be definitely "Yes", because in a society of this type it would be obvious that the term "the oldest carpenter in Pinsk" is intended only to determine the person's identity (as the person who is known as the oldest carpenter in Pinsk in the real world) but not to determine his necessary qualities. Even though the term functions as a sort of name, it is undoubtedly a definite description. Would anyone claim that under such conditions the person's identity is not fixed? In general, since we have come to the conclusion that the very act of naming is a socio-cultural act, how could metaphysical issues of necessity and possibility depend on it?

The concepts of objects (I will refer mainly to individual objects) that we have in our minds are constantly changing. Let us focus for the moment on a particular person – myself, in the example – and imagine that all the details that were transmitted to me about the object are preserved in their entirety. In such a situation, at every stage, the concept includes more and more data that have accumulated about this object. These data have two aspects: external and internal. In the above example, the parents' concept of the baby at t1 is different from their concept of him at t2, after they acquired more data about him. At each stage at which some source is operating in regard to the object under discussion, my concept of that object becomes richer. This concept is therefore continually growing.

We all know, however, that this is not what happens in real life. The main reason for this is that things are forgotten. In real life we do not always remember from what source we received each datum, or when, where, and in what circumstances we obtained it. At some point, the identity of the object in my mind is "Someone/thing about which my reliable sources transmitted to me such and such data". A "reliable source" for this purpose is one that has been adopted by my cultural community, whether directly or indirectly. In the case under discussion, these reliable sources seem to belong to my individual system – my senses, my understanding, and the evidence I obtained through these sources – but the reason I believe the data provided by these sources is the fact that they serve as basic sources of my cultural system, as long as there are no other data that contradict them.

If any particular datum belonging to that concept is rejected, it is because another datum has been added to the mind from a source that is considered more reliable. If I read in the newspaper that my neighbor, who I had believed until then to be named Mark Jones, was convicted in court of being a conman whose real name is John Smith, then the concept of this object in my mind becomes "the person about whom reliable sources transmitted to me that he has properties A-B-C, but the newspaper transmits that the court transmits that he does not have property C (the possessor of the name 'Mark Jones') but rather property D". Here the system acts in an even more complicated way. Now I do not remember which reliable sources transmitted properties A-B-C, but I do remember the degree of reliability that I ascribed to them – high enough so that I would believe their data, but not high enough to continue to believe them when a source with greater status in the hierarchy (the court, as transmitted through the mediation of the newspaper and received by my basic cognitive tools) rejects these data. I thus give the court (as transmitted through the mediation of the newspaper and my basic cognitive tools) a higher position in my source model than the forgotten sources due to which I believed property C in the first place. However, my greater trust in this source is not only a result of my personal source model, it is also accepted in the source model of the general cultural system to which I belong. In general, I tend to forget the sources that transmitted data to me when I can assume that they were transmitted by h. System users therefore take it as a rebuttable presumption that the data transmitted by h belong to the cultural system and were received from its adopted sources. Therefore they are considered atemporally and impersonally "accepted". As soon as a particular datum is considered as if it had been transmitted by h, the speaking self no longer has to remember from whom or when it was actually received, and so he tends to forget this. This determination of identity, however, does not stem from any metaphysical importance of h, but only from its high position in the hierarchy of sources of my personal system, and its importance to my practical life. If, for example, I held a personal source model where h did not have a high position in its hierarchy, or did not belong to it at all, then the object would presumably obtain its identity in some other way. Mark Jones, for example, would be identified as "the neighbor across the hall", which is an important datum in my practical life. We may call this process "tagging".

This is how things are in people's personal systems, but they are a little different in a cultural system. Here h is necessarily a critically important source by virtue of the fact that a cultural system is a broad collective system. I know very well that I cannot always call Mark Jones "my neighbor" when I am talking to other people, so his name is important here. In the cultural communities in which most of us live, a person's name is the most useful means of identifying him – as well as for fixing his reference – since it belongs to the public sphere that is common to everyone. Since h is the source with the highest position in the hierarchy for identifying objects in that sphere, the point where h transmits a means of identification becomes the crucial point for fixing the object's reference. In this system we can therefore consider the moment when we are told a person's name to be the moment of his "baptism", at least within our personal systems. Nevertheless, even this fixing of the object's reference is not absolute. For example, we might find out that the name by which the person is known is not his real name (as in the case of Jones-Smith), or the person can change his name or adopt a pen name that is better known than his real name. In cases of this sort, as in one's personal system, the name will be redetermined on the basis of the new datum if the source transmitting it is more important than the one that transmitted the previous name. Nevertheless, the final step of the "baptism" is always completed by h's transmission of the datum. These are thus cases of a second "baptism", and more than two are also possible. In fact, these are all acts of tagging, while the word "baptism" is proper only for one of them – the act of naming. The very fact that there can be more than one "baptism" teaches us that none of them really serves as a rigid designator, in the strict sense of the word. The important point is that the later "baptism" is always based upon an earlier one, so that the first one remains the datum that properly fixes the object's reference for the future. But the first "baptism" is the individual person's acquaintance with the object, and so it fixes its identity only for the individual system, so, here again, it cannot serve as a rigid designator in the strict sense of the word. John Smith's parents came to know him when he was born at the hospital, his childhood friends became acquainted with him at school or in the neighborhood, his friends from work know him as an adult and first met him at their common workplace; I know him as my neighbor and first met him when he moved into the apartment across the hall; and so on. All of these persons have, therefore, a different "first baptism" of Smith according to different "baptismal properties". The only power of the object's name is derived from the fact that a person's name is more or less common to most of the community: At some stage we understand that many people know Smith, each of them by different "baptismal properties", but we allow ourselves to assume that all of them call him John Smith. This makes his name the most convenient property for identification, and that is what usually gives the naming the power of a second baptism. But this is just a fact on the communicative ("Gricean", if you will) level, stripped of any metaphysical aspect, and certainly not anything that turns it into a rigid designator in the strong sense of the word.

When people become famous through their penname or underground name, and these names become better known than their original ones (Molière, Max Stirner, Lewis Carroll, Mark Twain, O. Henry, Lenin, Stalin and George Orwell, to name just a few), we may consider the act of attaching these names as a third "baptism", no less powerful than the second. Furthermore, where famous people are concerned, their identity may be determined partly by their achievements, if these are considered by h to be their especially well-known qualities. Kripke raises this possibility in an example he presents concerning Gödel's identity, suggesting that it was established as "the man to whom the incompleteness of arithmetic is commonly attributed" (Kripke 1980: 88). Although he offers some reservations about this suggestion, he does conclude that it is possible, under the condition that the source h (in our terms) is not the factor that fixes Gödel's reference, but rather Gödel's parents, or whoever was first to transmit the datum of his name, somewhere back in an early link of the chain. Personally, I do not see any problem fixing a person's reference on the basis of the present situation, in which the chain of transmission has ended and the transmission of a datum by h which attributes an identifying property to Gödel leads to a new "baptism". This, too, should be recognized as a "third baptism" of a different type. This is just an example. We can imagine more complicated examples of "third baptisms", or fourth ones, or more.

I will summarize my conclusions up to this point as follows:

- There is never any one absolute "rigid designator" that fixes the reference of an individual object forever. The concept of an object is dynamic and determined in accordance with the person's memory of the data that have accumulated about the object.
- Among the various data that accumulate about an object, there are some that the system considers more important than others. Their degree of importance stems from both the reliability attributed to the source that transmits them and their usefulness in everyday life. These data are often used as properties by which the object is tagged, and thus become the determiners of the object's reference within that system.
- When an individual system is involved, the most rigid designator of an object is the system activator's first acquaintance with the object, through the object's unique properties as transmitted to her at that event. This may be considered the "first baptism" in that system. Afterwards she can tag them differently and consequently create other determination(s), in accordance with the importance of the data. Since the individual is part of a cultural system, at some stage she adopts the methods of fixing an object's reference that are accepted in her cultural system, as follows:
- When a cultural system is involved, an object's reference is initially fixed by naming it (and in this context we may accept Kripke's thesis). This is a "second baptism" for many of the members of the community already acquainted with the object. There can also be other ways of fixing the object's reference in which different names are attached to the object in place of the initial one. These are all acts of tagging, and in Kripke's terms can be considered third, fourth, or nth "baptisms". Thus, if the person becomes famous in the cultural community, then the accomplishments attributed to

that person may also serve to replace his original name. In all these cases the object's reference is fixed in virtue of the fact that these data are transmitted by h and are the ones the system considers important for publicly identifying the object.

This theory may be more complex and less elegant than Kripke's, but it seems more convincing. Aside from the fact that it solves some problems evoked by Kripke's theory and improves some parts of it, it also places other parts of the theory in a broader philosophical context – that of Source Theory.

The suggested theory of reference determination gives us a better understanding of why we tend to forget the data about the procedural (or "external") aspects of the transmission (the exact source, the time, the place, the circumstances) that determined the object's identity: These data are suppressed by the later "baptism". In parallel, the data about the procedural aspects of the new "baptism" are also quite often forgotten because they are perceived as atemporal and impersonal, since the new "baptism" involves the object's reference in the broader community system, as described above. From this point on, the object's rigid designator is therefore "the object to which source h ascribes such-and-such properties". Even if I later reject one or all of these properties because of data received from truth sources with greater authority in my hierarchy of sources – such as my personal sources – the objects' most rigid designator will remain "the object to which h ascribes such-and-such properties". But this designator is not absolutely rigid either. It will remain in place until another designator, more powerful than it, performs another "baptism".

In light of these remarks, it would be advisable to remove the aura of mystification from the act of naming, especially as it appears in Kripke's theory. From a source-theoretical standpoint, the act of naming is merely an ordinary act of attributing a property to an object by virtue of a datum transmitted by a source, and is thus no different from any other such attribution. What gives it its status as a rigid designator is its capacity to survive in our minds for a long time, which is derived from considerations of importance based mainly on personal and social convenience. Since fixing an object's reference is basically a psychological rather than a logical process, it is hard to see it as making any substantial contribution to the modal discussion of trans-world identity, or to any other metaphysical discussion.

The meanings of words in language

Nowadays many thinkers agree that the issue of meaning occupied philosophers in the last century out of all proportion to its true philosophical importance. And if that were not enough, this occupation produced a considerable number of scholastic discussions that would not have shamed the most meticulous medieval philosophers (such discussions, quite ironically, often include terms that are meaningless according to their own authors' criteria). However, there is indeed a real problem at the basis of this issue which is worth discussing. We will begin with the issue of naming individuals, as discussed in the previous section, after a few preliminary remarks.

Frege and his followers distinguished between the meaning (reference) of a word and the meaning of a sentence. Frege claimed that the meaning of a word is the object it denotes, while the meaning of a sentence is its truth value (Frege 1952b). In light of our discussion in Appendix I this statement is nonsensical, since we have shown that the difference between a word (or a phrase that is not a sentence) and a sentence is present only in the "psychological" aspects that involve the speaker's hypotheses about the hearer's knowledge and the like. In our view there is thus no place for such a distinction, and so we will discuss the meaning of a **datum,** whatever its linguistic form might be.

Frege, Russell and others established a theory of reference, which claims that the meaning of a word (or a name) is an object in the real world (Frege was more moderate on this issue, in his distinction between "sense" and "reference"). Russell claimed that the discussion was about objects that could be empirically known, and accused anyone who did not agree with him of lacking "a robust sense of reality" Russell 1920: 170). Aside from the problem that this philosophical trend involves a blurring of the boundaries between meaning and truth, it cannot hold from the standpoint of Source Theory. Source Theory does not recognize any principled superiority of the senses over other sources. If we accept the basic notions of the reference theory, the test should be not the relations between the word and the sense datum, but rather the relations between the word and a datum transmitted by any of the basic sources of the system in question. Just as Source Theory does not have a concept of pure truth but only "truth in a system", so it does not have a concept of pure meaning, but only "meaning in a (cultural) system".

The main opposition to the Russell and Frege's theories of reference is the later Wittgenstein's "meaning as use" theory (Wittgenstein 1953). In this view, meaning as external object is not workable, at least not as the only test, because there are many words which do not denote external objects. The meaning of a word is the way it is used in language, which is a "way of life" rather than a mental state, and is determined by following social rules, just as one follows the rules of a game. Wittgenstein also claims that the meanings of words in language are not fixed.

If we reformulate the controversy in terms of Source Theory, we find that it is limited to some very fine points, and may even disappear completely. The only assumption we need here is that language is a subsystem of the cultural system, activated by the individual. Russell bases meaning on truth, and truth is itself determined by the system's sources, so that the meaning of a word (as well as that of a sentence) is the object transmitted by the basic sources of the very same system. As with what was said above regarding proper names, this meaning is created by the fact that someone, some time in the past, determined that a particular object should have a particular name, and this meaning is transmitted from one speaker to another until it becomes the property of the community – which is the source h. When a person is born into a cultural system, he receives the meaning of the word from the sources who teach it to him, i.e., who transmit to him its meaning according to h. Since h is composed of many speakers, and many additional data about the object were added to the original data over the years, while some of the original data may have been forgotten, their meaning in spoken language is not fixed. Russell was very much aware of this, and the logical positivists even more so.

The later Wittgenstein speaks about obeying social rules, but even these rules are nothing but data, and the society in question is nothing but h. The data transmitted by h do not necessarily determine meaning, but rather methods of use. And when they do determine meaning, this meaning is not fixed.

Since Russell too is aware that objects are not fixed in natural language, it turns out that the only difference between Russell and Wittgenstein, in terms of Source Theory, is the question of whether h determines meaning through establishing a connection between a word and an object or through establishing the way a word is used without any necessary connection with an object.

It seems that the later Wittgenstein ignored Frege's remarks about the nature of concepts. In Frege's view, concepts are not the product of language; they are associated with the "physics" rather than the "psychology" of things. Accordingly, concepts are the general boundaries according to which various individual objects in the world are divided, and since objects are divided into such groups in actuality – without any connection to the way they are perceived – then these boundaries are "real". Language, conversely, is the expression of the human aspiration to create words suitable for the everyday needs of most of its speakers. Sometimes words embody the aspiration to reach the utopian, pure, sharp boundaries of the concepts, but sometimes they do not; and even when they do embody this aspiration, it is obviously pointless: If every attempt to define a word analytically makes use of more general words, and so on, then how can the most general words be defined? Plato tried to answer this question by looking for the "primary elements" (Plato 1997, p. 223, [Theaetetus, Steph. p. 201]) or the "most important (i.e. supreme) kinds" (Plato 1997, p. 275, 277 [Sophist, Steph. p. 253c, 254d]) of reality, which he took to be undefinable. But if the only way to understand words precisely is by analytic definition, those "primary" undefineable terms cannot be understood; and if they cannot be understood, neither can all the terms that are defined by them; thus, in a *reductio ad absurdum*, nothing is understandable (compare Wittgenstein 1953: 46). However, the linguistic difficulty in defining the primary elements or even understanding them in *language* does not negate the claim of Plato and his followers that the *world* is indeed divided in this basic way, whether or not we are able to express it in words.

Moreover, even if we give up the quest for "primary elements", we know that every general concept reflects a division of the world. If we imagine the world as the totality of all objects, it is possible to divide it in a variety of ways. Each division into two leaves us with some objects on one side of the boundary and other objects on the other side, whatever that boundary might be. Our ability to discover the line where the "boundary" lies – that is, the borders of the concept as opposed to what is not inside these borders – may be limited, but it is this aspiration that underlies the philosophical and scientific aspiration for exactness. Indeed, this very attempt may sometimes change the contours of the boundary, and there are also additional factors, especially cultural processes that affect natural language, that constantly change this contour, but none of this necessitates the conclusion that such a contour does not exist.

Wittgenstein's claim thus does not undermine the view of the world as divisible into primary kinds, secondary kinds, and so on, but only raises the question of the degree of fit between the this non-verbal metaphysical division and the division of concepts expressed by words in language. Natural language is indeed very dynamic, but this dynamic is closely connected with the state of our knowledge about the objects that language is supposed to represent. Furthermore, as mentioned previously, our concepts about the objects in our minds also change constantly. The fact that they are nonetheless relatively fixed does not mean that they determine absolute boundaries in some metaphysical sense, but only the conventions that are accepted by the cultural community at a particular time. Frege, Russell and the logical positivists can also agree with this. The main difference between them and the later Wittgenstein is on the question of how far we can rid ourselves of natural language and create a "scientific language" that better represents the conceptual division (which is actually metaphysical, even though some of the philosophers under discussion would not use that term). However, the naïve vision of creating a pure scientific language no longer fires the imagination of philosophers. It seems to me that at the present time it is enough to say that scientific language tries to refine the concepts of natural language as much as possible and make them as close as possible to a metaphysical conceptualization, but this process is endless, with a goal that is largely utopian.

In many areas of life the advancement of knowledge leads to changes in our concepts about objects, and thus the changes in the meanings of words reflect our increasing ability to define their boundaries precisely. Clearly, for example, the definition of gold according to Mendeleev's periodic table allows us to understand the concept of gold more precisely (within WRS). Even people who do not know this definition know, for example, that "fools' gold" is not gold, and that they have to beware of fakes, as long as they are members of this cultural system to one degree or another. In such cases, we can assume that the historical process has occurred largely the way Kripke described it. We can imagine that primitive people came upon a bright yellow metal and called it "gold". In Kripke's terms, this was its baptism. It is entirely possible that this metal was not even gold, but rather platinum or fools' gold, but the baptism took place anyway. (Indeed, Kripkean baptism does not necessarily have to be based on a *true* description of the object named! – compare Gettier 1963). Later generations discovered some of its chemical and physical properties and distinguished among different types of bright yellow metals, culminating in Mendeleev's definitive characterization. At present, no one knows which metal was called "gold" at the dawn of history, and very few (mainly historians of science) know which metals were called "gold" at different points in the development of science. The word "gold" in our language reflects the latest developments of science that have come to the notice of h.

This is even more true when we consider what Searle and others call "institutional facts" (in contrast to "brute facts" such as the nature of gold). In these cases, h is often not a source that presumes to transmit an outside fact, but the very creator of that fact. In this respect, the fact that a bachelor is an unmarried man is even more secure than the fact that gold is a metal: The latter required a long scientific development to be validated, while the latter was an unshakeable truth ever since h coined the term "bachelor".

In other areas of life we do not even try to reach such precision. For example, the fruits and vegetables that existed a hundred years ago were quite different from the ones with the same names today – now they are grown differently, which changes their taste and shape. Moreover, in the course of the centuries, new species of fruits and vegetables have been developed, with very different shapes and tastes, thus expanding the boundaries of the concept of each fruit or vegetable. We continue, however, to use the same names for them, since the process of change has been gradual and they are used in more or less the same way that they were used in the past. If a historian wants to know what the meaning of "tomato" was in an early twentieth-century text, he would have to find out the boundaries of the concept at that time through the use of evidence, but most language speakers are not the least bit interested in this topic. (To be sure, the meanings of linguistic expressions can sometimes change through deliberate manipulation; such changes are discussed below in Appendix IV.)

It is noteworthy that discussions parallel to those in the philosophy of language have also taken place in the philosophy of law. Here it was Hart (1961, Chapter 7) who noticed, more than any of his predecessors, that the legal terms used by legislators seem to have two circles of meaning: the hard circle, which he called the "core", and the soft circle, which he called the "penumbra". In the core, any speaker of the language can determine which objects fall under a legal term, while terms in the penumbra are subject to uncertainty. This area thus has an "open texture", where interpretation is required. This, says Hart, is where judicial discretion has to be involved. Several scholars (especially

Bix 1996; Marmor 2005) have noticed the connection between this view and that of Wittgenstein, but even in Hart's theory the core area is supposed to be determined not by pure metaphysical concepts, but rather by the accepted use of natural language. Hart did not discuss Wittgenstein's philosophy, but his theory offers some perhaps unintended answers to some of the questions Wittgenstein presented. Hart showed that the fact that linguistic expressions have a penumbra makes their borders less rigid, but does not annihilate them altogether. The fact that gray exists does not negate the existence of black and white; there is black, there is white, and there is also a gray area between them (this idea is largely the theoretical basis of fuzzy logic). Similarly, the fact that the boundaries are constantly moving does not negate the fact that they exist, since the boundaries at t3 were created by expanding or contracting the boundaries at t2, which for their part were created by expanding or contracting the boundaries at t1, and so on. In other words, it is the gradual historical evolution that determines the continuum of meaning of linguistic expressions, even though times change.

This leads to the same conclusion as that presented above. The later Wittgenstein was right in stating that the boundaries of linguistic expressions are not always clear, and even those that are clear are constantly changing, so words do not have fixed, eternal meanings. On many issues, however, everyday language does not aspire to any fixed meaning, and all we need is what is accepted at a given moment in our cultural system. In areas that are not philosophical or scientific, we do not aspire to precision, but only to effective use. When I go to the store to buy tomatoes, I am not interested in any pure – philosophical or scientific – concept of tomatoes, but only in an ingredient for salads. Even here, as mentioned above, the boundary has not shifted on the level of pure concepts. There is a pure concept of a tomato of the old sort, such that the tomatoes of the new sort are outside its boundaries; and there is a broader pure concept of tomatoes that includes both the old and the new sort. These have always been part of the extension of the concept, even before they actually existed. Natural language does not represent the world of pure concepts, but only the constant aspiration to represent them, and even this is true only in the areas in which people aspire to precision, such as philosophy and the sciences. Of course, this is not in Wittgenstein's line, but neither is it in Frege's: Frege spoke of "objective" concepts existing in the external world, and so could consider them pure and rigid; Wittgenstein spoke about concepts as created by language, and therefore saw them as vague and unstable.

As I suggested above, Source Theory helps us to eliminate most of this alleged controversy: for both Frege and the later Wittgenstein, concepts are ways of dividing the world, and there are numerous possible ways of doing so. The question is whether there is a single "right" way, and whether this way is attainable, in view of the fact that we acquire our concepts through our "deficient" ordinary language. Source Theory reminds us that all of our data, whether those of metaphysics and logic or those of language, whether "right" or "deficient", come from sources. The right data for the division of the world are those that are transmitted by the basic sources of the ideal system of the activator concerned – in the case of Western philosophers like Frege and Wittgenstein this is the source mechanism of WRS – and the deficient ones are those transmitted by other sources, in our case by h, insofar as h is not subordinate to the source mechanism of WRS. These sources are parts of the source model of the real system under discussion. The gap between Fregean concepts and Wittgensteinean concepts is just another manifestation of the gap between the real system and the ideal system that is almost taken for granted by Source Theory.

Philosophers and scientists try to use language to represent the world. Since Wittgenstein showed that many linguistic expressions do not play such a role, but are rather action rules for language users, we may take one of the following views: either these expressions somehow help us create the representations, or they do not. If they do, they are parts of the mechanism of representation even though they are not themselves representations; if they do not, then we should try to exclude them in disciplines that strive for precision. The problems involved in this striving for precision do not necessitate the defeatist conclusions of some philosophers (e.g., Rorty 1979), but only imply that we need to increase our efforts to figure out how to achieve precision in spite of the problems.

In the discussion above I addressed only semantic aspects of language, but the gist of my arguments applies, *mutatis mutandis*, to its syntactic and even pragmatic aspects as well. This issue deserves a more extensive discussion, which should be undertaken elsewhere, so I will only name a few points: The laws of syntax are data. They are transmitted to us explicitly only during late childhood and adolescence, in grammar classes at school, for example, but we begin to acquire them at much earlier stages. The sources that transmit them to us are not much different from those who transmit semantic relations, i.e., the community of the speakers of the language, especially those in our close environment. Even if the rules are not formulated explicitly by these sources, as they are presented to us in grammar classes and books, they are nevertheless parts of the content of what is said to us.

This is one of many examples of the fact that the term "transmission" does not refer only to plain and explicit conveyance of the contents but also to other forms, which are more complex and implicit. Even pragmatics, a discipline that explores the more fluid aspects of human language, has been shown in recent scholarship to be based on rules and compositionality which are transmitted in everyday speech. In both realms – syntax and pragmatics – it should be remembered that (unlike what Wittgenstein's *Investigations* implies) language rules are also kinds of objects, and we identify and acquire them through learning processes that are not far different from those through which we acquire data about word-object relations.

This discussion is not intended to decide controversies in the philosophy of language, but only to show how to apply Source Theory to these problems. Let us now try to formulate our conclusions in terms of Source Theory. The system of pure concepts is the ideal system of a cultural system. The world can be divided up in numberless ways, but the division that system users aspire to achieve is the one transmitted to them by the sources of their cultural system (in the case of WRS, the basic cognitive tools). In contrast, the division reflected by natural language belongs to that cultural system's real system, for which h is the principal source. The aspiration to achieve the ideal system is thus the one discussed above – that is, the attempt to bring the real system closer to the ideal one.

Moreover, Source Theory provides a simple explanation for the question of how meaning is possible at all. Since everything takes place within the same system, it is the same system that transmits both the data and the way that other data – linguistic expressions – should be used to represent them, as well as how other linguistic expressions should be used as aids in the act of representation. Linguistic representation is thus no longer mysterious, as it is merely the encounter between the data of sources within the same system, which is possible due to the obvious fact that the sources in a system influence one another mutually.

CHAPTER EIGHT

Summary and Perspective

The idea underlying Source Theory is amazingly simple – so simple that it's a bit surprising that it was never developed before, at least not as systematically as it should have been. Our thoughts are data; every datum has a source; we believe data when they come from a source we have adopted. Different people think different thoughts not necessarily because they have different premises, but because they think in different ways; *what* they think is often dependent on *how* they think. How people think should not be considered mysterious, however. In the ultimate analysis it can be explained as the different structures of a system – different sources or a different division of labor among the same sources. These simple claims ought to be used in any attempt to understand human thinking.

Indeed, Source Theory offers a theoretical model that can be applied to any systematic field of knowledge. Chapters 5–7 illustrate its application to three major branches of philosophy, but the book also includes occasional allusions to literature, anthropology, and cultural criticism, and it can also be useful for many other fields. This broad applicability is neither coincidental nor overly ambitious. It stems from the fact that each of these fields is actually a subsystem that is searching for the truth about a certain part of the world, and the truth can only be considered within a particular system. Therefore all researchers in all fields of knowledge who want to be aware of themselves and their working methods need a theoretical model to explain how they think. In fact, they need the foundation of epistemology as a whole, of which Source Theory is a part, since the goal of epistemology is to determine the limits of human knowledge and name the instruments that enable us to attain it within those limits. The advantage of Source Theory is that it provides clear, simple tools for achieving such awareness and even offers a rigorous calculus for this enterprise.

Since Source Theory is so widely applicable in almost all fields of knowledge, can it provide a foundation for the ideal of a unified science in the spirit of the

---

How to cite this book chapter:
Brown, B 2017 *Thoughts and Ways of Thinking: Source Theory and Its Applications.* Pp. 137–141. London: Ubiquity Press. DOI: https://doi.org/10.5334/bbh.i. License: CC-BY 4.0

logical positivists? I do not believe that it can, precisely for the reason mentioned above. Every epistemological theory is ostensibly a foundation for every science, but just as classical epistemological theory did not actually provide such a foundation, so Source Theory, as a part of epistemology, cannot do so either. The reason for this is that an epistemological theory provides the basic conditions for knowledge in general, but not for particular bodies of information – it provides a structure but not the content. A unified structure is not enough to generate a unified science; rather, such a science, if possible at all, would have to create its own unified database.

The theory of truth embodied in Source Theory is that there is no truth except for what accords with a system's adopted sources. As I explained, this is not an idealistic view, since Source Theory in its basic form does not deal with the issue of the existence or non-existence of an "external world". Rather, it is an internalist view, as it is called in the modern epistemological literature. Systems that are constructed from sources are indeed part of their users' "internal worlds", and we have no way of knowing for certain what relationship they have with the external world beyond them ("things in themselves", as Kant put it). This is not, however, a reason to deny the existence of such an external world or the plausibility of such an assumption (personally, I think there are good grounds for believing in the existence of the "external world", but I will leave that for another discussion). Moreover, almost all systems, possibly excluding those that are constructed on the basis of idealistic or skeptical theories, assume that an external world does exist and try to represent is as best they can. From this standpoint, almost all systems have at least the object of their aspiration in common.

As we have seen, Source Theory is a branch of epistemology, as it deals with the sources and justifications of the data we possess. Source Calculus, which I presented in Chapter Three, lays the foundations of this theory and provides the logical course of argumentation for it. We have seen that the ultimate justification in the chain of justifications for any given datum is the determination of the source from which it was taken and the adoption relation between the speaking self and that source. This is true of sources as well. At this point, we are confronted with a particular version of the infinite regress problem and the inevitable conclusion that the ultimate adoption of any source (or source model) is always arbitrary. It is this conclusion that led to the nihilistic absurdities. When we are confronted with two or more systems, we have no non-arbitrary way of deciding among them. The adoption of one of them is always just as arbitrary as the adoption of any other. And if we try to find a third source (or source model) to decide between two others, then the adoption of this third source would be equally arbitrary, so that we have no way out of this difficulty.

The nihilistic absurdities actually imply that no thought we have can be counted on to be true. This is a radically skeptical conclusion derived from understanding the concept of a system as a purely logical concept, like a sophisticated computer program. The pragmatist line of argumentation, however, limits the number of source models that can be used in practice, thus going from nihilism to relativism. In this view, not just any source model can actually serve as a way of thinking, but only those that are at the basis of active cultural systems that have proven themselves as traditions, and with which the individuals who are "candidates" for adopting them can have a psychological connection. Even though we are still left with a large number of systems, at least they are concrete rather than ethereal.

I know that many people will not be happy with this conclusion. On the one hand, there will be those who disapprove of the non-nihilistic relativism that remains and want to find a strong foundation of absolute justification for some system. On the other hand, there will be those who claim that my questions are better than my answers and choose to remain with the skeptical nihilism of Chapter Three. I will answer both of these groups with architectonic allegories.

My answer to the first group is that it is better to build several modest structures on solid ground than one great edifice on shaky earth. My answer to the second group is that it is better to build several modest structures on solid ground than not to build anything at all. Although the relativism of Source Theory leaves all systems in a very modest state, any artificial attempt to find an absolute justification for a system – even though all such justifications have been shown *a priori* to be impossible – does not provide such a system with epistemological strength. Such pseudo-justifications do not really "save" the systems under attack but rather render them unrespectable and leave their supporters without intellectual integrity. On the other hand, remaining in the nihilistic condition is not an option, either. The nihilistic absurdities, like all skeptical argumentation, make it impossible to think at all – not even skeptical thoughts are possible. If you think at all, you do so within some system, and so it is better for you to think in a system that you are actually capable of using.

Some people may claim that some meta-system must exist. They may also claim that not only is it impossible to justify a system outside a given system, but that the same would apply to any discussion of a system; the fact that I developed my arguments within the discourse of rational Western philosophy may demonstrate, they might say, that I myself recognize WRS as a default meta-system. Indeed, as I mentioned, my arguments in this book (above all the formalist line of argumentation of Chapter Three, but also the others) are constructed entirely through the use of WRS, but they are it meant to free us of this system and allow us to look at all the systems from a bird's eye view, which presents us with all the systems as equals from the standpoint of their degree of justification and internal logic. The WRS argumentation serves our purposes as a meta-system because it is most capable of making us understand the nature of sources, data, and systems, not because it is by any means more justifiable per se. The pragmatist line of argumentation, and especially the pragmatic guidelines, is based on the understanding that the adoption of a source model is a type of action, and so we should perform this action in the most prudent way. Even if this way is necessarily taken from the basic sources of a particular system or systems, there is no other alternative, and so it should be as close as possible to the way we make decisions on most of the issues that arise in the course of our daily lives. It is these ideas that led me to formulate the three guidelines of the pragmatic method (in Chapter Four), despite the philosophical difficulties they raise.

Indeed, the first and the third guidelines – conservatism and exhaustiveness – are very close to our simple, ordinary, pre-philosophical intuitions. They reflect the experiences we have all had when arguing with people holding different views. In some cases, we can see that there are people who share our system, and we can try to convince these people that our views are correct with arguments taken from the basic sources of that system. In other cases, however, we often feel that we there is no point in trying to conduct a dialogue this way, because the people we are facing seem to be "speaking a different language". These are the occasions in which we often say (in non-technical terms) that we simply have different *ways of thinking*. From the internal point of view, we clearly feel that our system is right and better than others, but it is difficult if not impossible to convey this feeling to those who do not belong to it but look at it from an external point of view. We see clearly that we cannot sway such people with arguments from our own system, but that we need to use arguments in which we try to enter into their system and manipulate the arguments so that they seem to be coming from within that system; without using this dishonest method we cannot change their minds. If we do not want to use such methods, we must simply give up trying to convince people with different ways of thinking, and focus on convincing people who share our own system, on developing it, and on making use of all the data that it can provide us.

The second guideline of the pragmatic method – separation – is much less intuitive. It asks us to give up the psychological harmony we aspire to in our daily lives, as part of our desire for ease. It asks us to compartmentalize our knowledge and ways of thinking, which is indeed difficult at first, but provides us with the satisfaction of clear-mindedness later on. Even though our goal is not satisfaction but truth, at the end of the day there is no greater satisfaction than that provided by clear understanding, including understanding the way we think. This satisfaction has greater advantages than those provided by false harmony.

The idea of looking at the various systems from a bird's eye view may seem tempting to many people. Actually, many relativists of different types, and especially of the postmodernist type, have such presumptions when they preach that we should not judge other cultures by the values of our own culture and the like. In truth, the attempt to look at cultures and values from a pseudo-neutral point of view can only work as an intellectual exercise. You can never remain in the meta-system for good. Actually, you may never use it for anything other than getting that bird's eye view on the variety of existing systems (unless you decide to adopt it as system-proper, not as meta-system, for the usual reasons people adopt systems). Every person is doomed to a particular system, or to particular systems, and can obtain his knowledge of the world only through them. All we can do is be aware of the systems we have adopted – and then re-affirm our allegiance to them or convert to other ones, but never try to surmount our dependence on a system. To stop thinking within a system (or systems) means to stop thinking.

When we applied the theory to the three disciplines we chose as examples, we were able investigate its usefulness not only in inter-system relations, but also in the relations between different subsystems within the same mother system. We have considered inter-system relations, comparing WRS with MRS and the various attempts to construct divisions of labor among them. Then we analyzed the ways of thinking in the legal subsystem of WRS by the judges and commentators who use it, and subsequently studied the ways of thinking embodied in spoken language. On the one hand, we must keep in mind that every individual has his or her own personal system – that is, his or her own way of thinking, which is distinct from that of others. On the other hand, people with the same cultural system also have a common real system, together with its common ideal system. "No man is an island" is true on the epistemic as well as the social level, and if we did not belong to cultural systems we would not be able to understand one another, argue with one another, or advance our shared systems.

To conclude, Source Theory is indeed an epistemological theory, but it also bears some moral, and possibly even existential, lessons. We began with a highly technical discussion, but ended up with messages of value for everyone. We think; we cannot help thinking; we think in a particular way (or ways); this way is the one in which we can really think and develop; it is the way we can help our culture and community develop. We should not go too far from our own culture; we should not look for ways that are alien to us and that we cannot really understand. If we want to broaden our horizons to include other ways of thinking, we should look for them nearby, in cultural traditions with which we are intimately familiar and to which we have a real psychological connection; we should continue to think within these traditions, and, through dialogues with their great past achievements and their present members, do our best to add our own links to the larger chain to which we belong.

Appendices

APPENDIX I

Sentential and Non-sentential Expressions of Data

When I say that a datum is an object of cognition, I do not necessarily mean sensory perception, but any sort of cognition from which people derive beliefs about the world. However, the term "datum" is presently known mainly from Russell's philosophy, which discussed "sense data", and so we can use these data as a point of origin for all the other sources.

Imagine that a group of people are watching a big volcano erupt. Each person in the group is asked to use exactly one sentence to tell a particular person about the event, where the only words the speakers are allowed to use are "thing" (or, in philosophical terminology, "entity"), "volcano", "big", and "erupt", together with the basic grammatical inflections, articles and connectives of ordinary language. Each person uses one of the following sentences to describe the event:

S1: A big volcano erupted.
S2: The big volcano erupted.
S3: The volcano that erupted was big.
S4: The big thing that erupted was a volcano.
S5: What erupted was a big volcano.

Clearly all these sentences describe the same event. What then is the difference among them? The answer is clear – each of them addresses the listener on the basis of a different presupposition about the state of her prior knowledge. These are the speaker's presuppositions for each sentence:

S1: The listener does not know which volcano is under discussion.
S2: The listener knows which volcano is under discussion, but does not know that it has erupted.
S3: The listener knows that a volcano erupted, but does not know how big it is.
S4: The listener knows that some big thing erupted, but does not know what.
S5. The listener knows that something erupted, but does not know what.

All the differences lead to sentences that are somewhat different linguistically. In practice, however, they all describe the same event. Frege (2007:17; 1964:13; 1979:3–7, 142–149), who was very careful to distinguish between "logic" and "psychology", would have called these differences "psychological" – that is, a case in which language reflects not only the world but also the cognitive state of the people involved in transmitting the information. Since Frege thought that logic should be divorced from psychology, he would have been careful to avoid allowing these differences to be expressed in the logical formulation of the sentences, and to make sure that the truth value of all of them would be the same.

The point of origin of a good logic must be that all the sentences listed above are merely **different linguistic expressions of the very same datum**. To borrow a term from Wittgenstein (even if we change its meaning somewhat), we can say that a datum is a mental object that claims to **depict** the world "outside" it. The picture described by sentences S1–S5 is exactly the same picture, and so all these sentences are linguistic expressions of the same datum (compare Brentano 1995, chapter 7 and appendix 9). One datum can thus appear in different types of sentences, where all these linguistic expressions are not the datum itself but only different ways of formulating it in words.

But now we must go a step further. A datum in and of itself does not have to be formulated as a sentence. It can be expressed as a phrase, such as "the eruption of the big volcano". As soon as this datum is present in my mind, even if I did not ascribe any predicate to it, I have a picture in my mind, and this picture too is the same as the one expressed by sentences S1–S5. We will therefore be very liberal in discussing the logical structure of data, and recognize all the forms – whether sentential or non-sentential – that express the same picture as linguistic forms of the datum itself. (On this issue I disagree with Davidson's critique of Hume; see Davidson 1989.) Nevertheless, as mentioned, when we introduce the Source Calculus we will confine ourselves to sentential forms, for simplicity.

Parenthetically, this discussion yields a corroborating proof for Russell's (1905) claim that sentences of the sort "The present king of France is bald" are false, as opposed to the claims of Strawson (1950), Geach (1950), and others. Questions of truth value should be decided only on the basis of whether or not a datum (in whatever grammatical form) has a corresponding object in the real world. This is the only way in which the concepts of truth and falsity are philosophically interesting. If logic has chosen to use other concepts of truth and falsity, which take the grammatical structure of sentences or some similar property associated with the data into account, then it has chosen philosophically uninteresting concepts, and these should be changed.

APPENDIX II

Forgetting as a Creative Function

A null datum is a datum in the same way that a null set is a set. A null datum should be treated as a datum even though it is null, not only because it changes a person's epistemic status, but because it has content that is grasped by a person.

One of the instances that manifest the "real" character of the null datum is the condition of forgetting. Consider a simple situation as an example. I remember Joe, but I have forgotten that he is an engineer. In this situation, before I forgot this detail, I remembered Joe as having properties A+B+C+engineer. After forgetting that he is an engineer, however, I remembered him as having only properties A+B+C. Thus at first I had a certain positive datum about Joe in my memory, while afterwards I had a different positive datum about him. The null datum thus changes the content of the positive datum, and so it itself becomes a grasped content which can be treated epistemically – the content of the *absence* of the property of being an engineer from the list of Joe's properties.

Now we can consider some more difficult cases. Let us say I have completely forgotten about Joe. Even this sort of forgetting should be considered the transmission of a datum – a null datum – not only because it changes the person's epistemic status but also because it has a grasped content – the content of Joe's absence. Indeed, just as forgetting a property can be said to transmit the content of the absence of that property (as we saw in the above example), so forgetting an object can be said to transmit the content of the absence of that object. If anyone asks me now if Joe exists, I could answer that I don't know, but my basic presumption would be that Joe does not exist as long as there is no evidence that he does. From this viewpoint, the erasure of a positive datum through forgetting is not very different from the situation in which it is nonexistent all along because it has never been transmitted. Just as in the latter case the basic presumption is that of absence, and the burden of proof is upon anyone who is trying to rebut it, so it is in the former case.

Moreover, no positive datum is transmitted to the mind of an adult in isolation; it is always an addition to a database in a particular area. For example, when I met Joe, he added an item to a datum I already had about the set of my acquaintances; when I forgot about him, this datum was changed. The new datum about the set of my acquaintances that was received after I forgot Joe is also a positive datum, but it is different from the one I had when Joe was still present in my memory. Thus my forgetting of Joe creates a change among my positive data, by changing one positive datum to another. Consequently, forgetting should be considered a datum even for those who consider only positive data to be important.

To be sure, a person can remember a datum he forgot, as if retrieving it from oblivion, but from an epistemological viewpoint (as opposed to the viewpoint of cognitive psychology) refreshing one's memory is merely another form of adding a new positive datum. In such a case we would therefore say that there have been two transmissions of data: the first, of a null datum, and the second, of a positive datum.

Freud (1935: 177–179) believed that no datum is ever lost from the data acquired in childhood (at least those that are not completely unimportant), and that even data that have been forgotten are not erased but are suppressed into the unconscious and remain there until they are retrieved. At first glance, this theory would seem to support the view I am presenting here, that a null datum is also a datum. However, the view I am presenting does not entail Freud's theory and is not dependent on it, since I have tried to show that even if a datum has been *completely* erased, it still has content that is grasped by the person, which changes his epistemic status, and should therefore be considered a datum. Moreover, Freud's theory has nothing to do with Source Theory, because we have already established that only conscious data are data. Thus from the standpoint of Source Theory, suppressing a datum into the subconscious is like erasing it. (I should mention that sources, in contrast to data, can be unconscious – that is, such that the subject cannot identify the source that transmitted data to him; I discuss this in Chapter Four).

In Source Theory, we consider forgetting a creative function, and so we may speak about the "power of forgetting" as a source. Forgetting is a source that loses data or parts of data that were previously transmitted by other sources. It turns positive data into null data. We can therefore consider the power of forgetting as the source for all functions whose input in a positive datum and whose output is a null one.

Some may argue that there is no power of forgetting at all, since forgetting is merely the non-use or inefficient use of the power of memory. However, such a claim is not obvious and requires proof. At first glance it would seem that any datum that has been stored in the memory could be expected to remain there unless some act has been performed to remove it. Such a claim, however, presumes the primacy of the positive source (memory) over the null one (forgetting) – a presumption that may follow our basic intuitions but is not more justified that presuming the primacy of positive integers over the null ones or of the state rest over the state of motion (even uniform). Indeed, we could just as well say that memory does not exist and that it is merely the non-use or inefficient use of the power of forgetting. Since neither of these claims has been proven, we will count both of these powers as sources.

What was said above about forgetting also applies, *mutatis mutandis*, to the addition of positive data. Transmitting a positive datum to the mind means adding a positive datum to a null one. To be sure, this does not mean that the mind was totally empty before this, since the new datum joins a database that already exists in the area it belongs to, but only that the mind was empty with respect to the specific content of this particular datum. As long as no new datum is transmitted, the subject can assume that its absence leaves the burden of proof on those who claim that it exists.

APPENDIX III

Creating Null Data out of Null Data

In the series of options presented at p. 8, option 1 relates to creating null data out of null data. One might attribute this function to memory. This possibility, however, is quite doubtful because, on the one hand, any state in which the output is a null datum is one in which the power of forgetting is operative, yet, on the other hand, any state in which the input and the output are the same is a state in which memory is operative (this doubt is a little bit reminiscent of the doubt regarding the value of 0/0 in arithmetic). I tend to think that this is actually an act of memory for two reasons. First, the definition of forgetting is the act of turning a positive datum into a null one, and here the input is not a positive datum. Second, if a person attests that he has no idea what the answer to a given question is, and he remains in the same state with regard to the same question, then it would be correct to say that he "preserves" the null datum, that is, that he "remembers" it, so to speak. If I once had a datum in my mind that there is no desk in my room, and later on I retrieve this datum from memory and I continue to believe that there is no desk there, then in both cases I had the same null datum about the desk. In spite of this apparently convincing argument, however, it is difficult to decide if a null datum can be created out of a null datum, and I am therefore leaving the matter for further consideration.

APPENDIX IV

Manipulative Changes in the Meanings of Words

The expansion and contraction of the meanings of linguistic expressions are not always natural developments, but can sometimes occur through deliberate manipulation. Data are not only informative, but also have other aspects, including emotive ones, and some words are data of this sort. Thus, someone who wants to influence the community to develop some emotional attitude toward a particular object can try to do so by using a word or phrase with the desired emotional charge to describe the object. It is often clear that the proposed use of the word is different from its accepted use, and so an expression is added to hint at the innovation in this use, such as "true" (as in: "true freedom is self-restraint"). It is generally impossible to give a word a meaning that is the exact opposite of the accepted one (e.g., Orwell's "War is peace"), and is equally difficult to give it an irrelevant meaning (e.g., "An apple is a poem"), except in poetry, where such combinations give the words their emotive power precisely because of the strangeness of the combination. In general, the expanded meaning is fairly close to the original one, so that the expansion occurs gradually and almost imperceptibly, without eliciting the hearer's resistance. There are many examples of this phenomenon, and I will not discuss it in detail here.

In terms of Source Theory, the process of manipulative change is interesting and complex. Sometimes the intention of the manipulative alteration is to change a particular aspect of the word's meaning within the system, but often enough it is to cover up a broader attempt to replace the entire system with another one. In more moderate cases, the intention is to change the system's division of labor, especially its hierarchy. In more extreme cases, it is a covert attempt to subordinate its basic sources to other sources that are not at the basis of the system. In either case, this is a change in the system and actually constitutes replacing its source mechanism with another one, and, as we have seen, even if two systems have the same sources and merely have a different division of labor among these sources, they are two different systems.

Sometimes it is indeed quite difficult to distinguish when a manipulative alteration of this sort merely leads to a change in the system's sources and when it attempts to replace them altogether. One of the tests of this distinction is the degree of emotional connection that the person who is trying to make this change feels toward the system in general, and toward its basic sources in particular. Even this issue is not always easy to determine, as such a connection is neither observable nor measurable. Clearly, a person's emotional connection to a system cannot be proven or measured by his rhetorical declarations and the like. Sometimes the test may have to be a practical one – to what extent the person decides the important questions of his practical life according to these sources.

Bibliography

Albalag, Isaac. *Tikkun Hade'ot [=Emendation of the Opinions]*. Jerusalem: Israel Academy of Sciences and Humanities, 1973 (Hebrew).

Al-Ghazali, Abu Hamid Muhammad. *The Incoherence of the Philosophers* (trans. Michael E. Marmura). Provo, UT: Brigham Young University Press, 2000.

Al-Ghazali, Abu Hamid Muhammad. *Deliverance from Error* (trans. Richard J. McCarthy). Louisville, KY: Fons Vitae, 1980.

Alston, William. *Perceiving God: The Epistemology of Religious Experience*. Ithaca, N.Y.: Cornell University Press, 1991.

Aquinas, Thomas. *Summa Theologica* (trans. Fathers of the English Dominican Province). London: Burns, Oates, & Washbourne, 1920. http://www.newadvent.org/summa/ (accessed August 2015); http://www.op.org/summa/ (accessed August 2015).

Armstrong, David M. *Belief, Truth and Knowledge*. Cambridge: Cambridge University Press, 1973.

Ascher, Saul. *Leviathan: oder, Über Religion in Rüchsicht des Judenthums*. Berlin: Franke, 1792.

Audi, Robert. The Place of Testimony in the Fabric of Knowledge and Justification. *American Philosophical Quarterly*. 1997; 34(4): 405–422.

Austin, John. *The Province of Jurisprudence Determined*. Cambridge: Cambridge University Press, 1995.

Barak, Aharon. *Judicial Discretion*. New Haven: Yale University Press, 1989.

Barak, Aharon. *Purposive Interpretation in Law*. Princeton, NJ: Princeton University Press, 2005.

Bentham, Jeremy. *A Fragment on Government*. Oxford: Blackwell, 1960.

Bentham, Jeremy. *Limits of Jurisprudence Defined*. New York: Columbia University Press, 1945.

Bix, Brian. *Law, Language, and Legal Determinacy*. Oxford: Clarendon Press, 1996.

BonJour, Laurence. Can Empirical Knowledge Have a Foundation? *American Philosophical Quarterly* 1978; *15*(1): 1–13.

Bradley, Owen. *A Modern Maistre*. Lincoln and London: University of Nebraska Press, 1999.

Brentano, Franz. *Psychology from an Empirical Standpoint,* 2nd revised edition (translated by Antos C. Rancurello, D. B. Terrell and Linda L. McAlister), London: Routledge 1995.

Brown, Benjamin. "Formalism Ve'arakhim: Sheloshah Degamim" ["Formalism and Values: Three Models"], in: Aviezer Ravitzky and Avinoam Rosenak (eds.), *'Iyunim Hadashim Baphilosophia shel Hahalakhah [New Streams in the Philosophy of Halakhah]*. Jerusalem: Hebrew University Magnes Press, 2008. pp. 233-258.

Carroll, Thomas D. The Traditions of Fideism. *Religious Studies*, 2008; *44*(1): 1–22.

Carroll, Thomas D. The Debate over "Wittgensteinian Fideism" and Phillips' Contemplative Philosophy of Religion. In: Ingolf U. Dalferth and Hartmut von Sass (eds.), *The Contemplative Spirit: D.Z. Phillips on Religion and the Limits of Philosophy*. Tübingen: Mohr Siebeck, 2010. pp. 99–114.

Chisholm, Roderick. Theory of Knowledge. In: R. Chisholm et al. (eds.) *Philosophy*. Englewood Cliffs, NJ: Prentice Hall, 1964.

Chisholm, Roderick. *Theory of Knowledge*. 2nd edition. Englewood Cliffs: Prentice Hall, 1977.

Coady, CAJ. *Testimony: A Philosophical Study*. Oxford: Clarendon Press, 1992.

Coleridge, Samuel Taylor. *Biographia Literaria*. (J. Shawcross, ed.). Oxford and London: Dent, 1939.

Davidson, Donald. A Coherence Theory of Truth and Knowledge. In: Ernest LePore (ed.), *Truth and Interpretation: Perspectives on the Philosophy of Donald Davidson*. New York: Blackwell,1989. pp. 307–319.

Dawkins, Richard. *The God Delusion*. Boston: Houghton Mifflin, 2006.

Descartes, René. Rules for the Direction of the Mind. In: E. S. Haldane, G. R. T. Ross (eds.)*The Philosophical Works of Descartes*. Cambridge: Cambridge University Press, 1934.

Dretske, Fred I. *Knowledge and the Flow of Information*. Cambridge, MA: MIT Press, 1995.

Dummett, Michael. Testimony and Memory. In: Bimal Krishna Matilal and Arindam Chakrabarti (eds.) *Knowing from Words*. Dordrecht: Kluwer Academic Publishers, 1994.

Dworkin, Ronald. *A Matter of Principle*. Cambridge, MA: Harvard University Press, 1985.

Dworkin, Ronald. *Taking Rights Seriously*. Cambridge, MA: Harvard University Press, 1978.

Flew, Antony, Hare, Richard Mervyn, Mitchell, Basil. *New Essays in Philosophical Theology*. New York: Macmillan, 1964.

Frazer, James George. *The Golden Bough: a Study of Magic and Religion (I–XIII)*. New York: MacMillan, 1951.

Frege, Gottlob. *The Basic Laws of Arithmetic: Exposition of the System* (trans. Montgomery Furth). Berkeley: University of California Press, 1964.

Frege, Gottlob. *The Foundations of Arithmetic: A Logical-Mathematical Investigation into the Concept of Number*. New York: Pearson, 2007.

Frege, Gottlob. On Concept and Object. In: Peter Geach, Max Black (eds.) *Translations from the Philosophical Writings of Gottlob Frege*. Oxford: Basil Blackwell, 1952. pp. 42–55. http://mind.oxfordjournals.org/cgi/pdf_extract/LX/238/168 (accessed August 2015).

Frege, Gottlob. On Sense and Reference. In: Peter Geach, Max Black (eds.) *Translations from the Philosophical Writings of Gottlob Frege*. Oxford: Basil Blackwell, 1952. pp. 56–78. http://mind.ucsd.edu/syllabi/00-01/phil235/a_readings/frege_S&R.html (accessed August 2015).

Frege, Gottlob. *Posthumous Writings*. Chicago: University of Chicago Press, 1979.

Freud, Sigmund. *A General Introduction to Psychoanalysis*. New York: Washington Square Press, 1935.

Freud, Sigmund, Einstein, Albert. *Why War?* Paris: International Institute of Intellectual Co-operation, League of Nations, 1933. http://www.idst.vt.edu/modernworld/d/Einstein.html (accessed August 2015).

Geach, Peter T. Russell's Theory of Descriptions. *Analysis* 1950; *10*(4): 84–88. Reprinted in: Margaret MacDonald (ed.) *Philosophy and Analysis*. Oxford: Basil Blackwell, 1954. pp. 32–36.

Gettier, Edmund. Is Justified True Belief Knowledge? *Analysis* 1963; *23*(6): 121–123.

Hage, Jaap C. *Reasoning with Rules: An Essay on Legal Reasoning & Its Underlying Logic*. Dordrecht: Kluwer, 1996

HaGra (R. Eliyahu ben Shlomo Zalman of Vilna). *Sifra diTzni'uta im Beur HaGra ['The Book of Concealment' with the commentary of HaGra]*. Vilna (Vilnius) and Horodna: Menahem Mann and Simha Simmel's Press, 1820.

Halbertal, Moshe. *People of the Book: Canon, Meaning and Authority*. Cambridge: Harvard University Press, 1997.

Hart, Herbert Lionel Adolphus. *The Concept of Law*. Oxford: Oxford University Press, 1961.

Heelas, Paul, Lash, Scott, Morris, Paul (editors). *Detraditionalization: Critical Reflections on Authority and Identity*. Cambridge, MA: Blackwell, 1996.

Hobsbawm, Eric J. Introduction: Inventing Traditions. In: E. J. Hobsbawm (ed.) *The Invention of Tradition*. Cambridge: Cambridge University Press, 1989.

D'Holbach, Paul Henri Thiry, Baron. *Good Sense without God, or Freethoughts Opposed to Supernatural Ideas*. London: Stewart and Co., c.1900 (translator unknown) http://www.ftarchives.net/holbach/good/gcontents.htm (accessed August 2015); or http://www.gutenberg.org/files/7319/7319-h/7319-h.htm (accessed August 2015)

Huber, Max. *Die Staatsphilosophie von Joseph de Maistre in Lichte des Thomismus*. Basel: Helbig und Lichtenhahn, 1958.

Ibn Rushd (Averroes). *On the Harmony of Religions and Philosophy*. London: Luzac, 1961. http://www.fordham.edu/halsall/source/1190averroes.html (accessed August 2015).

Ibn Taymiyyah, Taqi Ad-Din. *Ibn Taymiyyah Expounds on Islam: Selected Writings of Shaykh Al-Islam Taqi Ad-Din Ibn Taymiyyah on Islamic Faith, Life and Society* (translated and compiled by Muhammad Abdul Haqq Ansari). 2000 (press and place of publication not specified). http://islamfuture.files.wordpress.com/2009/12/ibn-taymiyyah-expounds-on-islam.pdf (accessed August 2015).

John Paul II. *Fides et Ratio*. Encyclical letter. http://www.vatican.va/holy_father/john_paul_ii/encyclicals/documents/hf_jp-ii_enc_15101998_fides-et-ratio_en.html (accessed August 2015).

Kelsen, Hans. *General Theory of Law and State*. New York: Russell and Russell, 1961.

Kelsen, Hans. *Pure Theory of Law* (translated from the 2nd German ed. by Max Knight). Berkeley, CA: University of California Press, 1967.

Kierkegaard, Søren. *Journals and Papers* (edited and translated by Howard V. Hong and Edna H. Hong). Vols. 1–7. Bloomington and London: Indiana University Press 1967–78.

Kierkegaard, Søren. *Concluding Unscientific Postscript* (translated by Howard V. Hong and Edna H. Hong). Vols. 1–2. Princeton: Princeton University Press, 1982.

Kripke, Saul. *Naming and Necessity*. Cambridge, MA: Harvard University Press, 1980. http://socialistica.lenin.ru/analytic/txt/k/kripke_1.htm (accessed August 2015).

Lackey, Jennifer. *Learning From Words*. Oxford: Oxford University Press, 2008.

Lackey, Jennifer, Sosa, Ernest (editors). *The Epistemology of Testimony*. Oxford: Oxford University Press, 2006.

Lebrun, Richard. *Throne and Altar: The Political and Religious Thought of Joseph de Maistre*. Ottawa: University of Ottawa Press, 1965.

Lehrer, Keith. *Theory of Knowledge*. Oxon: Routledge, 1990.

Leibowitz, Yeshayahu. *Judaism, Human Values, & the Jewish State*. Cambridge, MA: Harvard University Press, 1992.

Lewis, David. *Convention: A Philosophical Study.* Cambridge, MA: Harvard University Press, 1969.

Loyola, Ignatius. *Letters of St. Ignatius of Loyola* (selected and translated by William J. Young). Chicago: Loyola University Press, 1959.

Luther, Martin. *Commentary to Saint Paul's Epistle to the Galatians.* London: B. Blake, 1833. http://books.google.com/books?id=sGXgZgVK-1kC&pg=PA172&lpg=PA172&dq=which+is+the+fountain+and+headspring+of+all+mischiefs.+For+reason+feareth+not+God+luther&source=bl&ots=R6dgL-z9e3&sig=L5cWjnoXXt8K0iX1OBbRjbfb7iU&hl=en&ei=R1uISpvuBNi1sga2sqnqBw&sa=X&oi=book_result&ct=result&resnum=1#v=onepage&q=&f=false (accessed August 2015).

Luther, Martin. *Luther's Works.* Vol. 51. *Sermons* (ed. and translated by John W. Doberstein (Helmut T. Lehmann, general editor). Philadelphia: Fortress Press,1959 3rd printing, 1973.

Maimonides, Moses. *The Guide of the Perplexed* (translated by Shlomo Pines). Chicago: University of Chicago Press, 1963.

Malcolm, Norman. *Wittgenstein: A Religious Point of View?* Ithaca: Cornell University Press, 1995.

Marmor, Andrei. *Interpretation and Legal Theory.* Portland: Hart Publishing, 2005.

Marmor, Andrei. *Philosophy of Law.* Princeton and Oxford: Princeton University Press, 2011.

Marmor, Andrei. *Social Conventions: From Language to Law.* Princeton and Oxford: Princeton University Press, 2009.

Mautner, Menachem. Three Approaches to Law and Culture. *Cornell Law Review.* 2011; 96(4): 839–866.

Nahman of Breslav (written by Rabbi Nathan Sternhartz). *Sichos HaRan.* In: Zvi Aryeh Rosenfeld (ed.) *Rabbi Nachman's Wisdom* (translated and annotated by Aryeh Kaplan). Brooklyn: The Breslov Research Institute, 1973.

Nielsen, Kai. *Atheism and Philosophy.* Amherst: Prometheus 2005.

Nielsen, Kai. *Naturalism and Religion.* Amherst: Prometheus 2001.

Neilsen, Kai. *Philosophy and Atheism.* Amherst: Prometheus 1985.

Nielsen, Kai, Phillips, Dewi Zephaniah (editors). *Wittgensteinian Fideism?* London: SCM Press, 2005.

Peterson, Michael L, VanArragon, Raymond J (editors). *Contemporary Debates in Philosophy of Religion.* Malden, MA: Blackwell, 2007.

Phillips, Dewi Zaphaniah. *Belief, Change and Forms of Life.* Hampshire and London: MacMillan, 1986.

Phillips, Dewi Zaphaniah. *Religion Without Explanation.* Oxford: Blackwell, 1976.

Phillips, Dewi Zaphaniah. *Wittgenstein and Religion.* Hampshire and London: MacMillan, 1993.

Plantinga, Alvin. *Warranted Christian Belief*. New York: Oxford University Press, 2000.
Plato. *Complete Works* (John M. Cooper, ed.). Indianapolis and Cambridge: Hackett Publishing Company, 1997.
Pollock, John. *Contemporary Theories of Knowledge*. Lanham: Rowman and Littlefield, 1989.
Raz, Joseph. *The Concept of a Legal System*. Oxford: Clarendon Press, 1970.
Raz, Joseph. *The Morality of Freedom*. Oxford: Clarendon Press, 1986.
Raz, Joseph. *Practical Reason and Norms*. Oxford: Oxford University Press, 1990.
Reid, Thomas. *Essays on the Intellectual Powers of Man*. In: Sir William Hamilton (ed.) *The Works of Thomas Reid*. 4th edition. London: Longmans, Green and Company, 1854.
Rorty, Richard. *Philosophy and the Mirror of Nature*. Princeton, NJ: Princeton University Press, 1979.
Rosenberg, Shalom. *Torah Umada' Behagut Hayehudit Hahadashah [Torah and Science in Modern Jewish Thought]*. Jerusalem: Israel Ministry of Education, 1988.
Rugai, Nick. *Computational Epistemology: From Reality to Wisdom*. 2nd edition. Raleigh NC: Kuku Press, 2013.
Russell, Bertrand. *Introduction to Mathematical Philosophy*. London: Allen and Unwin,, 1920. http://people.umass.edu/klement/imp/imp.html (accessed August 2015).
Russell, Bertrand. On Denoting. *Mind*. 1905; *14* (56): 479–493. Reprinted in: R. C. March (ed.) *Logic and Knowledge*. London: Allen and Unwin, 1956. pp. 39–56.
Russell, Bertrand. *Why I Am Not a Christian*. London: Unwin Books, 1967.
Saadia Gaon. *The Book of Beliefs and Opinions* (trans. Samuel Rosenblatt). New Haven: Yale University Press, 1948.
Shils, Edward. *Tradition*. Chicago: University of Chicago Press, 1980.
Sirat, Colette. *A History of Jewish Philosophy in the Middle Ages*. Cambridge: Cambridge University Press, 1985.
Sofer, Rabbi Moses. *Responsa Hatam Sofer* (I–VI). Bratislava 1841–1912.
Sosa, Ernest. How Do You Know? *American Philosophical Quarterly* 1974; *11*(2): 113–122. Reprinted in: G. S. Pappas and M. Swain. *Essays on Knowledge and Justification*. Ithaca: Cornell University Press, 1978. pp. 184–205.
Sosa, Ernest. The Raft and the Pyramid. *Midwest Studies in Philosophy, Vol. 5: Studies in Epistemology*. Minneapolis: University of Minneapolis Press, 1980. pp. 3–25.
Spinoza, Baruch. *The Letters* (trans. Samuel Shirley). Indianapolis and Cambridge: Hackett, 1995.
Steup, Matthias. *An Introduction to Contemporary Epistemology*. Upper Saddle River: Prentice Hall, 1966.

Stich, Stephen. Reflective Equilibrium, Analytic Epistemology, and the Problem of Cognitive Diversity. *Synthese.* 1988; *74* (3): 391–413

Strawson, Peter F. On Referring. *Mind.* 1950; *59* (235): 320–344.

Taliaferro, Charles, Draper, Paul, Quinn, Philip L. (editors). *A Companion to Philosophy of Religion.* 2nd edition. Malden Ma: Blackwell, 2010.

Wahlberg, Mats. *Revelation as Testimony: A Philosophical-Theological Study.* Cambridge: Eerdmans Publishing Co., 2014.

Weber, Max. *Economy and Society* (I–II). Berkeley: University of California Press, 1978

Wigmore, John Henry. *Evidence.* Revised edition (James H. Chadbourn, ed.). Boston: Little, Brown, 1981.

Williamson, Timothy. *Knowledge and Its Limits.* Oxford: Oxford University Press, 2000.

Winch, Peter. "Discussion of Malcolm's Essay". In: Norman Malcolm. *Wittgenstein: A Religious Point of View?* Ithaca: Cornell University Press, 1995. pp. 95–135.

Wittgenstein, Ludwig. *On Certainty.* Oxford: Basil Blackwell, 1969. http://budni.by.ru/oncertainty.html (accessed August 2015).

Wittgenstein, Ludwig. *Philosophical Investigations.* Oxford: Basil Blackwell, 1953. http://www.scribd.com/doc/2916793/Ludwig-Wittgenstein-Philosophical-Investigations (accessed August 2015).

Yabetz, R Joseph. *Or HaHayim [=The Light of Life].* Ferrara: Abraham Usque Press, 1554.

Zagzebski, Linda T. *Epistemic Authority: A Theory of Trust, Authority and Autonomy in Belief.* Oxford: Oxford University Press, 2012.

Index

A

absorption 29
abstraction 9, 10
activators 46
addition 29
adoption 17
  complementary
    compartmentalization 22, 33
  consistency mechanisms 33
  definitions 7
  direct 24, 37
  exclusive 17, 20
  external decision 23, 33
  full 7, 17, 20
  hierarchy 22, 23, 33
  indirect 24, 37
  justification 7, 34
  mediated 25, 35
  ordinary
    compartmentalization 21, 33
  partial 7, 19, 32
  rejection 7, 17, 23, 34
adoption axiom 38
adoption-inclusion relation
    theorem 27
adoption relation
    theorem 21
adoption restriction
    condition 7, 19
adoption sentences 17
adoption sign 17
Albalag, Isaac 97
Al-Ghazali, Abu Hamid
    Muhammad 81, 97
alleged subdatabases 27
alleged subsystems 27
Alston, William 93
anti-rationalism 78
Aquinas, Thomas 88, 89, 90
Ascher, Saul 95
Ash'arite theology (Islam) 81

associativity   29
atheism   75, 87
Audi, Robert   9
Austin, John   105
authority and its justification   104
authority justification
        principle   104
availability of cultural
        systems   58, 63
Averroes   88, 89, 90, 91
    see Ibn Rushd
axioms
    adoption   38
    distribution of conjunctive
        transmissions   16, 32
    distribution of implicative
        transmissions   16
    logicality of speaking self   30
    non-transmission   17
    self-adoption   19, 60, 68, 69
    self-credibility   15
    source   15
    sources of i   15
    speaking self   15

B

Barth, Karl   87
basic cognitive tools   7, 48, 61
    see also reason-religion conflict
belief   24
    direct   24, 38
    indirect   38
    technical and vivid   63
Bentham, Jeremy   105
Bible   56, 57, 83, 91, 94
    see also Torah
biconditional adoption distribution
        theorem   19
biconditional transmissions
        distribution theorem   16
Boethius of Dacia   97
Boxel, Hugo   x
Bradley, Owen   106

C

cannibalism   111
Catholicism
    detachment from Protestantism   57
    fideism   82, 83
causal-historical theory   121
chain of validity   105
Chisholm, Roderick   viii, 7
Christianity
    and Islam   57
    detachment from Judaism   56
    detachment of Catholicism and
        Protestantism   57
    double-faith theory   90
    fideism   82, 86
coherentist theory   35, 37, 41, 45
co-justified models   38
co-justified sources   38
Coleridge, Samuel Taylor   65
combinatory faculty   10
common final justification   38
Communist thought   55
communities   12, 48, 50, 51
    and language   119, 121, 122, 125
commutativity   29
compartmentalization
    complementary   22, 33
    external decision   23, 33
    hierarchy   22, 23, 33
    in philosophy of religion   81, 94
    laws of evidence as   113
    mediated adoption   25, 35
    ordinary   21, 33
    subdatabases   27
    subsystems   27
complementary
        compartmentalization   22, 33
computational cognitive sciences   ix
computational epistemology   ix
conditional adoption
    see partial adoption
conditional exclusive adoption   20
conditional rejection   7

conjunction   29
conjunctive adoption distribution theorem   19
conjunctive transmissions distribution axiom   16, 32
conservative rule   68, 100, 112, 140
conservative solution   71
considerations, in law   111
consistency mechanisms   33
consistency theorem   31, 34
constructive dilemma   29
contradictory data   31
conversion   58, 66
   conservative rule   68, 100, 112, 140
   exhaustiveness rule   71, 100, 140
   justification of   60, 66
Core (law)   133
creative functions   8
   abstraction   9, 10
   combinatory faculty   10
   elimination   9
   ex materia   8, 10
   ex nihilo   8, 10
   forgetting   9, 147
   judgment   9
   partitionary faculty   10
   preservation   9
cultural communities   51
   and language   119, 121, 122, 125
cultural systems   43
   and logical systems   46, 53, 66
   and personal systems   47
   availability   58, 63
   conservative rule   68, 100, 112, 140
   convertibility   58
   defeasibility   52, 53
   detachability   54
   exhaustiveness rule   71, 100, 140
   individual psychological attachment to   58, 69
   language as a subsystem   119
   law as a subsystem   103, 119
   literature   64
   openness   53
   pragmatic guidelines   66, 139
   purest utilization principle   100
   real and ideal systems   47, 49, 53
   separation rule   68, 100, 140
   technical belief and vivid belief   63
culture   50
custom   108

D

data
   see also null data
   contradictory   31
   definitions   5
   in source calculus   11
   sentential and non-sentential expressions of   145
Data
   meaning data   120
databases   6, 14, 26
datasets   14
Davidson, Donald   146
Dawkins, Richard   78
deciding sources   23
decisions
   judicial   114, 117
   normative practical   70
decision theorem   34, 42
defeasibility   23, 52, 53
deities   55
De Morgan's theorems   29
Descartes, René   vii, 7
detachability   54
direct adoption   24, 37
direct belief   24, 38
direct transmissions   13
disjunctive syllogism   29
distribution   29
distribution of conjunctive transmissions   16, 32
distribution of disjunctive transmissions   16
distribution of implicative transmissions   16

division of labor   7, 17
   see also compartmentalization
double-faith theory   88
double negation   29
double-truth theory   97
Dretske, Fred I.   ix
Dummett, Michael   9
Dworkin, Ronald   115
dynamism of real systems   53

E

elimination   9
Eliyahu ben Shlomo Zalman of Vilna
   ('the Vilna Gaon')   85
epistemic authority theory   93
epistemology   vii, viii, 138
  computational   ix
  epistemological viewpoint   51
  Foundationalism
    (epistemology)   35
  religious   93
evidence law   113
excluded middle, law of   28
exclusive adoption   17
  conditional   20
exhaustiveness rule   71, 100, 140
ex materia creation   8, 10
ex nihilo creation   8, 10
exportation   30
external decision   23, 33
external justification   37

F

fideism   78
final justification   7, 35
Flew, Antony   78
forgetting   6, 9, 147, 151
Formalism (legal)   104
formalistic and non-formalistic legal
   systems   112, 117
formalist line of argumentation   ix, 1
  see also source calculus

foundationalist theory   44
Frazer, James George   55
Frege, Gottlob   vii, 2, 121, 124, 130,
   131, 132, 134, 146
Freud, Sigmund   106, 148
full adoption   7, 17, 20
full rejection   7
functioning, test of   3

G

Gaon of Vilna   85
  see Eliyahu ben Shlomo Zalman
Geach, Peter T.   146
generative sources
  see ex nihilo creation
gold   132
grammar   135
Greeks, ancient   vii

H

Hage, Jaap C.   108
HaGra   85
  see Eliyahu ben Shlomo Zalman
Hart, Herbert L. A.   103, 105, 115,
   117, 133
hasidic movement   85
Heelas, Paul   50
hierarchy   22, 23, 33
Hobsbawm, Eric   50, 113
Holbach, Paul Henri Thiry,
   Baron d'   75
holy individuals (*Tzadikim*)   86
holy texts
  Bible   56, 57, 83, 91, 94
  in fideism   78
  Oral Torah   56
  Qur'an   80
  Talmud   56
  Torah   56, 85, 96, 97
Hume, David   146
hypothetical syllogism   28

I

Ibn Rushd   88, 89, 90, 91
Ibn Taymiyyah, Taqi Ad-Din Ahmed   80
ideal systems   47, 49, 53
identity, law of   28
imagination   7, 10, 49
implicative adoption distribution theorem   19
implicative transmissions distribution axiom   16
indirect adoption   24, 37
indirect adoption theorem   24
indirect belief   24, 38
indirect transmissions   14
infinite regress problem   ix, 36, 37, 41, 44, 104, 138
inner consistency   69
institutional facts   133
internality of justification of adoption theorem   39, 40, 41
internal justification   37
Islam   57
   double-faith theory   89, 90, 91
   fideism   80

J

James, William   3
Jewish Bible   56, 57, 91, 94
   see also Torah
Judaism
   and Islam   57
   detachment of Christianity from   56
   double-faith theory   89, 90, 91
   double-truth theory   97
   fideism   81, 85
   orthopistism   95
   orthopraxy   94, 97
   separationist approach   94
judgment   9
judicial decisions   114, 117
judicial process   112
justification   7, 34
   external   37
   final   7, 35
   internal   37
   of conversion   60, 66
   self-justification   36, 37

K

Kant, Immanuel   96, 138
Kelsen, Hans   104
Kierkegaard, Søren   86
Kripke, Saul   121, 128, 129, 132

L

language   vii, viii, 119
   as a subsystem   119
   meaning of words   120, 129, 153
   naming individual objects   121
   pragmatic aspects   135
   syntax   135
Laplace, Pierre Simon   78
law
   see philosophy of law
law of excluded middle   28
law of identity   28
law of non-contradiction   28, 31
laws of evidence   113
legal interpretation   114, 117
legal philosophy
   see philosophy of law
legal process   107
Leibowitz, Yeshayahu   94
Lewis, David   48, 120
liar paradox   19
libertarian solution   71
linguistic turn   viii
literature   64
logical calculus   1
logicality of speaking self axiom   30
logical systems   46, 53, 66
logic, rules of   27

Loyola, Ignatius   83
Luther, Martin   82

M

magic   55
Maimonides, Moses   91
Maistre-Bradley theory   106
Maistre, Joseph de   106
Malcolm, Norman   87
manipulative changes in meanings of words   153
Marmor, Andrei   48, 120
Marxism   55
material equivalence   30
material implication   30
meaning data   120
meaning of words   120, 129
   manipulative changes in   153
mediated adoption   25, 35
medieval period
   see Middle Ages
memory
   see forgetting
meta-systems   139
Middle Ages
   double-faith theory   88
   double-truth theory   97
   irrational character of religion   55
   reason-religion conflict   74
   religious rationalism   55, 74, 88
Mill, John Stuart   122
misidentification of source   49, 51
modus ponens   28
modus tollens   28
Monotheist Religious System (MRS)   51, 73
   double-faith theory   88
   double-truth theory   97
   fideism   78
   orthopistism   95
   orthopraxy   94, 97
   separationist approach   94
Morality and Law   105

morality-religion conflict
   see reason-religion conflict
MRS
   see Monotheist Religious System (MRS)

N

Nahman of Breslav   85
naming individual objects   121
native systems   66
negative obligations   70
negative permissions   70
New Testament   56, 83
Nielsen, Kai   78
nihilism   66
nihilistic absurdities   ix, 40, 43, 112, 138, 139
non-contradiction, law of   28, 31
non liquet state   16, 32, 39, 72, 101
non-transmission axiom   17
normative discourse   67
normative practical decisions   70
normative relativism   111
null data   8
   and forgetting   147, 151
   creating out of null data   151

O

objects   9
obligations   70
   in law   108
onomatopoeias   120
openness (of systems)   53
operation failure   52
operators   46
Oral Torah   56
orthopistism   95
orthopraxy   94, 97
Orwell, George   65, 153

P

Paine, Thomas   106
paradox   2

partial adoption   7, 19, 32
  complementary compartmentalization   22, 33
  external decision   23, 33
  hierarchy   22, 23, 33
  mediated   25, 35
  ordinary compartmentalization   21, 33
  rejection   7, 17, 23, 34
partial adoption distribution theorem   20
partitionary faculty   10
part-whole relation   9
penumbra (law)   117, 133
permissions   70
personal systems   47
Phillips, Dewi Z.   78, 87
philosophy of language   119
  language as a subsystem   119
  meaning of words   120, 129, 153
  naming individual objects   121
  pragmatic aspects   135
  syntax   135
philosophy of law   103
  authority and its justification   104
  formalism and non-formalism   104, 112, 117
  judicial process   112
  law as a subsystem   103, 119
  legal process   107
  meaning of legal terms   133
philosophy of religion   xii, 73
  adoption of reason and rejection of religion   75, 87
  adoption of religion and rejection of reason   78
  atheism   75, 87
  double-faith theory   88
  double-truth theory   97
  fideism   78
  orthopistism   95
  orthopraxy   94, 97
  separationist approach   94
Plantinga, Alvin   93

Plato   131
pleasure, test of   3
positive data and forgetting   147
positive obligations   70
positive permissions   70
pragmatic aspects of language   135
pragmatic guidelines   66, 139
  conservative rule   68, 100, 112, 140
  exhaustiveness rule   71, 100, 140
  purest utilization principle   100
  separation rule   68, 100, 140
pragmatist line of argumentation   ix, 2, 139
  see also cultural systems
precedent   108
preservation   9
presumptions, in law   110
primary sources   24
prohibitions   70
  in law   108
propositions   9
Protestantism
  detachment from Catholicism   57
  fideism   82
psychological attachment to systems   58, 69
  and conversion   58, 66, 68, 71
  availability   58, 63
  degrees of   62, 64
  literature   64
  technical belief and vivid belief   63
  two or more systems   62, 68, 100
psychological viewpoint   51
purest utilization principle   100
Pure Theory of Law   104

Q

Qur'an   80

R

radical religious approach   78
radical secular approach   75, 87

rationalism 55, 74, 88
   see also anti-rationalism, religious
rational system viii, ix
Raz, Joseph 105
real systems 47, 49, 53
   dynamism of 53
reason-religion conflict xii, 73
   adoption of reason and rejection of religion 75, 87
   adoption of religion and rejection of reason 78
   atheism 75, 87
   double-faith theory 88
   double-truth theory 97
   fideism 78
   orthopistism 95
   orthopraxy 94, 97
   separationist approach 94
recognition, rule of 103, 105
reference determination 121
reference theory 130
reform movement, Jewish 95
Reid, Thomas 7
rejection 7, 17, 23, 34
rejection sign 17
relativism 66, 111
religion xii, 73
   deities 55
   detachment of Catholicism and Protestantism 57
   detachment of Christianity from Judaism 56
   double-faith theory 88
   double-truth theory 97
   fideism 78
   irrational character of 55
   magic 55
   orthopistism 95
   orthopraxy 94, 97
   rejection of 75, 87
   religious rationalism 55, 74, 88
   separationist approach 94
religious epistemology 93
Roman Empire 54
rule of recognition 103, 105
rule-skepticism 117
rules of logic 27
Russell, Bertrand vii, 2, 75, 77, 121, 130, 132, 146

S

Saadia Gaon 88, 89, 90, 91
sacrificium intellectus 83
sanctions, in law 108
Schiller, F. C .S. 3
Schopenhauer, Arthur 67
scientific systems 53
Searle, John 133
secondary sources 24
self-adoption axiom 19, 60, 68, 69
self-correction in science 53
self-credibility axiom 15
self-justification 36, 37
senses 18, 22
Senses
   see also Basic cognitive tools
sentences 5, 6
   adoption 17
   transmission 13
sentence variables 13
separationist approach 94
separation rule 68, 100, 140
Shils, Edward 50
Siger de Brabant 97
simplification 29
source axiom 15
source calculus ix, xii, 4, 11, 37, 38, 41, 122, 138
   adoption 17
   contradictory data 31
   databases and systems 26
   data, sources and transmission 11
   justification 34
   nihilistic absurdities ix, 40, 43, 112, 138, 139
   subordination to logic 27
source models 7, 18

co-justified   38
sources
   definitions   5
   in source calculus   11
sources of i axiom   15
speaking self   12, 13
   logicality of speaking self axiom   30
   speaking self's claim of
      transmission theorem   16
   undecidedness of speaking self
      theorem   39
speaking self axiom   15
Spinoza, Baruch   x, 93
Strawson, Peter F.   146
subdatabases   27
   alleged   27
   compartmentalized   27
subjective solution   71
subordinate sources   22
subsystems   27
   compartmentalized   27
superior sources   22
suspension of disbelief   65
syntax   135
systems   7, 26
   see also cultural systems

T

Tagging (language)   126
Talmud   56
tautology   30
technical belief   63
tertiary sources   24
Tertullian   79
testimony   6, 61
   witnesses   47
test of functioning   3
test of pleasure   3
theorems
   adoption-inclusion relation   27
   adoption relation   21
   biconditional adoption
      distribution   19

biconditional transmissions
      distribution   16
   conjunctive adoption
      distribution   19
   consistency   31, 34
   decision   34, 42
   implicative adoption
      distribution   19
   indirect adoption   24
   internality of justification of
      adoption   39, 40, 41
   partial adoption distribution   20
   speaking self's claim of
      transmission   16
   undecidedness of speaking
      self   39
Thomas Aquinas   88, 89, 90
Torah   81, 85, 96, 97
   Oral   56
   See also Jewish Bible. *See*
totality problem   69
tradition   50
transmission
   by virtue of adoption   24
   by virtue of full adoption   24
   definitions   5
   failure   52
   in source calculus   11
   in virtue of partial adoption   25
   sentences   13
   sign   12
transposition   30
truth sources
   definitions   5
   in source calculus   11
truth systems   7, 26
type of sources   48
Tzadikim (holy individuals)   86

U

unconditional adoption
   see full adoption
unconditional rejection   7

unconscious datum   5
undecidedness of speaking self theorem   39
unified science   138
users   46

V

variables, sentence   13
vivid belief   63

W

Weber, Max   104, 111
Western Rational Legal Subsystem   103
Western Rational Tradition (WRS)   51, 73
   adoption of reason and rejection of religion   75, 87
   atheism   75, 87
   double-faith theory   88
   double-truth theory   97
   orthopistism   95
   orthopraxy   94, 97
   separationist approach   94
WFF rules   14
Whitehead, Alfred North   2
Winch, Peter   87
wishful thinking   49
Wittgenstein, Ludwig   xi, 67, 78, 87, 119, 130, 131, 132, 134, 135
written law   108
WRS
   see Western Rational Tradition (WRS)

Y

Yabetz, R. Joseph   81

Z

Zagzebski, Linda T.   93

www.ingramcontent.com/pod-product-compliance
Ingram Content Group UK Ltd.
Pitfield, Milton Keynes, MK11 3LW, UK
UKHW051517160125
4144UKWH00041BA/494